Prayer Book and Psalms

Pocket Edition

HOLY TRINITY PUBLICATIONS
The Printshop of St Job of Pochaev
Holy Trinity Monastery
Jordanville, New York

Printed with the blessing of His Eminence,
Metropolitan Hilarion, First Hierarch
of the Russian Orthodox Church Outside of Russia

Edited Compilation:
Prayer Book and Psalms—Pocket Edition
© 2019 Holy Trinity Monastery
Text: *Prayer Book*, 4th Edition
© 2005 Holy Trinity Monastery
Psalm text: *A Psalter for Prayer*, 2nd Edition
© David Mitchell James 2011

PRINTSHOP OF
SAINT JOB OF POCHAEV

An imprint of

HOLY TRINITY PUBLICATIONS
Holy Trinity Monastery
Jordanville, New York 13361-0036
www.holytrinitypublications.com

ISBN: 978-0-88465-344-8

Library of Congress Control Number 2019940249

Prayers for the Living and for the Departed, and the
Psalms taken from: *A Psalter for Prayer*,
trans. David Mitchell James
(Jordanville, NY: Holy Trinity Publications, 2019).

Contents

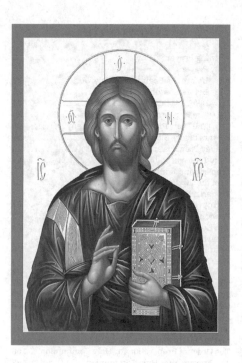

Morning Prayers

Having risen from sleep, before any other action, stand reverently, considering thyself to be in the presence of the All-seeing God, and, having made the sign of the cross, say:

In the name of the Father and of the Son and of the Holy Spirit. Amen.

Then pause a moment, until all thy senses are calmed and thy thoughts forsake all things earthly; and then make three bows, saying with each bow:

The Prayer of the Publican:

O God, be merciful to me, a sinner.

The Beginning Prayer:

O Lord Jesus Christ, Son of God, for the sake of the prayers of Thy most pure Mother and all the saints, have mercy on us. Amen.

Glory to Thee, our God, glory to Thee.

O Heavenly King, Comforter, Spirit of Truth, Who art everywhere present and fillest all things, Treasury of good things and Giver of life: Come and dwell in us, and cleanse us of all impurity, and save our souls, O Good One.

Holy God, Holy Mighty, Holy Immortal, have mercy on us. *Thrice.*

Glory to the Father and to the Son and to the Holy Spirit, both now and ever and unto the ages of ages. Amen.

O Most Holy Trinity, have mercy on us. O Lord, blot out our sins. O Master, pardon our iniquities. O Holy One, visit and heal our infirmities for Thy name's sake.

Lord, have mercy. *Thrice.*

Glory to the Father and to the Son and to the Holy Spirit, both now and ever and unto the ages of ages. Amen.

Our Father, Who art in the heavens, hallowed be Thy name. Thy kingdom come, Thy will be done, on earth as it is in heaven. Give us this day our daily bread, and forgive us our debts, as we forgive our debtors; and lead us not into temptation, but deliver us from the evil one.

Troparia to the Holy Trinity:

Having risen from sleep, we fall down before Thee, O Good One, and we cry aloud the angelic hymn to Thee, O Mighty One: Holy, Holy, Holy art Thou, O God; through the Theotokos, have mercy on us.

Glory to the Father and to the Son and to the Holy Spirit.

From bed and sleep hast Thou raised me up, O Lord: enlighten my mind and heart, and open my lips that I may hymn Thee, O Holy Trinity: Holy, Holy, Holy art Thou, O God; through the Theotokos, have mercy on us.

Both now and ever and unto the ages of ages. Amen.

Suddenly the Judge shall come, and the deeds of each shall be laid bare; but with fear do we cry at midnight: Holy, Holy, Holy art Thou, O God; through the Theotokos, have mercy on us.

Lord, have mercy. *Twelve.*

Prayer of St Basil the Great to the Most Holy Trinity:

As I rise from sleep, I thank Thee, O Holy Trinity, for through Thy great goodness and patience Thou wast not angry with me, an idler and sinner, nor hast Thou destroyed me with mine iniquities, but hast shown Thy usual love for mankind; and when I was prostrate in despair, Thou hast raised me up to keep the morning watch and glorify Thy power. And now enlighten my mind's eye, and open my mouth that I may meditate on Thy words and understand Thy commandments and do Thy will and hymn Thee in heartfelt confession and sing praises to Thine all-holy name: of the Father and of the Son and of the Holy Spirit, now and ever and unto the ages of ages. Amen.

O come let us worship God, our King.

O come let us worship and fall down before Christ, our King and God.

O come let us worship and fall down before Christ Himself, our King and God.

Psalm 50

Have mercy upon me, O God, after Thy great goodness, and according to the multitude of Thy mercies do away mine offenses. Wash me thoroughly from my wickedness, and cleanse me from my sin. For I know my fault, and my sin is ever before me. Against Thee only have I sinned, and done evil before Thee, that Thou mightest be justified in Thy words, and prevail when Thou art judged. For behold, I was conceived in wickedness, and in sins did my mother bear me. For behold, Thou hast loved truth; the hidden and secret things of Thy wisdom hast Thou revealed unto me. Thou shalt sprinkle me with hyssop, and I shall be made clean; Thou shalt wash me, and I shall become whiter than snow. Thou shalt give joy and gladness to my hearing; the bones that have been humbled will rejoice. Turn Thy face from my sins, and put out all my misdeeds. Make me a clean heart, O God, and renew a right spirit within me. Cast me not away from Thy presence, and take not Thy Holy Spirit from me. O give me the comfort of Thy salvation, and stablish me with Thy governing Spirit. Then shall I teach Thy ways unto the wicked, and the ungodly shall be converted unto Thee. Deliver me from blood-guiltiness, O God, the God of my salvation, and my tongue shall rejoice in Thy righteousness. O Lord, open Thou my lips, and my mouth shall show forth Thy praise. For if

Thou hadst desired sacrifice, I would have given it; but Thou delightest not in burnt offerings. The sacrifice unto God is a contrite spirit; a contrite and humble heart God shall not despise. O Lord, be favorable in Thy good will unto Zion, and let the walls of Jerusalem be builded up. Then shalt Thou be pleased with the sacrifice of righteousness, with oblation and whole-burnt offerings; then shall they offer young bullocks upon Thine altar.

The Creed:

I believe in one God, the Father Almighty, Maker of heaven and earth, and of all things visible and invisible; and in one Lord Jesus Christ, the Son of God, the Only-begotten, begotten of the Father before all ages; Light of Light, true God of true God; begotten, not made; of one essence with the Father; by Whom all things were made; Who for us men and for our salvation, came down from the heavens and was incarnate of the Holy Spirit and the Virgin Mary and became man; and was crucified for us under Pontius Pilate and suffered and was buried; and arose on the third day according to the Scriptures; and ascended into the heavens and sitteth at the right hand of the Father; and shall come again, with glory, to judge both the living and the dead; Whose kingdom shall have no end; and in the Holy Spirit, the Lord, the Giver of Life; Who proceedeth from the Father; Who with the Father and the Son together is worshipped and glorified; Who spake by the prophets. In One Holy, Catholic and Apostolic Church. I confess one baptism for the remission of sins. I look for the resurrection of the dead and the life of the age to come. Amen.

Prayer I, of St Macarius the Great:

O God, cleanse me, a sinner, for I have never done anything good in Thy sight; but deliver me from the evil one, and let Thy will be done in me, that I may open mine unworthy mouth without condemnation and praise Thy holy name: of the Father and of the Son and of the Holy Spirit, now and ever and unto the ages of ages. Amen.

Prayer II, of the same saint:

Having risen from sleep, I offer unto Thee, O Saviour, the midnight hymn, and falling down I cry unto Thee: Grant me not to fall asleep in the death of sin, but have compassion on me, O Thou Who wast voluntarily crucified, and hasten to raise me who am reclining in idleness and save me in prayer and intercession; and after the night's sleep shine upon me a sinless day, O Christ God, and save me.

Prayer III, of the same saint:

Having risen from sleep, I hasten to Thee, O Master, Lover of mankind, and by Thy loving-kindness, I strive to do Thy work, and I pray to Thee: Help me at all times, in everything, and deliver me from every worldly, evil thing and every impulse of the devil, and save me, and lead me into Thine eternal kingdom. For Thou art my Creator and the Giver and Provider of everything good, and in Thee is all my hope, and unto Thee do I send up glory, now and ever and unto the ages of ages. Amen.

Prayer IV, of the same saint:

O Lord, Who in Thine abundant goodness and Thy great compassion hast granted me, Thy servant, to go through the time of the night that is past without attack from any opposing evil: Do Thou Thyself, O Master, Creator of all things, vouchsafe me by Thy true light and with an enlightened heart to do Thy will, now and ever and unto the ages of ages. Amen.

Prayer V, of St Basil the Great:

O Lord Almighty, God of hosts and of all flesh, Who dwellest on high and lookest down on things that are lowly, Who searchest the heart and innermost being and clearly foreknowest the secrets of men; O unoriginate and everlasting Light, with Whom is no variableness, neither shadow of turning: Do Thou, O Immortal King, receive our supplications which we, daring because of the multitude of Thy compassions, offer Thee at the present time from defiled lips; and forgive us our sins, in deed, word and thought, whether committed by us knowingly or in ignorance, and cleanse us from every defilement of flesh and spirit. And grant us to pass through the night of the whole present life with watchful heart and sober thought, ever expecting the coming of the bright and appointed day of Thine Only-begotten Son, our Lord and God and Saviour, Jesus Christ, whereon the Judge of all shall come with glory to reward each according to his deeds. May we not be found fallen and idle, but watching and upright in activity, ready to accompany Him into the joy and divine palace of His glory, where there is the ceaseless sound of those who keep festival and the unspeakable delight of those who behold the ineffable beauty of Thy countenance. For Thou art the true Light Who enlightenest and sanctifiest all, and all creation doth hymn Thee unto the ages of ages. Amen.

Prayer VI, likewise by St Basil:

We bless Thee, O Most High God and Lord of mercy, Who ever doest with us things both

great and inscrutable, both glorious and awesome,
of which there is no measure; Who grantest to us
sleep for rest from our infirmities and relaxation
from the labors of our much-toiling flesh. We thank
Thee that Thou hast not destroyed us with our iniquities, but hast shown Thy loving-kindness to man
as usual, and while we were lying in despair upon
our beds, Thou hast raised us up that we might
glorify Thy dominion. Wherefore, we implore Thy
boundless goodness: Enlighten the eyes of our
understanding and raise up our minds from the
heavy sleep of indolence; open our mouths and fill
them with Thy praise, that we may be able steadily
to hymn and confess Thee, Who art God glorified
in all and by all, the unoriginate Father, with Thine
Only-begotten Son and Thine All-holy and good
and life-creating Spirit, now and ever and unto the
ages of ages. Amen.

Prayer VII, to the Most Holy Theotokos:

I sing of Thy grace, O Sovereign Lady, and I pray
Thee to grace my mind. Teach me to step aright
in the way of Christ's commandments. Strengthen
me to keep awake in song, and drive away the sleep
of despondency. O Bride of God, by Thy prayers
release me, bound with the bonds of sin. Guard me
by night and by day, and deliver me from foes that
defeat me. O bearer of God the Life-giver, enliven
me who am deadened by passions. O bearer of

the Unwaning Light, enlighten my blinded soul. O marvelous palace of the Master, make me to be a house of the Divine Spirit. O bearer of the Healer, heal the perennial passions of my soul. Guide me to the path of repentance, for I am tossed in the storm of life. Deliver me from eternal fire, from wicked war and from hell. Let me not be exposed to the rejoicing of demons, guilty as I am of many sins. Renew me, grown old from senseless sins, O Most Immaculate One. Present me untouched by all torments, and pray for me to the Master of all. Vouchsafe me to find the joys of heaven with all the saints. O Most Holy Virgin, hearken unto the voice of Thine unprofitable servant. Grant me torrents of tears, O Most Pure One, to cleanse my soul from impurity. I offer the groans of my heart to Thee unceasingly; strive for me, O Sovereign Lady. Accept my service of supplication and offer it to compassionate God. O Thou Who art above the angels, raise me above this world's confusion. O Light-bearing heavenly tabernacle, direct the grace of the Spirit in me. I raise my hands and lips in Thy praise, defiled as they are by impurity, O All-immaculate One. Deliver me from soul-corrupting evils, and fervently intercede with Christ, to Whom is due honor and worship, now and ever and unto the ages of ages. Amen.

Prayer VIII, to our Lord Jesus Christ:

O my plenteously-merciful and all-merciful God, Lord Jesus Christ, through Thy great love Thou didst come down and become incarnate so that Thou mightest save all. And again, O Saviour, save me by Thy grace, I pray Thee. For if Thou shouldst save me for my works, this would not be grace or a gift, but rather a duty; yea, Thou Who art great in compassion and ineffable in mercy. For he that believeth in Me, Thou hast said, O my Christ, shall live and never see death. If, then, faith in Thee saveth the desperate, behold, I believe, save me, for Thou art my God and Creator. Let faith instead of works be imputed to me, O my God, for Thou wilt find no works which could justify me. But may my faith suffice instead of all works, may it answer for and acquit me, may it make me a partaker of Thine eternal glory. And let Satan not seize me and boast, O Word, that he hath torn me from Thy hand and fold. But whether I desire it or not, save me, O Christ my Saviour, forestall me quickly, quickly, for I perish. Thou art my God from my mother's womb. Vouchsafe me, O Lord, to love Thee now as fervently as I once loved sin itself, and also to work for Thee without idleness, diligently, as I worked before for deceptive Satan. But supremely shall I work for Thee, my Lord and God, Jesus Christ, all the days of my life, now and ever and unto the ages of ages. Amen.

Prayer IX, to the Holy Guardian Angel:

O holy angel who standeth by my wretched soul and my passionate life, forsake me not a sinner, nor shrink from me because of mine intemperance. Give no place for the cunning demon to master me through the violence of my mortal body, strengthen my poor and feeble hand, and guide me in the way of salvation. Yea, O holy angel of God, guardian and protector of my wretched soul and body, forgive me all wherein I have offended thee all the days of my life; and if I have sinned during the past night, protect me during the present day, and guard me from every temptation of the enemy, that I may not anger God by any sin. And pray to the Lord for me, that He may establish me in His fear, and show me, His servant, to be worthy of His goodness. Amen.

Prayer X, to the Most Holy Theotokos:

O my Most Holy Lady Theotokos, through Thy holy and all-powerful prayers, banish from me, Thy lowly and wretched servant, despondency, forgetfulness, folly, carelessness and all filthy, evil and blasphemous thoughts from my wretched heart and my darkened mind. And quench the flame of my passions, for I am poor and wretched, and deliver me from many cruel memories and deeds, and free me from all their evil effects. For blessed art Thou by all generations and glorified

is Thy most honorable name unto the ages of ages.
Amen.

Prayer for the Salvation of the Nation:

O Lord Jesus Christ our God, forgive our iniquities. Through the intercessions of Thy most pure
Mother, grant our rulers peaceful governance so
that in their calm we may also live a peaceable life
in all godliness and modesty. Amen.

Prayerful Invocation of the Saint
Whose Name we bear:

Pray unto God for me, O holy God-pleaser N., for
I fervently flee unto thee, the speedy helper and
intercessor for my soul.

Song to the Most Holy Theotokos:

O Theotokos and Virgin, rejoice, Mary, full of grace,
the Lord is with Thee; blessed art Thou among
women and blessed is the Fruit of Thy womb, for
Thou hast borne the Saviour of our souls.

Troparion to the Cross:

Save, O Lord, Thy people, and bless Thine inheritance; grant Thou victory to Orthodox Christians
over enemies; and by the power of Thy Cross do
Thou preserve Thy commonwealth.

*Then offer a brief prayer for the health and sal-
vation of thy spiritual father, thy spouse, thy parents
and thy other relatives; for those in authority, for*

*benefactors and for others known to thee: the ailing,
or those passing through sorrows.*

And if it be possible, read this commemoration:

For the Living:

Remember, O Lord Jesus Christ our God, Thy
mercies and bounties which are from everlasting,
and through which Thou didst deign to become
man and suffer crucifixion and death for the salvation of those who rightly believe in Thee, and, having risen from the dead, didst ascend into heaven,
and sittest at the right hand of God the Father, and
regardest the humble entreaties of those who call
upon Thee with their whole heart. Incline Thine
ear, and hearken unto the humble prayer of Thine
unworthy servant, and receive it as a fragrance
of spiritual incense, which I offer unto Thee for
all people. And among the first remember Thy
Holy, Catholic and Apostolic Church, which Thou
hast purchased by Thy precious Blood. Confirm,
strengthen, extend, and increase her, and keep
her in peace, and for ever proof against the power
of hell. Calm the dissensions of the Churches, and
foil the plans of the powers of darkness; dispel the
prejudice of the nations, and quickly ruin and root
out the risings of heresy, and frustrate them by the
power of Thy Holy Spirit. *Bow.*

Save, O Lord, and have mercy upon the holy
Eastern Orthodox Patriarchs and the Orthodox
episcopate of the [N.] Church, His Holiness, the

most reverend [N.], Patriarch of [N.], and His Grace, the right reverend [N.], Bishop of [N.], the priests and deacons, and all who serve in the Church, and whom Thou hast ordained to feed Thy spiritual flock; and by their prayers have mercy on me and save me, a sinner. *Bow.*

Save, O Lord, and have mercy upon the leaders of our country, and upon all in authority throughout the whole world: commanders-in-chief of armies and navies and air forces, governors of provinces and cities, and all in civil authority; protect their power with peace, and subdue under their feet every enemy and foe, and speak peace and blessing in their hearts for Thy holy Church, and for all Thy people, and grant that, in their calm, we, too, may lead a quiet and peaceful life, in true faith, with all piety and honesty. *Bow.*

Save, O Lord, and have mercy upon my spiritual father, [N.], and by his prayers forgive me my sins. *Bow.*

Save, O Lord, and have mercy upon my parents, [N.] and [N.], my brothers and sisters, and all my relatives and the neighbors of my family and friends, and grant them Thy worldly and spiritual blessings. *Bow.*

Save, O Lord, and have mercy upon the old and the young, the poor and destitute, the orphans and widows, lepers, epileptics and spastics, and those in sickness and sorrow, misfortune and tribulation, captives and exiles, in mines and prisons and reformatories, and especially upon those of Thy servants that are suffering persecution for Thy sake and for the Orthodox faith from godless peoples, apostates and heretics. Visit, strengthen, comfort and heal them, and by Thy power quickly grant them relief, freedom and deliverance. *Bow.*

Save, O Lord, and have mercy upon those whom I have purposely or inadvertently offended or scandalized in my madness and folly, and whom I have turned from the way of salvation, and whom I have led into evil and harmful deeds. By Thy divine Providence restore them to the way of salvation. *Bow.*

Save, O Lord, and have mercy upon those who hate and offend me, and do me harm, and let them not perish through me, a sinner. *Bow.*

Ilumine with the light of grace all apostates from the Orthodox faith, and those blinded by pernicious heresies, and draw them to Thyself, and unite them to Thy Holy, Catholic, and Apostolic Church. *Bow.*

For the Departed:

Remember, O Lord, the souls of Thy servants who have departed in sleep, my parents, [NN.], and all my relatives according to the flesh; forgive them their every transgression, voluntary and involuntary; grant them the Kingdom and a share in Thine eternal joy, and the delight of Thy blessed and everlasting life. *Bow.*

Remember, O Lord, all monks and nuns and members of our brotherhood who have departed in sleep with the hope of resurrection and eternal life, and all Orthodox Christians who lie here and in all the world, and with Thy Saints give them rest where the light of Thy countenance shineth, and have mercy upon us, for Thou art good and lovest mankind. Amen. *Bow.*

Grant, O Lord, remission of all sins unto our fathers, brothers and sisters departed in the faith and hope of resurrection, and grant them memory eternal. *Bow.*

Final Prayer:

It is truly meet to bless Thee, the Theotokos, ever-blessed and most blameless and Mother of our God. More honorable than the Cherubim and beyond compare more glorious than the Seraphim, Who without corruption gavest birth to God the Word, the very Theotokos, Thee do we magnify.

Glory to the Father and to the Son and to the Holy Spirit, both now and ever and unto the ages of ages. Amen.

Lord, have mercy. *Thrice.*

O Lord, bless. *And the dismissal:* O Lord Jesus Christ, Son of God, for the sake of the prayers of Thy most pure Mother, our holy and God-bearing fathers and all the saints, have mercy on us. Amen.

Daily Prayers

Before the Beginning of Any Work:

O Lord, bless. *Or:*

O Lord Jesus Christ, Only-begotten Son of Thine unoriginate Father, Thou hast said with Thy most pure lips: For without Me, ye can do nothing. My Lord, O Lord, in faith having embraced Thy words, I fall down before Thy goodness; help me, a sinner, to accomplish through Thee this work which I am about to begin, in the name of the Father and of the Son and of the Holy Spirit. Amen.

After the Completion of Any Work:

Glory to Thee, O Lord. *Or:*

Thou art the fullness of all good things, O my Christ; fill my soul with joy and gladness, and save me, for Thou alone art plenteous in mercy.

Before Lessons:

O Heavenly King, Comforter, Spirit of Truth, Who art everywhere present and fillest all things, Treasury of good things and Giver of life: Come and dwell in us, and cleanse us of all impurity, and save our souls, O Good One.

Or:

O Most-good Lord! Send down upon us the grace of Thy Holy Spirit, Who granteth gifts and strengtheneth the powers of our souls, so that by attending to the teaching given us, we may grow to the glory of Thee, our Creator, to the comfort of our parents and to the service of the Church and our native land.

After Lessons:

It is truly meet to bless Thee, the Theotokos, ever-blessed and most blameless and Mother of our God. More honorable than the Cherubim and beyond compare more glorious than the Seraphim, Who without corruption gavest birth to God the Word, the very Theotokos, Thee do we magnify.

Or:

We thank Thee, O Creator, that Thou hast vouch-safed us Thy grace to attend instruction. Bless our leaders, parents and instructors who are leading us to an awareness of good, and grant us power and strength to continue this study.

Before Breakfast, Noon and Evening Meals:

Our Father, Who art in the heavens, hallowed be Thy name. Thy kingdom come, Thy will be done, on earth as it is in heaven. Give us this day our daily bread, and forgive us our debts, as we forgive our debtors; and lead us not into temptation, but deliver us from the evil one.

Or:

The eyes of all look to Thee with hope, and Thou givest them their food in due season. Thou openest Thy hand and fillest every living thing with Thy favor.

After Breakfast, Noon and Evening Meals:

We thank Thee, O Christ our God, that Thou hast satisfied us with Thine earthly gifts; deprive us not of Thy heavenly kingdom, but as Thou camest among Thy disciples, O Saviour, and gavest them peace, come to us and save us.

The Prayer of the Optina Elders:

Grant unto me, O Lord, that I may meet all that this new day brings with peace of soul. Grant me to submit myself completely to Thy Holy Will. ~ Instruct and support me in all things in every hour of this day. Teach me to accept calmly whatever news I receive today, in the firm conviction that Thy Holy Will governs all. ~ Govern Thou my thoughts and feelings in all I do and say. When things unforeseen occur, let me not forget that everything is sent from Thee. ~ Teach me to behave sincerely and reasonably with each member of my family, that I may not upset or grieve anyone. ~ Grant me, Lord, the strength to bear the fatigue of the day, and all that occurs therein. ~ Guide Thou my will and teach me to pray, to believe, to hope, to endure, to forgive, and to love. Amen.

The Daily Prayer of Fr Parfeny of Kiev-Pechersk:

Translated by Fr Lazarus (Moore)

O Lord Jesus Christ, Son of God, do not allow vanity, selfishness, sensuality, carelessness or anger to have dominion over me and snatch me from Thy love.

O my Lord, my Creator, all my hope. Leave me not without a share in blessed eternity. Grant that I may follow Thy holy example, and be obedient to the authorities placed over me. Grant me that purity of spirit, that simplicity of heart, which make us worthy of Thy love.

To Thee, O my God, I lift up my soul and my heart; do not allow Thy creature to perish, but deliver me from the one supreme evil—sin. Grant, O Lord, that I may bear disturbances and sufferings of the soul with the same patience as I receive pleasures of the heart with joy. If Thou wilt O Lord, Thou canst purify and sanctify me. Here and now I surrender myself to Thy goodness, beseeching Thee to root out of me all that is opposed to Thee, and unite me to the company of Thine elect.

O Lord, take from me idleness of spirit, which wastes Thy time, and vain thoughts which hinder Thy Presence and distract my attention in prayer. And if when I am praying, my attention is diverted from Thee by my thoughts, help me so that this distraction may not be voluntary, and that in turning away my mind I may not turn away my heart from Thee.

I confess to Thee my Lord God, all the sins of my wickedness committed now and previously before Thee. Forgive me, for Thy holy Name's sake and save my soul which Thou hast redeemed with Thy precious Blood. I entrust myself to Thy mercy. I surrender myself to Thy will; deal with me according to Thy goodness and not according to my malice and wickedness. Teach me, O Lord, so to arrange my affairs, that they may promote the glory of Thy holy Name.

Have mercy, O Lord, on all Christians; hear the desire of all who cry to Thee, and deliver them from all evil. Save Thy servants (Names) and send them joy, comfort in their troubles, and Thy holy mercy.

O Lord, I pray Thee especially for those who in some way have wronged, offended or saddened me, or have done me some evil. Do not punish them on my account who am also a sinner, but pour upon them Thy goodness.

O Lord, I pray Thee for all whom I, sinful as I am, have grieved, offended, or scandalized, by word, deed, or thought, consciously or unconsciously.

O Lord God, forgive us our sins and mutual offenses; expel from our hearts all indignation, scorn, anger, resentment, altercation and all that can hinder charity and lessen brotherly love.

Have mercy, O Lord, on those who have entrusted me, sinful and unworthy, to pray for them. Have mercy, O Lord, on everyone who asks for Thy help.

O Lord, make this day a day of Thy mercy, and grant to each according to his faith. Be the Shepherd of those who have gone astray, the Guide and Light of unbelievers, the Teacher of the foolish, the Father of orphans, the Helper of the oppressed, the Healer of the sick, the Comforter of the dying. And lead us all to the desired end, to Thee, our haven and blessed rest. Amen.

Prayers before Sleep

In the name of the Father and of the Son and of the Holy Spirit. Amen.

O Lord Jesus Christ, Son of God, for the sake of the prayers of Thy most pure Mother, of our holy and God-bearing fathers and all the saints, have mercy on us. Amen.

Glory to Thee, our God, glory to Thee.

O Heavenly King, Comforter, Spirit of Truth, Who art everywhere present and fillest all things, Treasury of good things and Giver of life: Come and dwell in us, and cleanse us of all impurity, and save our souls, O Good One.

Holy God, Holy Mighty, Holy Immortal, have mercy on us. *Thrice.*

Glory to the Father and to the Son and to the Holy Spirit, both now and ever and unto the ages of ages. Amen.

O Most Holy Trinity, have mercy on us. O Lord, blot out our sins. O Master, pardon our iniquities. O Holy One, visit and heal our infirmities for Thy name's sake.

Lord, have mercy. *Thrice.*

Glory to the Father and to the Son and to the Holy Spirit, both now and ever and unto the ages of ages. Amen.

Our Father, Who art in the heavens, hallowed be Thy name. Thy kingdom come, Thy will be done, on earth as it is in heaven. Give us this day our daily bread, and forgive us our debts, as we forgive our debtors; and lead us not into temptation, but deliver us from the evil one.

Troparia:

Have mercy on us, O Lord, have mercy on us; for at a loss for any defense, this prayer do we sinners offer unto Thee as Master: Have mercy on us.

Glory to the Father and to the Son and to the Holy Spirit.

Lord, have mercy on us, for we have hoped in Thee; be not angry with us greatly, neither remember our iniquities; but look upon us now as Thou art compassionate, and deliver us from our enemies, for Thou art our God, and we, Thy people; all are the works of the Thy hands, and we call upon Thy name.

Both now and ever and unto the ages of ages. Amen.

The door of compassion open unto us, O Blessed Theotokos, for hoping in Thee, let us not perish; through Thee may we be delivered from adversities, for Thou art the salvation of the Christian race.

Lord, have mercy. *Twelve times.*

Prayer I, of St Macarius the Great:

O Eternal God and King of all creation, Who hast vouchsafed me to arrive at this hour, forgive me the sins that I have committed this day in deed, word and thought; and cleanse, O Lord, my lowly soul of all impurity of flesh and spirit, and grant me, O Lord, to pass the sleep of this night in peace; that, rising from my lowly bed, I may please Thy most holy name all the days of my life and thwart the enemies, fleshly and bodiless, that war against me. And deliver me, O Lord, from vain thoughts and evil desires which defile me. For Thine is the kingdom and the power and the glory: of the Father and of the Son and of the Holy Spirit, now and ever and unto the ages of ages. Amen.

Prayer II, of St Antiochus:

O Ruler of all, Word of the Father, O Jesus Christ, Thou Who art perfect: For the sake of the plenitude of Thy mercy, never depart from me, but always remain in me Thy servant. O Jesus, Good Shepherd of Thy sheep, deliver me not over to the sedition of the serpent, and leave me not to the will of Satan, for the seed of corruption is in me. But do Thou, O Lord, worshipful God, holy King, Jesus Christ, as I sleep, guard me by the Unwaning Light, Thy Holy Spirit, by Whom Thou didst sanctify Thy disciples. O Lord, grant me, Thine unworthy servant, Thy salvation upon my bed. Enlighten

my mind with the light of understanding of Thy
Holy Gospel; my soul, with the love of Thy Cross;
my heart, with the purity of Thy word; my body,
with Thy passionless Passion. Keep my thought in
Thy humility, and raise me up at the proper time
for Thy glorification. For most glorified art Thou,
together with Thine unoriginate Father and the
Most-holy Spirit, unto the ages of ages. Amen.

Prayer III, to the Holy Spirit:

O Lord, Heavenly King, Comforter, Spirit of
Truth, show compassion and have mercy on
me, Thy sinful servant, and loose me from mine
unworthiness, and forgive all wherein I have
sinned against Thee today as a man, but even
worse than a man, as a beast; my sins voluntary
and involuntary, known and unknown, whether
from youth and from evil suggestion, or whether
from brazenness and despondency. If I have sworn
by Thy name or blasphemed it in my thought; or
reproached anyone or slandered anyone in mine
anger or grieved anyone or have become angry
about anything; or have lied or slept needlessly
or if a beggar hath come to me and I disdained
him; or if I have grieved my brother or have quar-
reled or have condemned anyone; or if I have
been boastful or prideful or angry; if, as I stood at
prayer, my mind hath been distracted by the wiles
of this world or by thoughts of depravity; if I have

overeaten or have drunk excessively or laughed frivolously; if I have thought evil or seen the beauty of another and been wounded thereby in my heart; if I have said improper things or derided my brother's sin when mine own sins are countless; if I have been neglectful of prayer or have done some other wrong that I do not remember, for all of this and more than this have I done: have mercy, O Master my Creator, on me Thy downcast and unworthy servant, and loose me and remit and forgive me, for Thou art good and the Lover of mankind, so that, lustful, sinful and wretched as I am, I may lie down and sleep and rest in peace. And I shall worship and hymn and glorify Thy most honorable name, together with the Father and His Only-begotten Son, now and ever and unto the ages of ages. Amen.

Prayer IV, of St Macarius the Great:

What shall I offer Thee, or what shall I give Thee, O greatly-gifted, immortal King, O compassionate Lord Who lovest mankind? For though I have been slothful in pleasing Thee and have done nothing good, Thou hast led me to the close of this day that is past, establishing the conversion and salvation of my soul. Be merciful to me, a sinner, bereft of every good deed, raise up my fallen soul which hath become defiled by countless sins, and take away from me every evil thought of this visible life. Forgive my sins, O Only Sinless One, in which I have sinned against Thee this day, known or unknown, in word and deed and thought and in all my senses. Do Thou Thyself protect and guard me from every opposing circumstance, by Thy Divine authority and power and inexpressible love for mankind. Blot out, O God, blot out the multitude of my sins. Be pleased, O Lord, to deliver me from the net of the evil one, and save my passionate soul, and overshadow me with the light of Thy countenance when Thou shalt come in glory; and cause me, uncondemned now, to sleep a dreamless sleep, and keep Thy servant untroubled by thoughts, and drive away from me all satanic deeds; and enlighten for me the eyes of my heart with understanding, lest I sleep unto death. And send me an angel of peace, a guardian and guide of my soul and body, that he may deliver me from mine enemies; that, rising from my bed, I may offer Thee prayers of thanksgiving. Yea, O Lord, hearken unto me, Thy sinful and wretched servant, in confession and conscience; grant me, when I arise, to be instructed by Thy sayings; and through Thine angels cause demonic despondency to be driven far from me: that I may bless Thy holy name and glorify and extol the most pure Theotokos Mary, whom Thou hast given to us sinners as a protectress, and accept Her who prayeth for us. For I know that She exemplifieth Thy love for mankind and prayeth for us without ceasing.

Through Her protection and the sign of the precious Cross and for the sake of all Thy saints, preserve my wretched soul, O Jesus Christ our God: for holy art Thou and most glorious forever. Amen.

Prayer V:

O Lord our God, as Thou art good and the Lover of mankind, forgive me wherein I have sinned today in word, deed and thought. Grant me peaceful and undisturbed sleep; send Thy guardian angel to protect and keep me from all evil. For Thou art the Guardian of our souls and bodies and unto Thee do we send up glory: to the Father and to the Son and to the Holy Spirit, now and ever and unto the ages of ages. Amen.

Prayer VI:

O Lord our God, in Whom we believe and Whose name we invoke above every name, grant us, as we go to sleep, relaxation of soul and body, and keep us from all dreams and dark pleasures; stop the onslaught of the passions and quench the burnings that arise in the flesh. Grant us to live chastely in deed and word, that we may obtain a virtuous life and not fall away from Thy promised blessings; for blessed art Thou forever. Amen.

Prayer VII, of St John Chrysostom:
(A prayer for each hour of the day and night.)

O Lord, deprive me not of Thy heavenly good things. O Lord, deliver me from the eternal torments. O Lord, if I have sinned in mind or thought, in word or deed, forgive me. O Lord, deliver me from all ignorance, forgetfulness, faintheartedness and stony insensibility. O Lord, deliver me from every temptation. O Lord, enlighten my heart, which evil desire hath darkened. O Lord, as a man I have sinned, but do Thou, as the compassionate God, have mercy on me, seeing the infirmity of my soul. O Lord, send Thy grace to my help, that I may glorify Thy holy name. O Lord Jesus Christ, write me, Thy servant, in the Book of Life, and grant me a good end. O Lord my God, even though I have done nothing good in Thy sight, yet grant me by Thy grace to make a good beginning. O Lord, sprinkle into my heart the dew of Thy grace. O Lord of heaven and earth, remember me, Thy sinful servant, shameful and unclean, in Thy kingdom. Amen.

O Lord, accept me in repentence. O Lord, forsake me not. O Lord, lead me not into temptation. O Lord, grant me good thoughts. O Lord, grant me tears and remembrance of death and compunction. O Lord, grant me the thought of confessing my sins. O Lord, grant me humility, chastity and obedience. O Lord, grant me patience, courage and meekness. O Lord, implant in me the root of good, Thy fear in my heart. O Lord, vouchsafe me to love Thee with all my soul and thoughts and in all things to do Thy will. O Lord, protect me from evil men and demons and passions and from every other unseemly thing. O Lord, Thou knowest that Thou doest as Thou wilt: Thy will be done also in me a sinner; for blessed art Thou unto the ages of ages. Amen.

Prayer VIII, to our Lord Jesus Christ:

O Lord Jesus Christ, Son of God, for the sake of Thy most honorable Mother and Thy bodiless angels, Thy Prophet and Forerunner and Baptist, the God-inspired apostles, the radiant and victorious martyrs, the holy and God-bearing fathers, and through the intercessions of all the saints, deliver me from the besetting presence of the demons. Yea, my Lord and Creator, Who desirest not the death of a sinner, but rather that he be converted and live, grant conversion also to me, wretched and unworthy; rescue me from the mouth of the pernicious serpent, who is ravening to devour me and take me down to hades alive. Yea, my Lord, my Comfort, Who for my miserable sake wast clothed in corruptible flesh, draw me out of misery, and grant comfort to my miserable soul. Implant in my heart to fulfill Thy commandments and to forsake evil deeds and to obtain Thy blessings; for in Thee, O Lord, have I hoped, save me. Amen.

Prayer IX, to the Most Holy Theotokos:

O Good Mother of the Good King, Most Pure and Blessed Theotokos Mary, do Thou pour out the mercy of Thy Son and our God upon my passionate soul, and by Thine intercessions guide me unto good works, that I may pass the remaining time of my life without blemish and attain paradise through Thee, O Virgin Theotokos, Who alone art pure and blessed.

Prayer X, to the Holy Guardian Angel:

O angel of Christ, my holy guardian and protector of my soul and body, forgive me all wherein I have sinned this day, and deliver me from all the wickedness of mine enemy against me, lest I anger my God by any sin. Pray for me, a sinful and unworthy servant, that thou mayest show me forth worthy of the kindness and mercy of the All-holy Trinity and of the Mother of my Lord Jesus Christ and of all the saints. Amen.

Kontakion to the Theotokos:

To Thee, the Champion Leader, we Thy servants dedicate a feast of victory and of thanksgiving as ones rescued out of sufferings, O Theotokos; but as Thou art one with might which is invincible, from all dangers that can be do Thou deliver us, that we may cry to Thee: Rejoice, Thou Bride Unwedded!

Most glorious, Ever-Virgin, Mother of Christ

God, present our prayer to Thy Son and our God, that through Thee He may save our souls.

All my hope I place in Thee, O Mother of God: keep me under Thy protection.

O Virgin Theotokos, disdain not me a sinner, needing Thy help and Thy protection, and have mercy on me, for my soul hath hoped in Thee.

My hope is the Father, my refuge is the Son, my protection is the Holy Spirit: O Holy Trinity, glory to Thee.

It is truly meet to bless Thee, the Theotokos, ever-blessed and most blameless, and Mother of our God. More honorable than the Cherubim and beyond compare more glorious than the Seraphim, Who without corruption gavest birth to God the Word, the very Theotokos, Thee do we magnify.

Glory to the Father and to the Son and to the Holy Spirit, both now and ever and unto the ages of ages. Amen.

Lord, have mercy. *Thrice.*

O Lord, bless. *And the dismissal:*

O Lord Jesus Christ, Son of God, for the sake of the prayers of Thy most pure Mother, our holy and God-bearing fathers and all the saints, have mercy on us. Amen.

Prayer of St John of Damascus:
To be said while pointing at thy bed.

O Master, Lover of mankind, is this bed to be my coffin or wilt Thou enlighten my wretched soul with another day? Behold, the coffin lieth before me; behold, death confronteth me. I fear, O Lord, Thy judgment and the endless torments, yet I cease not to do evil. My Lord God, I continually anger Thee and Thy most pure Mother and all the Heavenly Hosts and my holy guardian angel. I know, O Lord, that I am unworthy of Thy love for mankind, but am worthy of every condemnation and torment. But, O Lord, whether I will it or not, save me. For to save a righteous man is no great thing and to have mercy on the pure is nothing wonderful, for they are worthy of Thy mercy. But on me, a sinner, show the wonder of Thy mercy; in this reveal Thy love for mankind, lest my wickedness prevail over Thine ineffable goodness and merciful kindness; and order my life as Thou wilt.

And when about to lie down in bed, say this:

Enlighten mine eyes, O Christ God, lest at any time I sleep unto death, lest at any time mine enemy say: I have prevailed against him.

Glory to the Father and to the Son and to the Holy Spirit.

Be my soul's helper, O God, for I pass through the midst of many snares; deliver me out of them, and save me, O Good One, for Thou art the Lover of mankind.

Both now and ever and unto the ages of ages. Amen.

The most glorious Mother of God, more holy than the holy angels, let us hymn unceasingly with our hearts and mouths, confessing Her to be the Theotokos, for truly She gaveth birth to God incarnate for us and prayeth unceasingly for our souls.

Then kiss thy cross, and make the sign of the cross [with the cross] from the head to the foot of the bed, and likewise from side to side, while saying the:

Prayer to the Honorable Cross:

L et God arise and let His enemies be scattered, and let them that hate Him flee from before His face. As smoke vanisheth so let them vanish; as wax melteth before the fire, so let the demons perish from the presence of them who love God and who sign themselves with the sign of the Cross and say in gladness: Rejoice, most venerable and life-giving Cross of the Lord, for Thou drivest away the demons by the power of our Lord Jesus Christ, Who was crucified on thee, Who went down to hades and trampled on the power of the devil and gave us thee, His venerable Cross, for the driving away of every adversary. O most venerable and life-giving Cross of the Lord, help me together with the holy Lady Virgin Theotokos and with all the saints, unto the ages of ages. Amen.

Or:

Compass me about, O Lord, with the power of Thy precious and life-giving Cross and preserve me from every evil.

Then, instead of asking forgiveness of anyone else:

Remit, pardon, forgive, O God, our offenses, both voluntary and involuntary, in word and deed, in knowledge and ignorance, by day and by night, in mind and thought; forgive us all things, for Thou art good and the Lover of mankind.

Prayer:

O Lord, Lover of mankind, forgive those who hate and wrong us. Do good to those who do good. Grant our brethren and kindred their saving petitions and life eternal; visit the infirm and grant them healing. Guide those at sea. Journey with those who travel. Help Orthodox Christians to struggle. To those who serve and are kind to us grant remission of sins. On those who have charged us, the unworthy, to pray for them, have mercy according to Thy great mercy. Remember, O Lord, our fathers and brethren departed before us, and grant them rest where the light of Thy countenance shall visit them. Remember, O Lord, our brethren in captivity, and deliver them from every misfortune. Remember, O Lord, those who bear fruit and do good works in Thy holy churches, and grant them their saving petitions and life eternal.

Remember also, O Lord, us Thy lowly and sinful and unworthy servants, and enlighten our minds with the light of Thy knowledge, and guide us in the way of Thy commandments; through the intercessions of our most pure Lady, the Theotokos and Ever-Virgin Mary, and of all Thy saints, for blessed art Thou unto the ages of ages. Amen.

Daily Confession of Sins:

I confess to Thee, my Lord God and Creator, to the one Holy Trinity glorified and worshipped, to the Father, Son and Holy Spirit, all my sins which I have committed in all the days of my life and at every hour, at the present time and in the past, day and night, by deed, word, or thought: gluttony, drunkenness, secret eating, idle talking, despondency, indolence, contradiction, disobedience, slandering, condemning, negligence, self-love, acquisitiveness, extortion, lying, dishonesty, mercenariness, jealousy, envy, anger, remembrance of wrongs, hatred, bribery; and by all my senses: sight, hearing, smell, taste, touch; and by the rest of my sins, of the soul together with the bodily, through which I have angered Thee, my God and Creator, and dealt unjustly with my neighbor. Sorrowing for these, I stand guilty before Thee, my God, but I have the will to repent. Only help me, O Lord my God, with tears I humbly entreat Thee. Forgive my past sins through Thy compassion, and absolve from all these which I have said in Thy presence, for Thou art good and the Lover of mankind.

When giving thyself up to sleep, say:

Into Thy hands, O Lord Jesus Christ my God, I commit my spirit. Do Thou bless me, do Thou have mercy on me, and grant me life eternal. Amen.

Sunday Troparia and Kontakia

First Tone:

Troparion: When the stone had been sealed by the Jews, and the soldiers were guarding Thine immaculate Body, Thou didst arise on the third day, O Saviour, granting life unto the world. Wherefore, the Hosts of the heavens cried out to Thee, O Life-giver: Glory to Thy resurrection, O Christ. Glory to Thy kingdom. Glory to Thy dispensation, O only Lover of mankind.

Kontakion: As God, Thou didst arise from the tomb in glory, and Thou didst raise the world together with Thyself. And mortal nature praiseth Thee as God, and death hath vanished. And Adam danceth, O Master, and Eve, now freed from fetters, rejoiceth as she crieth out: Thou art He, O Christ, Who grantest unto all resurrection.

Second Tone:

Troparion: When Thou didst descend unto death, O Life Immortal, then didst Thou slay hades with the lightning of Thy Divinity. And when Thou didst also raise the dead out of the nethermost depths, all the hosts of the heavens cried out: O Life-giver, Christ our God, glory be to Thee.

Kontakion: Thou didst arise from the tomb, O omnipotent Saviour, and hades was terrified on beholding the wonder; and the dead arose, and creation at the sight thereof rejoiceth with Thee. And Adam also is joyful, and the world, O my Saviour, praiseth Thee forever.

Third Tone:

Troparion: Let the heavens be glad; let earthly things rejoice; for the Lord hath wrought might with His arm. He hath trampled down death by death; the firstborn of the dead hath He become. From the belly of hades hath He delivered us and hath granted to the world great mercy.

Kontakion: Thou didst arise today from the tomb, O Merciful One, and didst lead us out of the gates of death. Today Adam danceth and Eve rejoiceth; and together with them both the prophets and the patriarchs unceasingly praise the divine might of Thine authority.

Fourth Tone:

Troparion: Having learned the joyful proclamation of the resurrection from the angel and having cast off the ancestral condemnation, the women disciples of the Lord spake to the apostles exultantly: Death is despoiled and Christ God is risen, granting to the world great mercy.

Kontakion: My Saviour and Redeemer hath, as God, raised up the earthborn from the grave and from their fetters, and He hath broken the gates of hades, and, as Master, hath risen on the third day.

Fifth Tone:

Troparion: Let us, O faithful, praise and worship the Word, Who is co-unoriginate with the Father and the Spirit, and Who was born of the Virgin for our salvation; for He was pleased to ascend the cross in the flesh and to endure death and to raise the dead by His glorious resurrection.

Kontakion: Unto hades, O my Saviour, didst Thou descend, and having broken its gates as One omnipotent, Thou, as Creator, didst raise up the dead together with Thyself; and Thou didst break the sting of death and didst deliver Adam from the curse, O Lover of mankind. Wherefore, we all cry unto Thee: Save us, O Lord.

Sixth Tone:

Troparion: Angelic hosts were above Thy tomb, and they that guarded Thee became as dead. And Mary stood by the grave seeking Thine immaculate Body. Thou didst despoil hades and wast not tempted by it. Thou didst meet the Virgin and didst grant us life. O Thou Who didst rise from the dead, O Lord, glory be to Thee.

Kontakion: Having by His life-bestowing hand raised up all the dead out of the dark abysses, Christ God, the Giver of Life, hath bestowed resurrection upon the fallen human race; for He is the

Saviour of all, the Resurrection and the Life and the God of all.

Seventh Tone:

Troparion: Thou didst destroy death by Thy Cross; Thou didst open paradise to the thief. Thou didst change the lamentation of the myrrh-bearers, and Thou didst command Thine apostles to proclaim that Thou didst arise, O Christ God, and grantest to the world great mercy.

Kontakion: No longer will the dominion of death be able to keep men captive; for Christ hath descended, demolishing and destroying the powers thereof. Hades is bound; the prophets rejoice with one voice, saying: A Saviour hath come for those who have faith. Come forth, ye faithful, for the resurrection.

Eighth Tone:

Troparion: From on high didst Thou descend, O Compassionate One; to burial of three days hast Thou submitted, that Thou mightest free us from our passions. O our Life and Resurrection, O Lord, glory be to Thee.

Kontakion: Having arisen from the tomb, Thou didst raise up the dead and didst resurrect Adam. Eve also danceth at Thy resurrection, and the ends of the world celebrate Thine arising from the dead, O Greatly-merciful One.

Daily Troparia and Kontakia

MONDAY—The Bodiless Hosts: Troparion, Fourth Tone: Supreme commanders of the heavenly hosts, we unworthy ones implore you that by your supplications ye will encircle us with the shelter of the wings of your immaterial glory, and guard us who fall down before you and fervently cry: Deliver us from dangers, since ye are the marshals of the hosts on high.

Kontakion, Second Tone: Supreme commanders of God and ministers of the Divine Glory, guides of men and leaders of the angels, ask for what is to our profit and for great mercy, since ye are the supreme commanders of the bodiless hosts.

TUESDAY—St John the Forerunner: Troparion, Second Tone: The memory of the righteous is celebrated with hymns of praise, but the Lord's testimony is sufficient for thee, O Forerunner; for thou hast proved to be truly even more venerable than the prophets, since thou wast granted to baptize in the running waters Him Whom they proclaimed. Wherefore, having contested for the truth, thou didst rejoice to announce the good tidings even to those in hades: that God hath appeared in the flesh, taking away the sin of the world and granting us great mercy.

Kontakion, Second Tone: O Prophet of God and Forerunner of grace, having obtained thy head from the earth as a most sacred rose, we ever receive healings; for again, as of old in the world, thou preachest repentance.

WEDNESDAY and FRIDAY—the Cross: Troparion, First Tone: Save, O Lord, Thy people, and bless Thine inheritance; grant Thou victory to Orthodox Christians over enemies; and by the power of Thy Cross do Thou preserve Thy commonwealth.

Kontakion, Fourth Tone: O Thou Who wast lifted up willingly on the cross, bestow Thy mercies upon the new community named after Thee, O Christ God; gladden with Thy power the Orthodox Christians, granting them victory over enemies. May they have as Thy help the weapon of peace, the invincible trophy.

THURSDAY—the Holy Apostles and St Nicholas: Troparion to the Apostles, Third Tone: O holy apostles, intercede with the merciful God, that He grant unto our souls forgiveness of offenses.

Troparion to St Nicholas, Fourth Tone: The truth of things revealed thee to thy flock as a rule of faith, an icon of meekness and a teacher of temperance; therefore thou hast achieved the heights by humility, riches by poverty. O Father and Hierarch Nicholas, intercede with Christ God that our souls be saved.

Kontakion to the Holy Apostles, Second Tone: The firm and divine-voiced preachers, the chief of Thy disciples, O Lord, Thou hast taken to Thyself for the enjoyment of Thy blessings and for repose; their labors and death didst Thou accept as above every sacrifice, O Thou Who alone knowest our hearts.

Kontakion to St Nicholas, Third Tone: In Myra, O Saint, thou didst prove to be a minister of things sacred: for having fulfilled the Gospel of Christ, O righteous one, thou didst lay down thy life for thy people and didst save the innocent from death. Wherefore, thou wast sanctified as a great initiate of the grace of God.

SATURDAY—All Saints and the Departed:
Troparion to All Saints, Second Tone: O apostles, martyrs and prophets, hierarchs, monastics and righteous ones; ye who have accomplished a good labor and kept the Faith, who have boldness before the Saviour; O good ones, intercede for us, we pray, that our souls be saved.

Troparion for the Departed, Eighth Tone: O Thou Who by the depth of Thy wisdom, out of love for mankind, dost provide all things and grantest unto all that which is profitable, O only Creator: Grant rest, O Lord, to the souls of Thy servants, for in Thee have they placed their hope, O our Creator and Fashioner and God.

Kontakion for the Departed, Eighth Tone:
With the saints give rest, O Christ, to the souls of
Thy servants, where there is neither sickness, nor
sorrow, nor sighing, but life everlasting.

Kontakion to the Martyrs, Eighth Tone: To
Thee, O Lord, the Planter of creation, the world
doth offer the God-bearing martyrs as the first
fruits of nature. By their intercessions preserve
Thy Church, Thy commonwealth, in profound
peace, through the Theotokos, O Greatly-merciful
One.

Troparia and Kontakia of the Twelve Great Feasts

September 8th
The Nativity of the Most Holy Theotokos
Troparion, Fourth Tone:

Thy nativity, O Theotokos Virgin, hath proclaimed joy to all the world; for from Thee hath dawned the Sun of Righteousness, Christ our God, annulling the curse and bestowing the blessing, abolishing death and granting us life eternal.

Kontakion, Fourth Tone:

Joachim and Anna were freed from the reproach of childlessness and Adam and Eve from the corruption of death by Thy holy nativity, O Immaculate One, which Thy people, redeemed from the guilt of offenses, celebrate by crying to Thee: The barren woman giveth birth to the Theotokos, the nourisher of our life.

September 14th
The Elevation of the Precious and
Life-giving Cross of the Lord
Troparion, First Tone:

S ave, O Lord, Thy people, and bless Thine inheritance; grant Thou unto Orthodox Christians victory over enemies; and by the power of Thy Cross do Thou preserve Thy commonwealth.

Kontakion, Fourth Tone:

O Thou Who wast lifted up willingly on the cross, bestow Thy mercies upon the new community named after Thee, O Christ God; gladden with Thy power the Orthodox Christians; granting them victory over enemies. May they have as Thy help the weapon of peace, the invincible trophy.

November 21st
The Entry of Our Most Holy Lady
Theotokos and Ever-Virgin Mary
into the Temple
Troparion, Fourth Tone:

T oday is the prelude of God's goodwill and the heralding of the salvation of mankind. In the temple of God, the Virgin is presented openly, and She proclaimeth Christ unto all. To Her, then, with a great voice let us cry aloud: Rejoice, O Thou fulfillment of the Creator's dispensation.

Kontakion, Fourth Tone:

The most pure temple of the Saviour, the most precious bridal-chamber and Virgin, the sacred treasury of the glory of God, is on this day brought into the house of the Lord, bringing with Her the grace that is in the Divine Spirit. And the angels of God chant praise unto Her: She is the heavenly tabernacle.

December 25th
The Nativity of Our Lord God and Saviour Jesus Christ
Troparion, Fourth Tone:

Thy Nativity, O Christ our God, hath shined upon the world the light of knowledge; for thereby they who worshipped the stars were taught by a star to worship Thee, the Sun of Righteousness, and to know Thee, the Dayspring from on high. O Lord, glory be to Thee.

Kontakion, Third Tone:

Today the Virgin giveth birth to Him Who is transcendent in essence, and the earth offereth a cave to Him Who is unapproachable. Angels with shepherds give glory; with a star the Magi do journey; for our sake a young Child is born, Who is pre-eternal God.

January 6th
The Theophany of Our Lord God and Saviour Jesus Christ
Troparion, First Tone:

When Thou wast baptized in the Jordan, O Lord, the worship of the Trinity was made manifest; for the voice of the Father bare witness to Thee, calling Thee His beloved Son. And the Spirit in the form of a dove confirmed the certainty of the word. O Christ our God, Who hast appeared and hast enlightened the world, glory be to Thee.

Kontakion, Fourth Tone:

Thou hast appeared today unto the whole world, and Thy light, O Lord, hath been signed upon us who with knowledge chant unto Thee: Thou hast come, Thou hast appeared, O Light Unapproachable.

February 2nd
The Meeting of the Lord
Troparion, First Tone:

Rejoice, Thou Who art full of grace, O Virgin Theotokos, for from Thee hath risen the Sun of Righteousness, Christ our God, enlightening those in darkness. Rejoice, Thou also, O righteous elder, as thou receivest in thine arms the

Redeemer of our souls, Who also granteth unto us the resurrection.

Kontakion, First Tone:

Thou who didst sanctify the Virgin's womb by Thy birth and didst bless Symeon's hands as was meet, by anticipation didst even now save us, O Christ God. But grant peace in the midst of wars unto Thy commonwealth, and strengthen Orthodox Christians whom Thou hast loved, O only Lover of mankind.

March 25th
The Annunciation of the
Most Holy Theotokos
Troparion, Fourth Tone:

Today is the fountainhead of our salvation and the manifestation of the mystery which is from eternity. The Son of God becometh the Virgin's Son, and Gabriel proclaimeth the good tidings of grace; wherefore, we also cry to the Theotokos with him: Rejoice, Thou who art full of grace, the Lord is with Thee.

Kontakion, Eighth Tone:

To Thee, the Champion Leader, we Thy servants dedicate a feast of victory and of thanksgiving as ones rescued out of sufferings,

O Theotokos; but as Thou art one with might which is invincible, from all dangers that can be do Thou deliver us, that we may cry to Thee: Rejoice, Thou Bride Unwedded.

The Sunday before Great and Holy Pascha
The Entry of the Lord into Jerusalem,
Palm Sunday
Troparion, First Tone:

In confirming the common resurrection, O Christ God, Thou didst raise up Lazarus from the dead before Thy Passion. Wherefore, we also, like the children bearing the symbols of victory, cry to Thee, the Vanquisher of death: Hosanna in the highest; blessed is He Who cometh in the name of the Lord.

Another Troparion, Fourth Tone:

As by baptism we were buried with Thee, O Christ our God, so by Thy resurrection we were deemed worthy of immortal life; and praising Thee, we cry: Hosanna in the highest; blessed is He Who cometh in the name of the Lord.

Kontakion, Sixth Tone:

Being borne upon a throne in heaven and upon a colt on the earth, O Christ God, Thou didst accept the praise of the angels and the laudation of the children as they cry to Thee: Blessed is He Who cometh to recall Adam.

Forty days after Great and Holy Pascha
The Ascension of the Lord
Troparion, Fourth Tone:

T hou hast ascended in glory, O Christ our God, having gladdened Thy disciples with the promise of the Holy Spirit; and they were assured by the blessing that Thou art the Son of God, the Redeemer of the world.

Kontakion, Sixth Tone:

W hen Thou didst fulfill Thy dispensation for our sake, uniting things on earth with the heavens, Thou didst ascend in glory, O Christ our God, departing not hence, but remaining inseparable from us, and crying unto those who love Thee: I am with you, and no one shall be against you.

Fifty days after Great and Holy Pascha
Pentecost Sunday
Troparion, Eighth Tone:

B lessed art Thou, O Christ our God, Who hast shown forth the fishermen as supremely wise, by sending down upon them the Holy Spirit and through them didst draw the world into Thy net. O Lover of mankind, glory be to Thee.

Kontakion, Eighth Tone:

O nce, when He descended and confounded the tongues, the Most High divided the nations; and when He distributed the tongues of fire, He called all men into unity; and with one accord we glorify the All-Holy Spirit.

August 6th
The Transfiguration of the Lord
Troparion, Seventh Tone:

T hou wast transfigured on the mountain, O Christ our God, showing to Thy disciples Thy glory as each one could endure; shine forth Thou on us, who are sinners all, Thy light ever-unending, through the prayers of the Theotokos, O Light-giver, glory to Thee.

Kontakion, Seventh Tone:

O n the mount Thou wast transfigured, and Thy disciples, as much as they could bear, beheld Thy glory, O Christ God; so that when they should see Thee crucified, they would know Thy passion to be willing, and would preach to the world that Thou, in truth, art the Effulgence of the Father.

August 15th
The Dormition of The Most Holy Theotokos
Troparion, First Tone:

In giving birth Thou didst preserve Thy virginity; in Thy dormition Thou didst not forsake the world, O Theotokos. Thou wast translated unto life, since Thou art the Mother of Life; and by Thine intercessions dost Thou deliver our souls from death.

Kontakion, Second Tone:

The grave and death could not hold the Theotokos, Who is sleepless in Her intercessions and an unfailing hope in Her mediations. For as the Mother of Life, She was translated unto life by Him Who dwelt in Her ever-virgin womb.

Troparia, Kontakia, Prayers and Stichera from the Triodion

The Sunday of the Publican and the Pharisee
After the Matins Gospel, **Eighth Tone:**

The doors of repentance do Thou open to me, O Giver of life, for my spirit waketh at dawn toward Thy holy temple, bearing a temple of the body all defiled. But in Thy compassion, cleanse it by the loving-kindness of Thy mercy.

Theotokion: Guide me in the paths of salvation, O Theotokos, for I have defiled my soul with shameful sins and have wasted all my life in slothfulness, but by Thine intercessions deliver me from all uncleanness.

Sixth Tone: Have mercy on me, O God, according to Thy great mercy; and according to the multitude of Thy compassions, blot out my transgressions.

When I think of the multitude of evil things I have done, I, a wretched one, I tremble at the fearful day of judgment; but trusting in the mercy of Thy loving-kindness, like David do I cry unto Thee: Have mercy on me, O God, according to Thy great mercy. [*Note: These penitential songs the Church*

*chanteth on the Sunday of the Publican and the
Pharisee and the Sundays thereafter through the
Fifth Sunday of Great Lent.*]

Kontakion, Fourth Tone: Let us flee the brag-
ging of the Pharisee and learn the humility of the
Publican, while crying out unto the Saviour with
groanings: Be gracious unto us, O Thou Who alone
dost readily forgive.

The Sunday of the Prodigal Son

Kontakion, Third Tone: Having foolishly aban-
doned Thy paternal glory, I squandered on vices
the wealth which Thou gavest me. Wherefore,
I cry unto Thee with the voice of the prodigal: I
have sinned before Thee, O compassionate Father.
Receive me as one repentant, and make me as one
of Thy hired servants.

Meat-Fare Saturday

Troparion, Eighth Tone: O Thou, Who by the
depth of Thy wisdom, dost provide all things out of
love for mankind and grantest unto all that which
is profitable, O only Creator: Grant rest, O Lord,
to the souls of Thy servants, for in Thee have they
placed their hope, O our Creator and Fashioner
and God.

Kontakion, Eighth Tone: With the saints give
rest, O Christ, to the souls of Thy servants, where
there is neither sickness, nor sorrow, nor sighing,
but life everlasting.

Meat-Fare Sunday

Kontakion, First Tone: When Thou, O God, shalt come to earth with glory, and all things tremble, and the river of fire floweth before the Judgment Seat and the books are opened, and the hidden things made public, then deliver me from the unquenchable fire and deem me worthy to stand at Thy right hand, O most righteous Judge.

Cheese-Fare Saturday

Troparion, Fourth Tone: O God of our fathers, Who ever dealest with us according to Thy kindness, take not Thy mercy from us, but through their intercessions guide our life in peace.

Kontakion, Eighth Tone: Thou hast made the assembly of the God-bearers illustrious as preachers of piety and silencers of ungodliness, O Lord, and they shine upon the world. By their supplications keep in perfect peace those who glorify and magnify Thee, that they may chant and sing unto Thee: Alleluia.

Cheese-Fare Sunday

Kontakion, Sixth Tone: O Thou guide unto wisdom, bestower of prudence, instructor of the foolish and defender of the poor: Establish and grant understanding unto my heart, O Master. Grant me speech, O Word of the Father; for behold, I shall not keep my lips from crying unto Thee: O Merciful One, have mercy on me who have fallen.

The Prayer of St Ephraim the Syrian:

O Lord and Master of my life, give me not a spirit of idleness, despondency, ambition and idle talking. *Prostration.*

But rather a spirit of chastity, humble-mindedness, patience and love bestow upon me Thy servant. *Prostration.*

Yea, O Lord King, grant me to see my failings and not to condemn my brother; for blessed art Thou unto the ages of ages. Amen. *Prostration.*

O God, cleanse me a sinner. (*Twelve times, with a reverence each time, and then repeat the entire prayer.*)

O Lord and Master of my life. . . . and the rest, with a prostration at the end.

[*Note: This prayer is read at the hours of Wednesday and Friday of Cheese-Fare Week and in all of the Holy Great Lent, except on Saturdays and Sundays.*]

The First Week of Great Lent
Kontakion of the Great Canon, Sixth Tone:

My soul, my soul, arise! Why sleepest thou? The end draweth nigh, and thou shalt be confounded; arouse thyself, then, that Christ God may spare thee, for He is everywhere present and filleth all things.

First Saturday of Great Lent

Troparion, Second Tone: Great are the achievements of faith! In the fountain of flame, as in refreshing water, the holy martyr Theodore rejoiced; for having been made a whole-burnt offering in the fire, he was offered as sweet bread unto the Trinity. By his prayers, O Christ God, save our souls.

Kontakion, Eighth Tone: Having received the Faith of Christ in thy heart as a breastplate, thou didst trample upon the enemy hosts, O great champion; and thou hast been crowned eternally with a heavenly crown, as thou art invincible.

First Sunday of Great Lent

Troparion, Second Tone: We worship Thine immaculate Icon, O Good One, asking the forgiveness of our failings, O Christ God; for of Thine Own will Thou wast well-pleased to ascend the cross in the flesh, that Thou mightest deliver from slavery to the enemy those whom Thou hadst fashioned. Wherefore, we cry to Thee thankfully: Thou didst fill all things with joy, O our Saviour, when Thou camest to save the world.

Kontakion, Eighth Tone: The Uncircumscribable Word of the Father was circumscribed when He took flesh of Thee, O Theotokos; and when He had restored the defiled image to its ancient state, He suffused it with divine beauty. As for us, confessing our salvation, we record it in deed and word.

The Second Sunday of Great Lent

Troparion, Eighth Tone: Light of Orthodoxy, pillar and teacher of the Church, adornment of monastics, invincible champion of theologians, O Gregory, thou wonderworker, boast of Thessalonica, herald of grace, ever pray that our souls be saved.

Kontakion, Eighth Tone: O sacred and divine organ of wisdom, clear trumpet of theology: we praise thee with one accord, O Gregory of divine speech; but as a mind standing before the Primordial Mind, direct our mind to Him, O father, that we may cry: Rejoice, O herald of grace!

Kontakion of the Sunday, Fourth Tone: The season of the virtues hath now been revealed, and judgment is at the doors; therefore let us arise and keep the Fast, offering tears of compunction together with our alms, and let us cry: Our sins are more than the sands of the sea; but do Thou pardon us, O Creator of all, that we may receive incorruptible crowns.

The Third Sunday of Great Lent
The Veneration of the Cross

Troparion, First Tone: Save, O Lord, Thy people, and bless Thine inheritance; grant Thou victory unto Orthodox Christians over enemies; and by the power of Thy Cross do Thou preserve Thy commonwealth.

Kontakion, Fourth Tone: O Thou Who wast

lifted up willingly on the cross, bestow Thy mercies upon the new community named after Thee, O Christ God; gladden with Thy power the Orthodox Christians, granting them victory over enemies. May they have as Thy help the weapon of peace, the invincible trophy.

Another Kontakion, Seventh Tone: No longer doth the flaming sword guard the gate of Eden, for a strange extinction hath come upon it, even the tree of the cross. The sting hath been taken from death and the victory from hades. And Thou, my Saviour, didst appear unto those in hades, saying: Enter ye again into paradise.

The Fourth Sunday of Great Lent
St John of the Ladder

Troparion, Third Tone: Having raised up a sacred ladder by thy words, thou wast shown forth unto all as a teacher of monastics, and thou dost lead us, O John, from the purification that cometh through godly discipline unto the light of divine vision. O righteous father, do thou entreat Christ God that we be granted great mercy.

Kontakion, First Tone: Offering teachings from thy book as ever-blossoming fruits, O wise one, thou dost sweeten the hearts of those who attend to them with vigilance, O blessed one; for it is a ladder that, from earth unto the heavenly and abiding glory, doth lead the souls of those who with faith do honor thee.

The Fifth Saturday of Great Lent
The Laudation of the Theotokos

Troparion, Eighth Tone: When the bodiless one learned the secret command, in haste he came and stood before Joseph's dwelling and spake unto the Maiden Who knew not wedlock: The One Who hath bowed the heavens by His descent is held and contained, unchanging, wholly in Thee. Seeing Him receiving the form of a servant in Thy womb, I stand in awe and cry to Thee: Rejoice, Thou Bride Unwedded!

Kontakion, Eighth Tone: To Thee, the Champion Leader, we Thy servants dedicate a feast of victory and of thanksgiving, as ones rescued out of sufferings, O Theotokos; but as Thou art one with might which is invincible, from all dangers that can be do Thou deliver us, that we may cry to Thee: Rejoice, Thou Bride Unwedded!

The Fifth Sunday of Great Lent
St Mary of Egypt

Troparion, Fifth Tone: Enlightened by the grace of the Cross, thou wast shown forth as a radiant lamp of repentance, dispelling the darkness of the passions, O all-holy one. Wherefore, thou didst appear as an angel in the flesh unto the sacred Zosimas in the wilderness; O Mary, our righteous mother, do thou intercede with Christ for us.

Kontakion, Third Tone: Thou who once of old wast filled with all manner of fornication, art now seen today to be a bride of Christ by thy repentance. Thou didst love and emulate the life of the angels. By the Cross thou didst annihilate the hordes of demons; for this cause thou art a bride now in the kingdom of the heavens, O Mary, thou all-modest one.

Another Kontakion, Fourth Tone: Having escaped the darkness of sin and having illumined thy heart with the light of repentance, O glorious one, thou didst come to Christ and didst offer to Him His immaculate and holy Mother as a merciful intercessor. Hence, thou hast found remission of thy transgressions, and thou ever rejoicest with the angels.

Lazarus Saturday

Troparion, First Tone: In confirming the common resurrection, O Christ God, Thou didst raise up Lazarus from the dead before Thy Passion. Wherefore, we also, like the children bearing the symbols of victory, cry to Thee, the Vanquisher of death: Hosanna in the highest; blessed is He Who cometh in the name of the Lord.

Kontakion, Second Tone: Christ, the Joy of all, the Truth, the Light, the Life, the Resurrection of the world, hath, of His goodness, appeared to those on earth and become the archetype of the resurrection, granting divine forgiveness unto all.

The Entry of the Lord into Jerusalem, Palm Sunday

Troparion, First Tone: In confirming the common resurrection... [*See the Troparion for Lazarus Saturday.*]

Another Troparion, Fourth Tone:
As by baptism we were buried with Thee, O Christ our God, so by Thy resurrection we were deemed worthy of immortal life; and praising Thee, we cry: Hosanna in the highest; blessed is He Who cometh in the name of the Lord.

Kontakion, Sixth Tone: Being borne upon a throne in heaven and upon a colt on the earth, O Christ God, Thou didst accept the praise of the angels and the laudation of the children as they cry to Thee: Blessed is He Who cometh to recall Adam.

Passion Week Troparia and Kontakia

Holy and Great Monday
At Matins:

Troparion, Eighth Tone: Behold, the Bridegroom cometh at midnight, and blessed is that servant whom He shall find watching; but unworthy is he whom He shall find heedless. Beware, therefore, O my soul, lest thou be weighed down with sleep; lest thou be given up to death and be shut out from the kingdom. But rouse thyself and cry: Holy, Holy, Holy art Thou, O God; through the Theotokos, have mercy on us. *Thrice.*

Kontakion, Eighth Tone: Jacob lamented the loss of Joseph, but that noble one was seated in a chariot and honored as a king; for by not being enslaved then to the pleasures of the Egyptian woman, he was glorified by Him Who beholdeth the hearts of men and Who bestoweth an incorruptible crown.

Holy and Great Tuesday
At Matins:

Troparion, Eighth Tone: Behold, the Bridegroom cometh . . . [*See Monday, above.*]

Kontakion, Second Tone: Having realized the hour of the end, O my soul, and having feared at the cutting down of the fig tree, labor with the talent that was given thee, O hapless one, and be watchful and cry: Let us not remain outside the bridal-chamber of Christ.

Holy and Great Wednesday
At Matins:

Troparion, Eighth Tone: Behold, the Bridegroom cometh . . . [*See Monday.*]

Kontakion, Second Tone: Having transgressed more than the harlot, O Good One, I have in no wise brought forth streams of tears for Thee; but in silence I supplicate Thee and fall down before Thee, kissing Thine immaculate feet with love, so that, as Master that Thou art, Thou mayest grant me the forgiveness of debts, as I cry to Thee, O Saviour: From the mire of my deeds do Thou deliver me.

Holy and Great Thursday
At Matins:

Troparion, Eighth Tone: When the glorious disciples were enlightened at the washing of the feet, then Judas the ungodly one was stricken and darkened with the love of silver. And unto the lawless judges did he deliver Thee, the Righteous Judge. Behold, O lover of money, him that for the sake thereof did hang himself; flee from that insatiable soul who dared such things against the Master. O Thou Who art good unto all, Lord, glory be to Thee.

Kontakion, Second Tone: Taking the bread into his hands, the betrayer stretcheth them forth secretly and receiveth the price of Him that, with His Own hands, fashioned man. And Judas, the servant and deceiver, remained incorrigible.

Holy and Great Friday

Troparion, Eighth Tone: When the glorious disciples . . . [See Thursday.]

Kontakion, Eighth Tone: Come, let us all praise Him Who was crucified for us, for Mary beheld Him on the Tree and said: Though Thou endurest the Cross, Thou art My Son and My God.

Holy and Great Saturday

At Vespers and Saturday Matins:

Troparia, Second Tone: The noble Joseph, having taken Thy most pure Body down from the Tree and wrapped It in pure linen and covered It with spices, laid It in a new tomb.

When Thou didst descend unto death, O Life Immortal, then didst Thou slay hades with the lightning of Thy divinity. And when Thou didst also raise the dead out of the nethermost depths, all the Hosts of the heavens cried out: O Life-giver, Christ our God, glory be to Thee.

Unto the myrrh-bearing women did the angel cry out as he stood by the grave: Myrrh is meet for the dead, but Christ hath proved a stranger to corruption.

Kontakion, Second Tone: He that shut up the abyss is seen as one dead, and like a mortal, the Immortal One is wrapped in linen and myrrh and placed in a grave. And women came to anoint Him, weeping bitterly and crying out: This is the most blessed Sabbath day wherein Christ, having slept, shall arise on the third day.

The Hours of
Holy Pascha

If there be a priest: Blessed is our God....

But a layman saith: Through the prayers of our holy fathers, O Lord Jesus Christ our God, have mercy on us. Amen.

Christ is risen from the dead, trampling down death by death, and on those in the tombs bestowing life. *Thrice. Then we chant thrice:*

Having beheld the resurrection of Christ, let us worship the holy Lord Jesus, the only Sinless One. We worship Thy Cross, O Christ, and Thy holy resurrection we hymn and glorify; for Thou art our God, and we know none other beside Thee, we call upon Thy name. O come, all ye faithful, let us worship Christ's holy resurrection, for behold, through the Cross joy hath come to all the world. Ever blessing the Lord, we hymn His resurrection; for, having endured crucifixion, He hath destroyed death by death. *Thrice.*

The Hypakoe, *Eighth Tone, once:*

Forestalling the dawn, the women came with Mary and found the stone rolled away from the sepulcher and heard from the angel: Why seek ye among the dead, as though He were mortal, Him Who liveth in everlasting light? Behold the grave-clothes. Go quickly and proclaim to the world that the Lord is risen and hath slain death, for He is the Son of God Who saveth mankind.

The Kontakion, *Eighth Tone, once:*

Though Thou didst descend into the grave, O Immortal One, yet didst Thou destroy the power of hades and didst arise as victor, O Christ God, calling to the myrrh-bearing women: Rejoice! and giving peace unto Thine apostles: Thou Who dost grant resurrection to the fallen.

And these **Troparia***, once:*

In the grave bodily, but in hades with Thy soul as God; in Paradise with the thief, and on the throne with the Father and the Spirit wast Thou Who fillest all things, O Christ the Inexpressible.

Glory to the Father and to the Son and to the Holy Spirit.

How life-giving, how much more beautiful than Paradise, and truly more resplendent than any royal palace was Thy tomb shown to be, O Christ, the source of our resurrection.

Both now and ever and unto the ages of ages. Amen.

O sanctified and divine tabernacle of the Most High, rejoice! For through Thee, O Theotokos, joy is given to those who cry: Blessed art Thou among women, O All-spotless Lady.

Lord, have mercy. *Forty times.*

Glory to the Father and to the Son and to the Holy Spirit, both now and ever and unto the ages of ages. Amen.

More honorable than the Cherubim and beyond compare more glorious than the Seraphim, Who without corruption gavest birth to God the Word, the very Theotokos, Thee do we magnify.

In the name of the Lord, Father (Master), bless.

Priest: Through the prayers of our holy fathers, O Lord Jesus Christ our God, have mercy on us.

And we say: Amen. *And we chant thrice:* Christ is risen.... Glory, both now.

Lord, have mercy. *Thrice.* Bless.

And the dismissal by the priest.

But a layman saith: O Lord Jesus Christ our God, for the sake of the intercessions of Thy most pure Mother, of our holy and God-bearing fathers and all the saints, have mercy on us. Amen.

Troparia and Kontakia from the Pentecostarion

Friday of Bright Week
The Life-giving Spring

Troparion, Third Tone: As a life-giving fount, Thou didst conceive the Dew that is transcendent in essence, O Virgin Maid, and Thou didst pour forth for us the Immortal Nectar. And as ever-flowing streams from Thy fountain, Thou broughtest forth the Water that springeth up unto life everlasting; wherein, taking delight, we all cry out: Rejoice, O life-bearing fount.

Kontakion, Eighth Tone: From Thine unfailing fount, O Maiden full of grace, Thou dost reward me by pouring forth the unending streams of Thy grace that passeth human understanding. And since Thou didst bear the Word incomprehensibly, I entreat Thee to refresh me with Thy grace divine, that I may cry to Thee: Rejoice, O water of salvation.

Thomas Sunday

Troparion, Seventh Tone: While the tomb was sealed, Thou, O Life, didst shine forth from the grave, O Christ God. And while the doors were shut, Thou didst come unto Thy disciples, O Resurrection of all, renewing, through them, an upright Spirit in us, according to Thy great mercy.

Kontakion, Eighth Tone: With his searching right hand, Thomas didst probe Thy life-bestowing side, O Christ God; for when Thou didst enter while the doors were shut, he cried out unto Thee with the rest of the disciples: Thou art my Lord and my God.

Sunday of the Myrrh-Bearing Women

Troparion, Second Tone: When Thou didst descend unto death, O Life Immortal, then didst Thou slay hades with the lightning of Thy Divinity. And when Thou didst also raise the dead out of the nethermost depths, all the Hosts of the heavens cried out: O Life-giver, Christ our God, glory be to Thee.

The noble Joseph, taking Thine immaculate Body down from the Tree and having wrapped It in pure linen and spices, laid It in a new tomb. But on the third day Thou didst arise, O Lord, granting to the world great mercy.

Unto the myrrh-bearing women did the angel cry out as he stood by the tomb: Myrrh is meet for the dead, but Christ hath proved to be a stranger to corruption; so cry out: The Lord is risen, granting to the world great mercy.

Kontakion, Second Tone: When Thou didst cry, Rejoice, unto the myrrh-bearers, Thou didst make the lamentation of Eve, the first mother, to cease

by Thy resurrection, O Christ God. And Thou didst
bid Thine apostles to preach: The Saviour is risen
from the grave.

Sunday of the Paralytic

Kontakion, Third Tone: As of old Thou didst
raise the paralytic, O Lord, by Thy Divine presence;
raise my soul, which is paralyzed grievously by all
manner of sins and unseemly deeds, that being
saved I may cry out: O compassionate Christ, glory
be to Thy power.

Mid-Pentecost Wednesday

Troparion, Eighth Tone: In the midst of the
Feast, give Thou my thirsty soul to drink of the
waters of piety; for Thou, O Saviour, didst cry out
to all: Whosoever is thirsty, let him come to Me and
drink. Wherefore, O Well-spring of life, Christ our
God, glory be to Thee.

Kontakion, Fourth Tone: In the midst of the
Judaic feast, Thou didst say to those present, O
Christ God, Master and Creator of all: Come ye and
receive the Water of immortality. Wherefore, we
fall down before Thee, crying out in faith and saying: Grant us Thy mercy and compassion; for Thou
art the Well-spring of our life.

Sunday of the Samaritan Woman

Kontakion, Eighth Tone: Having come to the
well in faith, the Samaritan woman saw Thee, the

Water of Wisdom; whereof having drunk abundantly, she, the renowned one, inherited the kingdom on high forever.

Sunday of the Blind Man

Kontakion, Fourth Tone: Blinded in the eyes of my soul, I draw nigh unto Thee, O Christ, like the man blind from his birth, and in repentance I cry to Thee: Thou art the exceeding radiant Light of those in darkness.

The Ascension of the Lord

Troparion, Fourth Tone: Thou hast ascended in glory, O Christ our God, having gladdened Thy disciples with the promise of the Holy Spirit; and they were assured by the blessing that Thou art the Son of God, the Redeemer of the world.

Kontakion, Sixth Tone: When Thou didst fulfill Thy dispensation for our sake, uniting things on earth with the heavens, Thou didst ascend in glory, O Christ our God, departing not hence, but remaining inseparable from us, and crying unto those who love Thee: I am with you, and no one shall be against you.

The Sunday of the Holy Fathers of the First Ecumenical Council

Troparion, Eighth Tone: Most glorified art Thou, O Christ our God, Who hast established our holy fathers as luminous stars upon the earth and through them didst guide us all to the true Faith. O Most-merciful One, glory be to Thee.

Kontakion, Eighth Tone: The preaching of the apostles and the doctrines of the fathers confirmed the one Faith of the Church. And wearing the garment of truth, woven from the theology on high, she rightly divideth and glorifieth the great mystery of piety.

Pentecost Sunday

Troparion, Eighth Tone: Blessed art Thou, O Christ our God, Who hast shown forth the fishermen as supremely wise, by sending down upon them the Holy Spirit and through them didst draw the world into Thy net. O Lover of mankind, glory be to Thee.

Kontakion, Eighth Tone: Once, when He descended and confounded the tongues, the Most High divided the nations; and when He distributed the tongues of fire, He called all men into unity; and with one accord we glorify the All-Holy Spirit.

Sunday of All Saints

Troparion, Fourth Tone: Adorned in the blood of Thy martyrs throughout all the world, as in purple and fine linen, Thy Church, through them doth cry unto Thee, O Christ God: Send down Thy compassions upon Thy people; grant peace to Thy flock and to our souls great mercy.

Kontakion, Eighth Tone: To Thee, the Planter of creation, the world doth offer the God-bearing martyrs as the firstfruits of nature. By their intercessions preserve Thy Church, Thy commonwealth, in profound peace, through the Theotokos, O Greatly-merciful One.

Second Sunday After Pentecost
All Saints of Russia

Troparion, Eighth Tone: As a beautiful fruit of the sowing of Thy salvation, the land of Russia doth offer to Thee, O Lord, all the saints who have shone in her. By their intercessions preserve the Church and our land in profound peace, through the Theotokos, O Greatly-merciful One.

Kontakion, Third Tone: Today the choir of the saints who pleased God in the land of Russia doth stand before us in church and invisibly doth pray for us to God. With them the angels glorify Him, and all the saints of the Church of Christ keep festival with them; and they all pray together for us to the Eternal God.

The Order for Reading Canons and Akathists When Alone

Before beginning any rule of prayer and at its completion, the following reverences are made (prostrations or bows), which is called:

The Seven-Bow Beginning

1. O God, be merciful to me a sinner. *Bow.*

2. O God, cleanse me a sinner and have mercy on me. *Bow.*

3. Thou hast created me, O Lord, have mercy on me. *Bow.*

4. Countless times have I sinned, O Lord, forgive me. *Bow.*

5. My Most Holy Lady Theotokos, save me a sinner. *Bow.*

6. O angel, my holy guardian, protect me from all evil. *Bow.*

7. Holy Apostle (or Martyr, or Holy Father N.), pray to God for me. *Bow.*

Then: Through the prayers of our holy fathers, O Lord Jesus Christ our God, have mercy on us. Amen.

Glory to Thee, our God, glory to Thee.

O Heavenly King; Holy God *(thrice)* ... Glory

... Both now ... O Most Holy Trinity ... Lord, have mercy *(thrice)* ... Glory ... Both now ... Our Father ... Lord, have mercy *(twelve)* ... Glory ... Both now ... O come let us worship *(thrice)* ... Psalm 50 ... "Have mercy on me, O God" ... "I Believe"; *and the reading of the canons and akathists.*

The canons and akathists are read as follows:

A. If one canon or akathist is to be read, it is read straight through.

B. If more than one canon is to be read, the first ode of the first canon is read. If the refrain before the final or last two troparia is "Glory ... Both now," the *Glory* is replaced by the refrain of the canon, and the *Both now* is replaced by "O most holy Theotokos, save us" (this comes before a *Theotokion*, a troparion to the Mother of God). Then the first ode of the second canon is read, beginning with the refrain of the canon (the eirmos being omitted, since the eirmos of the first canon only is read or chanted), etc. *Glory* and *Both now* are used as refrains only before the last two troparia (or the last troparion) of the final canon to be read. Then the third ode of the first canon, beginning with the eirmos, etc. After the third ode: *Lord, have mercy (3), Glory ... Both now,* and the Sessional Hymn(s). When there is more than one canon, the kontakion of the second is read (and any additional ones are read) after the Sessional Hymns, and the *Glory ... Both now* is read before the final two verses, not after *Lord, have mercy,* as given above. Then odes

4, 5, and 6 are read. After the sixth ode: *Lord, have mercy (3), Glory ... Both now,* and the kontakion of the first canon. Then odes 7, 8, and 9 are read.

C. If an akathist is read with the canon(s), it is inserted after the sixth ode. All kontakia of the canon(s) are read after the third ode in this case.

After the ninth ode:

It is truly meet...

Trisagion through Our Father....

Have mercy on us, O Lord, have mercy on us... *and the rest of the Prayers before Sleep.*

If no other prayers are to be read, the closing is as follows:

It is truly meet...

The Prayer(s) following the canon(s).

Trisagion through Our Father...

Lord, have mercy, *thrice.*

Glory ... Both now...

More honorable than the Cherubim....

Through the prayers of our holy fathers, O Lord Jesus Christ our God, have mercy on us. Amen.

Those who are preparing for Holy Communion are obliged to read three canons and one akathist the evening before. Usually read are the *Supplicatory Canons to the Saviour* and *the Mother of God* and the *Canon to the Guardian Angel* (in that order), and either the *Akathist to the Saviour* or *to the Mother of God.* Those who desire to carry out this evening rule of prayer daily receive great spiritual benefit from doing so.

Supplicatory Canon to Our Lord Jesus Christ

Second Tone:

Ode I

Eirmos: In the deep of old the infinite Power overwhelmed Pharaoh's whole army, but the incarnate Word annihilated pernicious sin. Exceedingly glorious is the Lord, for gloriously is He glorified.

Refrain: *O sweetest Jesus, save us.*

Sweetest Jesus Christ, long-suffering Jesus, heal the wounds of my soul, Jesus, and make sweet my heart, O Greatly-merciful One, I pray Thee, Jesus my Saviour, that being saved by Thee, I may magnify Thee.

O sweetest Jesus, save us.

Sweetest Jesus Christ, open to me the door of repentance, O Jesus, Lover of mankind, and accept me, O Jesus my Saviour, as I fall down before Thee and fervently implore the forgiveness of my sins.

O sweetest Jesus, save us.

O sweetest Jesus Christ, Jesus, snatch me from the hand of deceitful Belial, O Jesus, and make me stand at the right hand of Thy glory, O Jesus my Saviour, delivering me from the lot of those on the left.

O Most Holy Theotokos, save us.

Theotokion: O Lady Who gavest birth to Jesus our God, pray for us worthless servants, that by Thy prayers, O Immaculate One, we who are defiled may be delivered from torment, O Spotless One, and enjoy everlasting glory.

Ode III

Eirmos: By establishing me on the rock of faith, Thou hast enlarged my mouth over mine enemies, and my spirit rejoiceth when I sing: There is none holy as our God, and none righteous beside Thee, O Lord.

O sweetest Jesus, save us.

Hearken, O my Jesus, Lover of mankind, unto Thy servant calling with compunction; and deliver me, O Jesus, from condemnation and torment, O only long-suffering sweetest Jesus, plenteous in mercy.

O sweetest Jesus, save us.

Receive Thy servant, O my Jesus, who falleth down with tears, O my Jesus, and save me as one repentant, O my Jesus, delivering me from Gehenna, O Master, sweetest Jesus, plenteous in mercy.

O sweetest Jesus, save us.

O my Jesus, the time Thou gavest me I have squandered in passions, O my Jesus. Reject me not, O my Jesus, but call me, I pray, O Master, sweetest Jesus, and save me.

O Most Holy Theotokos, save us.

Theotokion: O Virgin Who gavest birth to my Jesus, implore Him to deliver me from Gehenna.

Thou alone art the protectress of the afflicted, O Thou Who art full of divine grace. And vouchsafe me the life that ageth not, O All-blameless One.

Lord, have mercy. *Thrice.*

Glory to the Father and to the Son and to the Holy Spirit, both now and ever and unto the ages of ages. Amen.

Sessional Hymn: O Jesus my Saviour, Thou didst save the prodigal. Jesus my Saviour, Thou didst accept the harlot. And now have mercy on me, O Jesus plenteous in mercy; have compassion and save me, O Jesus my Benefactor, as Thou hadst compassion on Manasseh, my Jesus, only Lover of mankind.

Ode IV

Eirmos: From a Virgin didst Thou come, not as an ambassador, nor as an angel, but the very Lord Himself incarnate, and didst save me, the whole man. Wherefore, I cry to Thee: Glory to Thy power, O Lord.

O sweetest Jesus, save us.

Heal, O my Jesus, the wounds of my soul, O my Jesus, I pray, and snatch me from the hand of soul-corrupting Belial, O my compassionate Jesus, and save me.

O sweetest Jesus, save us.

I have sinned, O my sweetest Jesus; O Compassionate One, O my Jesus, save me who flee to Thy protection, O long-suffering Jesus, and vouchsafe me Thy kingdom.

O sweetest Jesus, save us.

No one hath sinned, O my Jesus, as have I, the wretched one; but now I fall down praying: Save me, O my Jesus, and grant me life, O my Jesus.

O Most Holy Theotokos, save us.

Theotokion: O All-hymned One, Who gavest birth to the Lord Jesus, implore Him to deliver from torment all who hymn Thee and call Thee truly the Theotokos.

Ode V

Eirmos: O Thou Who art the Light of those lying in darkness and the salvation of the despairing, O Christ my Saviour, I rise early to pray to Thee, O King of Peace. Enlighten me with Thy radiance, for I know none other God beside Thee.

O sweetest Jesus, save us.

Thou art the light of my mind, O my Jesus; Thou art the salvation of my despairing soul, O Saviour. O my Jesus, do Thou deliver me from torment and Gehenna, as I cry: Save me, the wretched one, O Christ my Jesus.

O sweetest Jesus, save us.

Utterly cast down to shameful passions, O my Jesus, I now cry: Stretch down to me a helping hand, O my Jesus, and pluck me out as I cry: Save me, the wretched one, O Christ my Jesus.

O sweetest Jesus, save us.

Carrying about a mind defiled, I call to Thee, O Jesus: Cleanse me from the dirt of sin, and redeem me who slipped down to the depths of evil through ignorance, and save me, O Saviour my Jesus, I pray.

O Most Holy Theotokos, save us.

Theotokion: O maiden Mother of God, Who gavest birth to Jesus, implore Him to save all Orthodox monastics and laity and to deliver from Gehenna those who cry: Beside Thee we know no certain protection.

Ode VI

Eirmos: Whirled about in the abyss of sin, I appeal to the unfathomable abyss of Thy compassion: From corruption raise me up, O God.

O sweetest Jesus, save us.

O my Jesus Christ plenteous in mercy, accept me who confess my sins, O Master, and save me, O Jesus, and snatch me from corruption, O Jesus.

O sweetest Jesus, save us.

O my Jesus, no one else hath been so prodigal as I, the wretched one, O Jesus, Lover of mankind, but do Thou Thyself save me, O Jesus.

O sweetest Jesus, save us.

O my Jesus, with my passions I have surpassed the harlot and the prodigal, Manasseh and the publican, O my Jesus, and the robber and the Ninevites, O Jesus.

O Most Holy Theotokos, save us.

Theotokion: O Thou Who didst give birth to my Jesus Christ, O Only Undefiled and Immaculate Virgin, cleanse me now, the defiled one, by the hyssop of Thine intercessions.

Ode VII

Eirmos: When the golden image was worshipped in the plain of Dura, Thy three children despised the godless order. Thrown into the fire, they were bedewed and sang: Blessed art Thou, O God of our fathers.

O sweetest Jesus, save us.

O Christ Jesus, no one on earth hath ever sinned, O my Jesus, as I, the wretched one and prodigal, have sinned. Wherefore, I cry to Thee, my Jesus, have compassion on me as I sing: Blessed art Thou, O God of our fathers.

O sweetest Jesus, save us.

O Christ Jesus, I cry: Nail me down with the fear of Thee, O my Jesus, and pilot me to Thy calm haven now, O my compassionate Jesus, that as one saved I may sing to Thee: Blessed art Thou, O God of our fathers.

O sweetest Jesus, save us.

O Christ Jesus, ten thousand times have I, the passionate one, promised Thee repentance, O my Jesus, but wretch that I am, I deceived Thee. Wherefore, I cry to Thee, my Jesus: Enlighten my soul which remaineth unfeeling; O Christ, the God of our fathers, blessed art Thou.

O Most Holy Theotokos, save us.

Theotokion: O Thou Who gavest birth to Jesus awesomely and above nature, O All-blameless One, implore Him, O Maiden, to forgive me all the sins that I have committed against my nature, that as one saved I may cry: Blessed art Thou Who didst give birth to God in the flesh.

Ode VIII

Eirmos: O ye works, praise the Lord God, Who descended into the fiery furnace with the Hebrew children and changed the flame into dew, and supremely exalt Him unto all ages.

O sweetest Jesus, save us.

I implore Thee, O my Jesus: As Thou didst redeem the harlot from many sins, O my Jesus, likewise redeem me, O Christ my Jesus, and cleanse my foul soul, O my Jesus.

O sweetest Jesus, save us.

O Jesus, having yielded to irrational pleasures, I have become irrational, O my Jesus; and wretch that I am, I have truly become like unto the beasts, O my Saviour. Wherefore, O Jesus, deliver me from irrationality.

O sweetest Jesus, save us.

Having fallen, O Jesus, into the hands of soul-corrupting thieves, I have been stripped now of my divinely-woven garment, O my Jesus, and I am lying all bruised with wounds. O my Christ, do Thou pour on me oil and wine.

O Most Holy Theotokos, save us.

Theotokion: O Theotokos Mary, Who ineffably didst carry the Christ, my Jesus and God: Do Thou ever implore Him to save from perils Thy servants and those who praise Thee, O Virgin Who knewest not wedlock.

Ode IX

Eirmos: God the Word, Who came forth from God and Who by ineffable wisdom came to renew Adam after his grievous fall to corruption through eating and Who ineffably took flesh from the holy Virgin for our sake, Him do we the faithful with one accord magnify with hymns.

O sweetest Jesus, save us.

I have surpassed, O my Jesus, Manasseh and the publican, the harlot and the prodigal, O compassionate Jesus, and the robber, O my Jesus, through all my shameful and unseemly deeds, O Jesus; but do Thou forestall me, O my Jesus, and save me.

O sweetest Jesus, save us.

By my passions, O my Jesus, have I, the wretched one, surpassed all those from Adam who have sinned both before the Law and in the Law, O Jesus, and after the Law and Grace, O my Jesus; but by Thy judgments save me, O my Jesus.

O sweetest Jesus, save us.

May I not be parted from Thine ineffable glory, my Jesus, nor may the portion on the left fall to me, O sweetest Jesus; but set me on the right hand with Thy sheep and give me rest, O Christ my Jesus, since Thou art compassionate.

O Most Holy Theotokos, save us.

Theotokion: O Theotokos, Who didst carry Jesus, O Only Unwedded Virgin Mary Who knewest not wedlock, O Pure One, invoke Him, Thy Son and

Creator, to deliver those who hasten to Thee from temptations and perils and the fire that is to come.

Prayer to Our Lord Jesus Christ

O Lord and Master, Jesus Christ my God, Who, for the sake of Thine ineffable love for mankind, at the end of the ages wast wrapped in flesh from the Ever-Virgin Mary, I glorify Thy saving providence and care for me, Thy servant, O Master. I praise Thee, for through Thee I have learned to know the Father; I bless Thee through Whom the Holy Spirit came into the world; I bow to Thy most pure Mother Who served for the dread mystery of Thine incarnation; I praise the angelic choir as the servants and singers of Thy majesty; I bless Saint John the Forerunner who baptized Thee, O Lord; I honor also the prophets who announced Thee; I glorify Thy holy apostles; I celebrate the martyrs; I glorify Thy priests; I venerate Thy saints and praise all Thy righteous ones. This such countless and unutterable divine choir I, Thy servant, in prayer offer to Thee, O All-compassionate God, and therefore I ask the forgiveness of my sins, which do Thou grant me for the sake of all Thy saints, but especially for the sake of Thy holy compassion, for blessed art Thou unto the ages. Amen.

Supplicatory Canon to the Most Holy Theotokos

Troparion, Fourth Tone: To the Theotokos let us run now most earnestly, we sinners all and wretched ones, and fall down in repentance calling from the depths of our souls: O Lady, come unto our aid, have compassion upon us; hasten Thou, for we are lost in a throng of transgressions. Turn not Thy servants away with empty hands, for Thee alone do we have as our only hope. *Twice.*

Glory to the Father and to the Son and to the Holy Spirit, both now and ever and unto the ages of ages. Amen.

Never, O Theotokos, will we cease to speak of Thy powers, unworthy as we are. For if Thou didst not intercede in prayer, who would have delivered us from so many dangers? Who would have kept us free until now? Let us never forsake Thee, O Lady, for Thou dost ever save Thy servants from all perils.

Canon, Eighth Tone:

Ode I

Eirmos: Having passed through the water as on dry land and having escaped the malice of the Egyptians, the Israelites cried aloud: Unto our God and Redeemer let us now sing.

Refrain: *O Most Holy Theotokos, save us.*

Distressed by many temptations, I flee to Thee, seeking salvation. O Mother of the Word and Virgin, from ordeals and afflictions deliver me.

O Most Holy Theotokos, save us.

Outbursts of passions trouble me and fill my soul with great despondency. Calm it, O Maiden, by the peace of Thy Son and God, O All-blameless One.

Glory to the Father and to the Son and to the Holy Spirit.

I implore Thee who gavest birth to the Saviour and God, O Virgin, to deliver me from perils. For, fleeing now unto Thee for refuge, I lift up both my soul and my reasoning.

Both now and ever and unto the ages of ages. Amen.

Ailing as I am in body and soul, do Thou vouchsafe me the divine visitation and Thy care, O Thou Who alone art the Mother of God, for Thou art good and the Mother of the Good.

Ode III

Eirmos: Of the vault of the heavens art Thou, O Lord, the Maker and Builder of the Church; do Thou establish in me love of Thee, O Summit of desire, O Support of the faithful, O only Lover of mankind.

O Most Holy Theotokos, save us.

I have chosen Thee to be the protection and

intercession of my life, O Virgin, Mother of God. Pilot me to Thy haven, O author of blessings, O support of the faithful, O Thou Only All-lauded One.

O Most Holy Theotokos, save us.

I pray Thee, O Virgin, to dispel the tumult of my soul and the storm of my grief; for Thou, O Bride of God, hast given birth to Christ, the Prince of Peace, O Only Immaculate One.

Glory to the Father and to the Son and to the Holy Spirit.

Since Thou broughtest forth Him Who is the Benefactor and Cause of good, from the wealth of Thy loving-kindness do Thou pour forth on all; for Thou canst do all things, since Thou didst bear Christ, the One Who is mighty in power; for blessed of God art Thou.

Both now and ever and unto the ages of ages. Amen.

I am tortured by grievous sicknesses and morbid passions: O Virgin, do Thou help me; for I know Thee to be an inexhaustible treasury of unfailing healing, O All-blameless One.

Lord, have mercy. *Thrice.*

Glory to the Father and to the Son and to the Holy Spirit, both now and ever and unto the ages of ages. Amen.

Sessional Hymn, Second Tone:

O fervent advocate, invincible battlement, fountain of mercy and sheltering retreat for the world, earnestly we cry to Thee: O Lady Theotokos, hasten Thou and save us from all imperilment; for Thou alone art our speedy protectress.

Ode IV

Eirmos: I have heard, O Lord, of the mystery of Thy dispensation, and I came to knowledge of Thy works and glorify Thy Divinity.

O Most Holy Theotokos, save us.

The turmoil of my passions and the storm of my sins do Thou bestill, Thou Who gavest birth to the Lord and Pilot, O Thou Bride of God.

O Most Holy Theotokos, save us.

O bestow on me, Thy supplicant, the abyss of Thy compassion; for Thou didst give birth to the Kind-hearted One and Saviour of all who hymn Thee.

O Most Holy Theotokos, save us.

While delighting in Thy gifts, O Spotless One, we sing a song of thanksgiving to Thee, knowing Thee to be the Mother of God.

Glory to the Father and to the Son and to the Holy Spirit.

As I lie on the bed of my pain and infirmity, do Thou help me, as Thou art a lover of goodness, O Theotokos, Who alone art Ever-Virgin.

Both now and ever and unto the ages of ages. Amen.

Having Thee as our staff and hope and as our salvation's unshaken battlement, from all manner of adversity are we then redeemed, O Thou All-lauded One.

Ode V

Eirmos: Enlighten us by Thy commands, O Lord, and by Thy lofty arm bestow Thy peace upon us, O Lover of mankind.

O Most Holy Theotokos, save us.

Fill my heart with gladness, O Pure One, by giving me Thine incorruptible joy, O Thou Who didst bear the Cause of gladness.

O most holy Theotokos, save us.

Deliver us from dangers, O Pure Theotokos, Who didst give birth to Eternal Redemption and the Peace that doth pass all understanding.

Glory to the Father and to the Son and to the Holy Spirit.

Dispel the darkness of my sins, O Bride of God, by the radiance of Thy splendor, for Thou didst bear the Light Divine and Pre-eternal.

Both now and ever and unto the ages of ages. Amen.

Heal, O Pure One, the infirmity of my soul, when Thou hast deemed me worthy of Thy visitation, and grant me health by Thine intercessions.

Ode VI

Eirmos: I will pour out my prayer unto the Lord, and to Him will I proclaim my grief; for with evils my soul is filled, and my life unto hades hath drawn nigh, and like Jonah I will pray: From corruption raise me up, O God.

O Most Holy Theotokos, save us.

My nature, held by corruption and death, hath He saved from out of death and corruption; for unto death He Himself hath submitted. Wherefore, O Virgin, do Thou intercede with Him Who is Thy Lord and Son, to deliver me from the enemies' wickedness.

O Most Holy Theotokos, save us.

I know Thee as the protection of my life and most safe fortification, O Virgin; disperse the horde of temptations, and drive away demonic vexation; unceasingly I pray to Thee: From corruption of passions deliver me.

Glory to the Father and to the Son and to the Holy Spirit.

We have acquired Thee as a wall of refuge and the perfect salvation of our souls and a relief in afflictions, O Maiden, and we ever rejoice in Thy light. O Sovereign Lady, do Thou also now save us from passions and dangers.

Both now and ever and unto the ages of ages. Amen.

Bedridden, I lie supine with sickness now, and there is no healing for my flesh; but to Thee, O Good One Who gavest birth to God and the Saviour of the world and the Healer of infirmities, I pray: From corruption of illness raise me up.

Kontakion, Sixth Tone:

O protection of Christians that cannot be put to shame, O mediation unto the Creator unfailing: Disdain not the suppliant voices of sinners; but be Thou quick, O Good One, to help us who in faith cry unto Thee: hasten to intercession, and speed Thou to make supplication, Thou who dost ever protect, O Theotokos, those who honor Thee.

Sticheron, same tone:

Entrust me not to human protection, O Most Holy Lady, but receive the supplication of Thy servant; for sorrow hath fettered me, I cannot endure the demon's darts; a shelter have I not, neither place to run, I the wretched one; always I am fleeing and no consolation have I but Thee, O Sovereign Lady of creation, hope and protection of the faithful; turn not away from my supplication, do that which will profit me.

Ode VII

Eirmos: Having gone down to Babylon from Judea, the children of old by their faith in the Trinity trod down the flame of the furnace while chanting: O God of our fathers, blessed art Thou.

O Most Holy Theotokos, save us.

Having willed to accomplish our salvation, O Saviour, Thou didst dwell in the womb of the Virgin and didst show Her to the world as the mediatress; O God of our fathers, blessed art Thou.

O Most Holy Theotokos, save us.

The Dispenser of mercy, Whom Thou didst bear, O Pure Mother, do Thou implore to deliver from transgressions and defilements of the soul those who with faith cry out: O God of our fathers, blessed art Thou.

Glory to the Father and to the Son and to the Holy Spirit.

A treasury of salvation and a fountain of incorruption is She who gave Thee birth; a tower of safety and a door of repentance hast Thou proved Her to those who shout: O God of our fathers, blessed art Thou.

Both now and ever and unto the ages of ages. Amen.

For weakness of body and sickness of soul, O Theotokos, do Thou vouchsafe healing to those who with love draw near to Thy protection, O Virgin, Who for us gavest birth to Christ the Saviour.

Ode VIII

Eirmos: The King of Heaven, Whom hosts of angels hymn, let us praise and supremely exalt unto all ages.

O Most Holy Theotokos, save us.

Disdain not those who need Thy help, O Virgin, and who hymn and supremely exalt Thee unto the ages.

O Most Holy Theotokos, save us.

Thou healest the infirmity of my soul and the pains of my body, O Virgin, that I may glorify Thee,

O Pure One, unto the ages of ages.

Glory to the Father and to the Son and to the Holy Spirit.

Thou pourest forth a wealth of healing on those who with faith hymn Thee, O Virgin, and who supremely exalt Thine ineffable Offspring.

Both now and ever and unto the ages of ages. Amen.

Thou drivest away the assaults of temptations and the attacks of the passions, O Virgin; wherefore do we hymn Thee unto all ages.

Ode IX

Eirmos: Truly we confess Thee to be the Theotokos, we who through Thee have been saved, O Pure Virgin; with the bodiless choirs, Thee do we magnify.

O Most Holy Theotokos, save us.

Turn not away from the torrent of my tears, O Virgin, Thou Who didst give birth to Christ, Who doth wipe away all tears from every face.

O Most Holy Theotokos, save us.

Fill my heart with joy, O Virgin, Thou Who didst receive the fullness of joy and didst banish the grief of sin.

O Most Holy Theotokos, save us.

Be the haven and protection and a wall unshaken, a refuge and shelter and the gladness, O Virgin, of those who flee unto Thee.

Glory to the Father and to the Son and to the Holy Spirit.

Illumine with the rays of Thy light, O Virgin, those who piously confess Thee to be the Theotokos, and do Thou banish away all darkness of ignorance.

Both now and ever and unto the ages of ages. Amen.

Theotokion: In a place of affliction and infirmity am I brought low; O Virgin, do Thou heal me, transforming mine illness into healthfulness.

Prayer to the Most Holy Theotokos:

O my Most Blessed Queen, O Theotokos my hope, guardian of orphans, intercessor for strangers, joy of the sorrowful, protectress of the wronged: Thou seest my misfortune, Thou seest mine affliction; help me, for I am weak; feed me, for I am a stranger. Thou knowest mine offense: absolve it as Thou wilt, for I have no other help beside Thee, no other intercessor, nor good consoler, except Thee, O Mother of God. Do Thou preserve and protect me unto the ages of ages. Amen.

Canon to the Guardian Angel

Troparion, Sixth Tone: O angel of God, my holy guardian, keep my life in the fear of Christ God; strengthen my mind in the true way, and wound my soul with heavenly love, so that, guarded by thee, I may obtain of Christ God great mercy.

Glory to the Father and to the Son and to the Holy Spirit, both now and ever and unto the ages of ages. Amen.

Theotokion: O Holy Lady, Mother of Christ our God, Thou didst inexplicably bear the Creator of all; with my guardian angel entreat always His goodness to save my soul, possessed by passions, and to grant me remission of sins.

Canon, Eighth Tone:
Ode I

Eirmos: Let us sing to the Lord, Who led His people through the Red Sea, for He alone is gloriously glorified.

Refrain: *O Lord Jesus Christ my God, have mercy on me.*

To Jesus: Vouchsafe me, Thy servant, O Saviour, worthily to sing a song and to praise the fleshless angel, my guide and guardian.

Holy angel of the Lord, my guardian, pray to God for me.

Alone I lie in folly and idleness, O my guide and guardian; forsake me not who am perishing.

Glory to the Father and to the Son and to the Holy Spirit.

Direct my mind by thy prayer to fulfill the commands of God, that I may obtain of God forgiveness of sins, and teach me to hate all wickedness, I pray thee.

Both now and ever and unto the ages of ages. Amen.

With my guardian angel, O Virgin, pray for me, Thy servant, to the Gracious One, and teach me to fulfill the commandments of Thy Son and my Creator.

Ode III

Eirmos: Thou art the support of those who flee unto Thee, O Lord, Thou art the light of those in darkness, and my spirit doth hymn Thee.

Refrain: *Holy angel of the Lord, my guardian, pray to God for me.*

All my thoughts and my soul I have committed unto thee, O my guardian; do thou deliver me from all attacks of the enemy.

Holy angel of the Lord, my guardian, pray to God for me.

The enemy troubleth and trampleth on me and teacheth me always to do his will, but do thou, O my guide, forsake me not who am perishing.

Glory to the Father and to the Son and to the Holy Spirit.

Grant me to sing a song with thanksgiving and fervor unto my Creator and God and to thee, my good angel guardian; O my deliverer, rescue me from foes that do me evil.

Both now and ever and unto the ages of ages. Amen.

Theotokion: Heal, O Immaculate One, the most painful wounds of my soul, and drive away the enemies that ever fight against me.

Lord, have mercy. *Thrice.*

Sessional Hymn, Second Tone:

Out of the love of my soul I cry to thee, O guardian of my soul, mine all-holy angel! Protect and guard me always from the hunting of the evil one, and guide me to the heavenly life, teaching and enlightening and strengthening me.

Glory to the Father and to the Son and to the Holy Spirit, both now and ever and unto the ages of ages. Amen.

Theotokion: O Theotokos Unwedded, O Most Pure One Who gavest birth without seed to the Master of all, together with my guardian angel entreat Him to deliver me from all perplexity and to grant my soul compunction and light and cleansing of sins, for Thou alone art quick to help.

Ode IV

Eirmos: I have heard, O Lord, of the mystery of Thy dispensation, and I came to knowledge of Thy works, and I glorify Thy Divinity.

Refrain: *Holy angel of the Lord, my guardian, pray to God for me.*

Pray thou to God, the Lover of mankind, and forsake me not, O my guardian, but ever keep my life in peace and grant me the invincible salvation.

Holy angel of the Lord, my guardian, pray to God for me.

As the defender and guardian of my life I received thee from God, O angel. I pray thee, O holy one, free me from all danger.

Glory to the Father and to the Son and to the Holy Spirit.

Cleanse my defilement by thy holiness, O my guardian, and may I be drawn from the left side by thy prayers and become a partaker of glory.

Both now and ever and unto the ages of ages.

Theotokion: Perplexity confronteth me from the evil surrounding me, O Most Pure One, but deliver me from it speedily, for I flee only to Thee.

Ode V

Eirmos: Awaking at dawn, we cry to Thee: O Lord, save us; for Thou art our God, beside Thee we know none other.

Refrain: *Holy angel of the Lord, my guardian, pray to God for me.*

As one having boldness toward God, O my holy guardian, do thou entreat Him to deliver me from the evils that afflict me.

Holy angel of the Lord, my guardian, pray to God for me.

O radiant light, illumine my soul with radiance, O my guide and guardian given me by God, O angel.

Glory to the Father and to the Son and to the Holy Spirit.

Keep me vigilant who sleep from the evil burden of sin, O angel of God, and raise me up to glorify Him through thy supplication.

Both now and ever and unto the ages of ages. Amen.

Theotokion: O Mary, Lady Theotokos Unwedded, O hope of the faithful, subdue the uprisings of the enemy, and gladden those who hymn Thee.

Ode VI

Eirmos: Grant me a garment of light, O Thou Who coverest Thyself with light as with a garment, O plenteously-merciful Christ our God.

Refrain: *Holy angel of the Lord, my guardian, pray to God for me.*

Free me from every temptation, and save me from sorrow, I pray thee, O holy angel, given to me as my good guardian by God.

Holy angel of the Lord, my guardian, pray to God for me.

Enlighten my mind, O good one, and illumine me, I pray thee, O holy angel, and teach me to think always profitably.

Glory to the Father and to the Son and to the Holy Spirit.

Abolish present disturbance from my heart, and

strengthen me to be vigilant in good, O my guardian, and guide me miraculously to quietness of life.

Both now and ever and unto the ages of ages. Amen.

Theotokion: The Word of God dwelt in Thee, O Theotokos, and showed Thee to men as the heavenly ladder; for by Thee the Most High descended to us.

Kontakion, Fourth Tone:

Show compassion to me, O holy angel of the Lord, my guardian, and leave me not, a defiled one, but illumine me with the light unapproachable, and make me worthy of the heavenly kingdom.

Ekos: Vouchsafe my soul, humiliated by many temptations, the ineffable glory, O holy intercessor and singer with the choirs of the fleshless hosts of God. Have mercy and guard me and illumine my soul with good thoughts, that I may be enriched by thy glory, O my angel; and subdue the enemies who wish me evil, and make me worthy of the heavenly kingdom.

Ode VII

Eirmos: Having gone down to Babylon from Judea, the children of old by their faith in the Trinity trod down the flame of the furnace while chanting: O God of our fathers, blessed art Thou.

Refrain: *Holy angel of the Lord, my guardian, pray to God for me.*

Be merciful to me and entreat God, O angel of the Lord; for I have thee as a defender for the whole of my life, a guide and guardian given me by God forever.

Holy angel of the Lord, my guardian, pray to God for me.

Leave not my wretched soul, which was given thee blameless by God, to be slain by robbers along the way, O holy angel, but guide it to the way of repentance.

Glory to the Father and to the Son and to the Holy Spirit.

My whole soul is disgraced by the evil thoughts and deeds I have brought upon me, but make haste, O my guide, and grant me healing with good thoughts, that I may be inclined always to the right way.

Both now and ever and unto the ages of ages. Amen.

O Wisdom of the Most High Personified, for the sake of the Theotokos, fill with wisdom and divine strength all who faithfully cry: O God of our fathers, blessed art Thou.

Ode VIII

Eirmos: The King of heaven, Whom hosts of angels hymn, let us praise and supremely exalt unto all ages.

Refrain: *Holy angel of the Lord, my guardian, pray to God for me.*

O good angel, sent by God, support me, thy servant, in my life and forsake me not unto the ages.

Holy angel of the Lord, my guardian, pray to God for me.

O most-blessed one, I hymn thee, O good angel, guide and guardian of my soul unto the ages.

Glory to the Father and to the Son and to the Holy Spirit.

Be unto me a protection and fortification in the judgment day of all men, in which all deeds, both good and evil, shall be tried by fire.

Both now and ever and unto the ages of ages. Amen.

Theotokion: Be unto me, Thy servant, a helper and a calmness, O Ever-Virgin Theotokos, and leave me not bereft of Thy protection.

Ode IX

Eirmos: Truly we confess Thee to be the Theotokos, we who through Thee have been saved, O pure Virgin; with the bodiless choirs, Thee do we magnify.

Refrain: *O Lord Jesus Christ my God, have mercy on me.*

Have mercy on me, O my only Saviour, for Thou art merciful and kind-hearted, and make me a member of the choirs of the righteous.

Holy angel of the Lord, my guardian, pray to God for me.

Grant me ever to think and do what is useful, O angel of the Lord, that I may be blameless and strong in infirmity.

Glory to the Father and to the Son and to the Holy Spirit.

As one having boldness toward the Heavenly King, do thou, with the rest of the bodiless ones, entreat Him to have mercy on me the wretched one.

Both now and ever and unto the ages of ages. Amen.

Theotokion: Having great boldness toward Him Who took flesh of Thee, O Virgin, deliver me from fetters, and grant me absolution and salvation through Thine intercessions.

Prayer to the Guardian Angel:

O holy angel, my good guardian and protector! With broken heart and ailing soul I stand before thee entreating: Hearken unto me, thy sinful servant (*Name*); with loud wailing and bitter weeping I cry: Remember not mine iniquity and unrighteousness, through which I, a wretched one, have angered thee every day and hour and have made myself loathsome before our Lord the Creator; show me loving-kindness and leave me not, the defiled, even until mine end. Awaken me from the sleep of sin, and enable me, through thine intercessions, to pass the remaining time of my life without stain and to bring forth fruits worthy of repentance; and above all preserve me from deadly falls into sin, lest I perish in despair and mine enemy rejoice in my ruin. I know truly and confess with my mouth that there is no other friend and intercessor, protector and champion, such as thou, O holy angel; for, standing before the throne of the Lord, thou interceedest for me, the useless and most sinful of all, lest the Most Good One take my soul in the day of my despair and in a day of evil doing. Cease not, therefore, to entreat mercy of my most kind-hearted Lord and God, that He forgive mine offenses, which I have committed throughout all my life, in deed, word and all my senses, and by judgments which He knoweth, that He save me; that He may chasten me here according to His ineffable mercy, but that He may not expose and put me to trial there in accordance with His simple justice; that He may deem me worthy to bring repentance and with penitence to worthily receive Divine Communion; for this above all I make entreaty, and I desire such a gift with all my heart. And in the terrible hour of death, be not far from me, my good guardian, driving away the demons of darkness, who have the power to terrify my trembling soul; defend me from their net, when I shall pass through the aerial tollhouses, in order that, being guarded by thee, I may attain the desired paradise, where the choirs of the saints and the celestial hosts unceasingly praise the all-honorable and majestic name in Trinity of God glorified: the Father, the Son and the Holy Spirit, to Whom is due honor and worship, unto the ages of ages. Amen.

Akathist to Our Sweetest Lord Jesus Christ

Kontakion 1

O Champion Leader and Lord, Vanquisher of hades, I, Thy creature and servant, offer Thee songs of praise, for Thou hast delivered me from eternal death; but as Thou hast unutterable loving-kindness, free me from every danger, as I cry:

Jesus, Son of God, have mercy on me!

Ekos 1

C reator of angels and Lord of hosts, as of old Thou didst open ear and tongue to the deaf and dumb, likewise open now my perplexed mind and tongue to the praise of Thy most holy name, that I may cry to Thee:

Jesus, Most-wonderful, Angels' Astonishment!

Jesus, Most-powerful, Forefathers' Deliverance!

Jesus, Most-sweetest, Patriarchs' Exaltation!

Jesus, Most-glorious, Kings' Stronghold!

Jesus, Most-beloved, Prophets' Fulfillment!

Jesus, Most-marvelous, Martyrs' Strength!

Jesus, Most-peaceful, Monks' Joy!

Jesus, Most-gracious, Presbyters' Sweetness!

Jesus, Most-merciful, Fasters' Abstinence!
Jesus, Most-tender, Saints' Rejoicing!
Jesus, Most-honorable, Virgins' Chastity!
Jesus, Everlasting, Sinners' Salvation!
Jesus, Son of God, have mercy on me!

Kontakion 2

A s when seeing the widow weeping bitterly, O
Lord, Thou wast moved with pity and didst
raise her son from the dead as he was being carried to burial, likewise have pity on me, O Lover of
mankind, and raise my soul, deadened by sins, as
I cry: Alleluia!

Ekos 2

S eeking to understand the incomprehensible,
Philip asked: Lord, show us the Father, and
Thou didst answer him: Have I been so long with
you and yet hast thou not known that I am in the
Father and the Father in Me? Likewise, O Incom-
prehensible One, with fear I cry to Thee:
    Jesus, Eternal God!
    Jesus, All-powerful King!
    Jesus, Long-suffering Master!
    Jesus, All-merciful Saviour!
    Jesus, my Gracious Guardian!
    Jesus, cleanse my sins!
    Jesus, take away mine iniquities!
    Jesus, pardon mine unrighteousness!

Jesus, my Hope, forsake me not!
Jesus, my Helper, reject me not!
Jesus, my Creator, forget me not!
Jesus, my Shepherd, destroy me not!
Jesus, Son of God, have mercy on me!

Kontakion 3

Thou Who didst clothe with power from on high Thine apostles who tarried in Jerusalem, O Jesus, clothe also me, stripped bare of all good works, with the warmth of Thy Holy Spirit, and grant that with love I may sing to Thee: Alleluia!

Ekos 3

In the abundance of Thy mercy, O Jesus, Thou hast called publicans and sinners and infidels. Now disdain me not who am like them, but as precious myrrh accept this song:

Jesus, Invincible Power!
Jesus, Infinite Mercy!
Jesus, Radiant Beauty!
Jesus, Unspeakable Love!
Jesus, Son of the Living God!
Jesus, have mercy on me a sinner!
Jesus, hear me who was conceived in sins!
Jesus, cleanse me who was born in sins!
Jesus, teach me who am worthless!
Jesus, enlighten my darkness!
Jesus, purify me who am unclean!

Jesus, restore me, a prodigal!
Jesus, Son of God, have mercy on me!

Kontakion 4

H aving an interior storm of doubting thoughts, Peter was sinking. But beholding Thee in the flesh walking on the waters, O Jesus, he confessed Thee to be the true God; and receiving the hand of salvation, he cried: Alleluia!

Ekos 4

W hen the blind man heard Thee, O Lord, passing by on the way, he cried: Jesus, Son of David, have mercy on me! And Thou didst call him and open his eyes. Likewise enlighten the spiritual eyes of my heart with Thy love as I cry to Thee and say:

Jesus, Creator of those on high!
Jesus, Redeemer of those below!
Jesus, Vanquisher of the power of hades!
Jesus, Adorner of every creature!
Jesus, Comforter of my soul!
Jesus, Enlightener of my mind!
Jesus, Gladness of my heart!
Jesus, Health of my body!
Jesus, my Saviour, save me!
Jesus, my Light, enlighten me!
Jesus, deliver me from all torments!
Jesus, save me despite mine unworthiness!
Jesus, Son of God, have mercy on me!

Kontakion 5

As of old Thou didst redeem us from the curse of the Law by Thy Divine-flowing Blood, O Jesus, likewise rescue us from the snares in which the serpent hath entangled us through the passions of the flesh, through lustful suggestions and through evil despondency, as we cry unto Thee: Alleluia!

Ekos 5

Having beheld the Creator in human form and knowing Him to be the Master, the Hebrew children hastened to please Him with branches, crying: Hosanna! But we offer Thee a song, saying:

Jesus, True God!

Jesus, Son of David!

Jesus, Most-glorious King!

Jesus, Blameless Lamb!

Jesus, Most-wonderful Shepherd!

Jesus, Guardian of mine infancy!

Jesus, Nourisher of my youth!

Jesus, Praise of mine old age!

Jesus, my Hope at death!

Jesus, my Life after death!

Jesus, my Comfort at Thy judgment!

Jesus, my Desire, put me not then to shame!

Jesus, Son of God, have mercy on me!

Kontakion 6

In fulfillment of the words and message of the God-bearing prophets, O Jesus, Thou didst appear on earth, and Thou Who art uncontainable didst dwell with men and didst take on our infirmities; being healed through Thy wounds, we have learned to sing: Alleluia!

Ekos 6

The light of Thy truth shone upon the world, and demonic delusion was driven away; for the idols have fallen, O our Saviour, unable to endure Thy strength. But we, having received salvation, cry to Thee:

Jesus, the Truth, dispelling falsehood!

Jesus, the Light, above all radiance!

Jesus, the King, surpassing all in strength!

Jesus, God, constant in mercy!

Jesus, Bread of Life, fill me who am hungry!

Jesus, Source of Knowledge, give me to drink who am thirsty!

Jesus, Garment of Gladness, cloth me, the corruptible!

Jesus, Shelter of Joy, cover me, the unworthy!

Jesus, Giver to those who ask, give me sorrow for my sins!

Jesus, Finder of those who seek, find my soul!

Jesus, Opener to those who knock, open my wretched heart!

Jesus, Redeemer of sinners, blot out my
transgressions!
Jesus, Son of God, have mercy on me!

Kontakion 7

Desiring to reveal the mystery hidden from the
ages, Thou wast led as a sheep to the slaughter, O Jesus, and as a lamb before its shearer. But
as God Thou didst rise from the dead and didst
ascend with glory to heaven, and along with Thyself Thou didst raise us who cry: Alleluia! *Thrice.*

Ekos 7

The Creator hath shown us a marvelous Creature, Who was incarnate of a Virgin without
seed, rose from the tomb without breaking the
seal and entered bodily the Apostles' room when
the doors were shut. Wherefore, marveling at this,
we sing:

Jesus, Infinite Word!
Jesus, Inscrutable Word!
Jesus, Incomprehensible Power!
Jesus, Inconceivable Wisdom!
Jesus, Inexpressible Divinity!
Jesus, Boundless Dominion!
Jesus, Invincible Kingdom!
Jesus, Endless Sovereignty!
Jesus, Supreme Strength!
Jesus, Power Eternal!

Jesus, my Creator, have compassion on me!
Jesus, my Saviour, save me!
Jesus, Son of God, have mercy on me!

Kontakion 8

Seeing God wondrously incarnate, let us shun the vain world and set our mind on things divine; for God came down to earth that He might raise to heaven us who cry to Him: Alleluia! *Thrice.*

Ekos 8

The Immeasurable One was below all things, yet in no way separated from things above, when He willingly suffered for our sake, and by His death our death didst put to death, and by His resurrection didst grant life to those who sing:

Jesus, Sweetness of the heart!
Jesus, Strength of the body!
Jesus, Radiance of the soul!
Jesus, Swiftness of the mind!
Jesus, Joy of the conscience!
Jesus, Well-known Hope!
Jesus, Memory before the ages!
Jesus, High Praise!
Jesus, my Supremely-exalted Glory!
Jesus, my Desire, reject me not!
Jesus, my Shepherd, seek me!
Jesus, my Saviour, save me!
Jesus, Son of God, have mercy on me!

Kontakion 9

All the angelic nature of heaven doth glorify unceasingly Thy most holy name, O Jesus, crying: Holy, Holy, Holy! But we sinners on earth with lips of dust cry: Alleluia! *Thrice.*

Ekos 9

We see most eloquent orators voiceless as fish concerning Thee, O Jesus our Saviour; for they are at a loss to say how Thou art perfect man, yet remainest God immutable; but we, marveling at this mystery, cry faithfully:

Jesus, God before the ages!
Jesus, King of kings!
Jesus, Master of rulers!
Jesus, Judge of the living and the dead!
Jesus, Hope of the hopeless!
Jesus, Comfort of those who mourn!
Jesus, Glory of the poor!
Jesus, condemn me not according to my deeds!
Jesus, cleanse me according to Thy mercy!
Jesus, drive from me despondency!
Jesus, enlighten the thoughts of my heart!
Jesus, grant me remembrance of death!
Jesus, Son of God, have mercy on me!

Kontakion 10

Desiring to save the world, O Sunrise of the East, Thou didst come to the dark Occident of our nature and didst humble Thyself even unto death; wherefore, Thy name is supremely exalted above every name, and from all the tribes of heaven and earth Thou dost hear: Alleluia!

Ekos 10

King Eternal, Comforter, true Christ! Cleanse us of every stain, as Thou didst cleanse the ten lepers; and heal us, as Thou didst heal the greedy soul of Zacchaeus the Publican, that we may shout to Thee in compunction, crying aloud:

Jesus, Treasury Incorruptible!

Jesus, Wealth Unfailing!

Jesus, Strong Food!

Jesus, Drink Inexhaustible!

Jesus, Garment of the poor!

Jesus, Protection of widows!

Jesus, Defender of orphans!

Jesus, Help of toilers!

Jesus, Guide of pilgrims!

Jesus, Pilot of voyagers!

Jesus, Calmer of tempests!

Jesus, God, raise me who am fallen!

Jesus, Son of God, have mercy on me!

Kontakion 11

Tenderest songs I, though unworthy, offer to Thee, and like the woman of Canaan, I cry unto Thee: O Jesus, have mercy on me!, for it is not a daughter, but my flesh cruelly possessed with passions and burning with fury. So grant healing to me who cry unto Thee: Alleluia.

Ekos 11

Having previously persecuted Thee, the Light-bestowing Lamp of those in the darkness of ignorance, Paul heeded the power of the voice of Divine enlightenment and understood the swiftness of the soul's conversion; thus also do Thou enlighten the dark eye of my soul, as I cry:

Jesus, my Most-mighty King!

Jesus, my Most-powerful God!

Jesus, my Immortal Lord!

Jesus, my Most-glorious Creator!

Jesus, my Most-kind Guide!

Jesus, my Most-compassionate Shepherd!

Jesus, my Most-merciful Master!

Jesus, my Most-gracious Saviour!

Jesus, enlighten my senses darkened by passions!

Jesus, heal my body scabbed with sins!

Jesus, cleanse my mind of vain thoughts!

Jesus, keep my heart from evil desires!

Jesus, Son of God, have mercy on me!

Kontakion 12

Grant me Thy grace, O Jesus, Absolver of all debts, and receive me who am repenting, as Thou didst receive Peter who denied Thee, and call me who am downcast, as of old Thou didst call Paul who persecuted Thee, and hear me crying to Thee: Alleluia! *Thrice.*

Ekos 12

Praising Thine incarnation, we all extol Thee, and we believe with Thomas that Thou art Lord and God, sitting with the Father and coming to judge the living and the dead. Vouchsafe me then to stand on Thy right hand, who now cry:

Jesus, King before the ages, have mercy on me!

Jesus, Sweet-scented Flower, make me fragrant!

Jesus, Beloved Warmth, make me fervent!

Jesus, Eternal Temple, shelter me!

Jesus, Garment of Light, adorn me!

Jesus, Pearl of Great Price, irradiate me!

Jesus, Precious Stone, illumine me!

Jesus, Sun of Righteousness, shine on me!

Jesus, Holy Light, make me radiant!

Jesus, from sickness of soul and body deliver me!

Jesus, from the hands of the adversary rescue me!

Jesus, from the unquenchable fire and other

eternal torments save me!
Jesus, Son of God, have mercy on me!

Kontakion 13

O most-sweet and all-compassionate Jesus!
Receive now this our small supplication, as
Thou didst receive the widow's two mites, and keep
Thine inheritance from all enemies, visible and
invisible, from foreign invasion, from disease and
famine, from all tribulations and mortal wounds,
and rescue from the torment to come all who cry to
Thee: Alleluia! *This kontakion we say thrice. Then:*

Ekos 1

C reator of angels and Lord of hosts, as of old
Thou didst open ear and tongue to the deaf
and dumb, likewise open now my perplexed mind
and tongue to the praise of Thy most holy name,
that I may cry to Thee:

Jesus, Most-wonderful, Angels' Astonishment!
Jesus, Most-powerful, Forefathers'
    Deliverance!
Jesus, Most-sweet, Patriarchs' Exaltation!
Jesus, Most-glorious, Kings' Stronghold!
Jesus, Most-beloved, Prophets' Fulfillment!
Jesus, Most-marvelous, Martyrs' Strength!
Jesus, Most-peaceful, Monks' Joy!
Jesus, Most-gracious, Presbyters' Sweetness!
Jesus, Most-merciful, Fasters' Abstinence!

Jesus, Most-tender, Saints' Rejoicing!
Jesus, Most-honorable, Virgins' Chastity!
Jesus, Everlasting, Sinners' Salvation!
Jesus, Son of God, have mercy on me!

Kontakion 1

O Champion Leader and Lord, Vanquisher of hades, I, Thy creature and servant, offer Thee songs of praise, for Thou hast delivered me from eternal death; but as Thou hast unutterable loving-kindness, free me from every danger, as I cry:

Jesus, Son of God, have mercy on me!

Prayer to Our Lord Jesus Christ:

To Thee, O Lord, the only Good One, Who rememberest not evils, I confess my sins; I fall down before Thee, unworthy that I am, crying out: I have sinned, O Lord, I have sinned, and I am not worthy to look upon the height of heaven for the multitude of mine iniquities. But, my Lord, O Lord, grant me tears of compunction, Thou Who alone art good and merciful, so that with them I may entreat Thee to cleanse me of all sin before the end; for frightful and terrible is the place that I must pass through when I have separated from this body, and a multitude of dark and inhuman demons awaiteth me, and there is no one to come to my help or to deliver me; wherefore, I fall down before Thy goodness: Deliver me not up to those who wrong me, nor let mine enemies triumph over me, O Good Lord, nor let them say: Thou hast come into our hands, and thou hast been delivered unto us. Neither, O Lord, forget Thy compassions, and render not unto me according to mine iniquities, and turn not Thy countenance away from me; but do Thou, O Lord, chasten me, but with mercy and compassion, and let not mine enemy rejoice over me, but quench his threatening against me, and bring to nought all his deeds. And grant me an unsullied way to Thee, O Good Lord, because, having sinned, I have not had recourse to any other physician, and have not stretched out my hands to a strange god. Therefore, reject not my supplication, but hearken unto me in Thy goodness, and strengthen my heart in Thy fear; and let Thy grace be upon me, O Lord, like a fire consuming the impure thoughts within me. For Thou, O Lord, art the Light above all lights, the Joy above all joys, the Repose above all repose, the True Life and the Salvation that abideth unto the ages of ages. Amen.

Akathist to Our Most Holy Lady the Theotokos

Kontakion 1

To Thee, the Champion Leader, we Thy servants dedicate a feast of victory and of thanksgiving as ones rescued out of sufferings, O Theotokos; but as Thou art one with might which is invincible, from all dangers that can be do Thou deliver us, that we may cry to Thee:

Rejoice, Thou Bride Unwedded!

Ekos 1

An archangel was sent from heaven to say to the Theotokos: Rejoice! And beholding Thee, O Lord, taking bodily form, he was amazed and with his bodiless voice he stood crying to Her such things as these:

Rejoice, Thou through Whom joy will shine forth!

Rejoice, Thou through Whom the curse will cease!

Rejoice, recall of fallen Adam!

Rejoice, redemption of the tears of Eve!

Rejoice, height inaccessible to human thought!

Rejoice, depth indiscernible even for the eyes of angels!

Rejoice, for Thou art the King's throne!

Rejoice, for Thou bearest Him Who beareth all!

Rejoice, star that causest the Sun to appear!

Rejoice, womb of the Divine Incarnation!

Rejoice, Thou through Whom creation is renewed!

Rejoice, Thou through Whom we worship the Creator!

Rejoice, Thou Bride Unwedded!

Kontakion 2

Seeing Herself to be chaste, the holy one said boldly to Gabriel: The marvel of thy speech is difficult for My soul to accept. How canst thou speak of a birth from a seedless conception? And She cried: Alleluia.

Ekos 2

Seeking to know knowledge that cannot be known, the Virgin cried to the ministering one: Tell Me, how can a son be born from a chaste womb? Then he spake to Her in fear, only crying aloud thus:

Rejoice, initiate of God's ineffable will!

Rejoice, assurance of those who pray in silence!

Rejoice, beginning of Christ's miracles!

Rejoice, crown of His dogmas!

Rejoice, heavenly ladder by which God came down!

Rejoice, bridge that conveyest us from earth to
   heaven!
Rejoice, wonder of angels sounded abroad!
Rejoice, wound of demons bewailed afar!
Rejoice, Thou Who ineffably gavest birth to the
   Light!
Rejoice, Thou Who didst reveal Thy secret to
   none!
Rejoice, Thou Who surpassest the knowledge
   of the wise!
Rejoice, Thou Who givest light to the minds of
   the faithful!
Rejoice, Thou Bride Unwedded!

Kontakion 3

The power of the Most High then overshadowed
the Virgin for conception and showed Her
fruitful womb as a sweet meadow to all who
wish to reap salvation, as they sing: Alleluia!

Ekos 3

Having received God into Her womb, the Virgin
hastened to Elizabeth whose unborn babe at
once recognized Her embrace, rejoiced, and with
leaps of joy as songs, cried to the Theotokos:
   Rejoice, branch of an Unfading Sprout!
   Rejoice, acquisition of Immortal Fruit!
   Rejoice, laborer Who laborest for the Lover of
      mankind!

Rejoice, Thou Who gavest birth to the Planter
of our life!

Rejoice, cornland yielding a rich crop of
mercies!

Rejoice, table bearing a wealth of forgiveness!

Rejoice, Thou Who makest to bloom the garden
of delight!

Rejoice, Thou Who preparest a haven for souls!

Rejoice, acceptable incense of intercession!

Rejoice, propitiation of all the world!

Rejoice, goodwill of God to mortals!

Rejoice, boldness of mortals before God!

Rejoice, Thou Bride Unwedded!

Kontakion 4

Having within, a tempest of doubting thoughts,
the chaste Joseph was troubled. For knowing
Thee to have no husband, he suspected a secret
union, O Blameless One. But having learned that
Thy conception was of the Holy Spirit, he said:
Alleluia!

Ekos 4

While the angels were chanting, the shepherds heard of Christ's coming in the flesh,
and having run to the Shepherd, they beheld Him
as a blameless Lamb that had been pastured in
Mary's womb, and singing to Her they cried:

Rejoice, Mother of the Lamb and the Shepherd!

Rejoice, fold of rational sheep!

Rejoice, torment of invisible enemies!

Rejoice, opening of the gates of paradise!

Rejoice, for the things of heaven rejoice with the earth!

Rejoice, for the things of earth join chorus with the heavens!

Rejoice, never-silent mouth of the apostles!

Rejoice, invincible courage of the passion-bearers!

Rejoice, firm support of faith!

Rejoice, radiant token of grace!

Rejoice, Thou through Whom hades was stripped bare!

Rejoice, Thou through Whom we are clothed with glory!

Rejoice, Thou Bride Unwedded!

Kontakion 5

Having sighted the divinely-moving star, the Magi followed its radiance; and holding it as a lamp, by it they sought a powerful King; and having reached the Unreachable One, they rejoiced, shouting to Him: Alleluia!

Ekos 5

The sons of the Chaldees saw in the hands of the Virgin Him Who with His hand made man. And knowing Him to be the Master, even though

He had taken the form of a servant, they hastened to serve Him with gifts and to cry to Her Who is blessed:

Rejoice, Mother of the Unsetting Star!

Rejoice, dawn of the mystic day!

Rejoice, Thou Who didst extinguish the furnace of error!

Rejoice, Thou Who didst enlighten the initiates of the Trinity!

Rejoice, Thou Who didst banish from power the inhuman tyrant!

Rejoice, Thou Who didst show us Christ the Lord, the Lover of mankind!

Rejoice, Thou Who redeemest from pagan worship!

Rejoice, Thou Who dost drag us from the works of mire!

Rejoice, Thou Who didst quench the worship of fire!

Rejoice, Thou Who rescuest from the flame of the passions!

Rejoice, guide of the faithful to chastity!

Rejoice, gladness of all generations!

Rejoice, Thou Bride Unwedded!

Kontakion 6

Having become God-bearing heralds, the Magi returned to Babylon, having fulfilled Thy prophecy; and having preached Thee to all as the

Christ, they left Herod as a babbler who knew not how to sing: Alleluia!

Ekos 6

By shining in Egypt the light of truth, Thou didst dispel the darkness of falsehood; for its idols fell, O Saviour, unable to endure Thy strength; and those who were delivered from them cried to the Theotokos:

Rejoice, uplifting of men!

Rejoice, downfall of demons!

Rejoice, Thou Who didst trample down the dominion of delusion!

Rejoice, Thou Who didst unmask the fraud of idols!

Rejoice, sea that didst drown the Pharaoh of the mind!

Rejoice, rock that dost refresh those thirsting for life!

Rejoice, pillar of fire that guidest those in darkness!

Rejoice, shelter of the world broader than a cloud!

Rejoice, sustenance replacing manna!

Rejoice, minister of holy delight!

Rejoice, land of promise!

Rejoice, Thou from Whom floweth milk and honey!

Rejoice, Thou Bride Unwedded!

Kontakion 7

When Symeon was about to depart this age of delusion, Thou wast brought as a Babe to him, but Thou wast recognized by him as perfect God also; wherefore, marveling at Thine ineffable wisdom, he cried: Alleluia!

Ekos 7

The Creator showed us a new creation when He appeared to us who come from Him. For He sprang from a seedless womb and kept it incorrupt as it was, that seeing the miracle we might sing to Her, crying out:

Rejoice, flower of incorruptibility!

Rejoice, crown of continence!

Rejoice, Thou from Whom shineth the Archetype of the resurrection!

Rejoice, Thou Who revealest the life of the angels!

Rejoice, tree of shining fruit whereby the faithful are nourished!

Rejoice, tree of goodly shade by which many are sheltered!

Rejoice, Thou Who hast carried in Thy womb the Redeemer of captives!

Rejoice, Thou Who gavest birth to the Guide of those astray!

Rejoice, supplication before the Righteous Judge!

Rejoice, forgiveness of many sins!
Rejoice, robe of boldness for the naked!
Rejoice, love that vanquishest all desire!
Rejoice, Thou Bride Unwedded!

Kontakion 8

Having beheld a strange nativity, let us estrange ourselves from the world and transport our minds to heaven; for the Most High God appeared on earth as a lowly man, because He wished to draw to the heights those who cry to Him: Alleluia!

Ekos 8

Wholly present was the Inexpressible Word among those here below, yet in no way absent from those on high; for this was a divine condescension and not a change of place, and His birth was from a God-receiving Virgin Who heard these things:

Rejoice, container of the Uncontainable God!
Rejoice, door of solemn mystery!
Rejoice, report doubtful to unbelievers!
Rejoice, undoubted boast of the faithful!
Rejoice, all-holy chariot of Him Who sitteth upon the Cherubim!
Rejoice, all-glorious temple of Him Who is above the Seraphim!
Rejoice, Thou Who hast united opposites!

Rejoice, Thou Who hast joined virginity and
   motherhood!

Rejoice, Thou through Whom transgression
   hath been absolved!

Rejoice, Thou through Whom paradise is
   opened!

Rejoice, key to the kingdom of Christ!

Rejoice, hope of eternal good things!

Rejoice, Thou Bride Unwedded!

Kontakion 9

All the angels were amazed at the great act of
Thine incarnation; for they saw the Unapproachable God as a man approachable to all,
abid-ing with us and hearing from all: Alleluia!

Ekos 9

We see most eloquent orators mute as fish
before Thee, O Theotokos, for they are at
a loss to tell how Thou remainest a Virgin and
couldst bear a child. But we, marveling at this mystery, cry out faithfully:

Rejoice, receptacle of the Wisdom of God!

Rejoice, treasury of His Providence!

Rejoice, Thou Who showest philosophers to be
   fools!

Rejoice, Thou Who exposest the learned as
   irrational!

Rejoice, for the clever critics have become
   foolish!

Rejoice, for the writers of myths have faded
away!

Rejoice, Thou Who didst rend the webs of the
Athenians!

Rejoice, Thou Who didst fill the nets of the
fishermen!

Rejoice, Thou Who drawest us from the depths
of ignorance!

Rejoice, Thou Who enlightenest many with
knowledge!

Rejoice, ship for those who wish to be saved!

Rejoice, harbor for sailors on the sea of life!

Rejoice, Thou Bride Unwedded!

Kontakion 10

Desiring to save the world, He Who is the Creator of all came to it according to His Own
promise, and He Who, as God, is the Shepherd, for
our sake appeared unto us as a man; for, like calling unto like, as God He heareth: Alleluia!

Ekos 10

A bulwark art Thou to virgins and to all who flee
unto Thee, O Virgin Theotokos; for the Maker
of heaven and earth prepared Thee, O Most Pure
One, dwelt in Thy womb and taught all to call to
Thee:

Rejoice, pillar of virginity!

Rejoice, gate of salvation!

Rejoice, leader of mental formation!

Rejoice, bestower of divine good!

Rejoice, for Thou didst renew those conceived in shame!

Rejoice, for Thou gavest understanding to those robbed of their minds!

Rejoice, Thou Who didst foil the corrupter of minds!

Rejoice, Thou Who gavest birth to the Sower of purity!

Rejoice, bridechamber of a seedless marriage!

Rejoice, Thou Who dost wed the faithful to the Lord!

Rejoice, good nourisher of virgins!

Rejoice, adorner of holy souls as for marriage!

Rejoice, Thou Bride Unwedded!

Kontakion 11

Every hymn is defeated that trieth to encompass the multitude of Thy many compassions; for if we offer to Thee, O Holy King, songs equal in number to the sand, nothing have we done worthy of that which Thou hast given us who shout to Thee: Alleluia!

Ekos 11

We behold the Holy Virgin, a shining lamp appearing to those in darkness; for, kindling the Immaterial Light, She guideth all to divine

knowledge, She illumineth minds with radiance
and is honored by our shouting these things:

Rejoice, ray of the noetic Sun!

Rejoice, radiance of the Unsetting Light!

Rejoice, lightning that enlightenest our souls!

Rejoice, thunder that terrifiest our enemies!

Rejoice, for Thou didst cause the Refulgent
Light to dawn!

Rejoice, for Thou didst cause the river of many
streams to gush forth!

Rejoice, Thou Who paintest the image of the
font!

Rejoice, Thou Who blottest out the stain of sin!

Rejoice, laver that washest the conscience
clean!

Rejoice, cup that drawest up joy!

Rejoice, aroma of the sweet fragrance of
Christ!

Rejoice, life of mystical gladness!

Rejoice, Thou Bride Unwedded!

Kontakion 12

When the Absolver of all mankind desired to
blot out ancient debts, of His Own will He
came to dwell among those who had fallen from
His grace; and having torn up the handwriting of
their sins, He heareth this from all: Alleluia!

Ekos 12

While singing to Thine Offspring, we all praise Thee as a living temple, O Theotokos; for the Lord Who holdeth all things in His hand dwelt in Thy womb, and He sanctified and glorified Thee and taught all to cry to Thee:

Rejoice, tabernacle of God the Word!
Rejoice, saint greater than the saints!
Rejoice, ark gilded by the Spirit!
Rejoice, inexhaustible treasury of life!
Rejoice, precious diadem of pious kings!
Rejoice, venerable boast of reverent priests!
Rejoice, unshakable fortress of the Church!
Rejoice, inviolable wall of the kingdom!
Rejoice, Thou through Whom victories are obtained!
Rejoice, Thou through Whom foes fall prostrate!
Rejoice, healing of my flesh!
Rejoice, salvation of my soul!
Rejoice, Thou Bride Unwedded!

Kontakion 13

O All-praised Mother Who didst bear the Word holiest of all the saints, accept now our offering, and deliver us from all misfortune, and rescue from the torment to come those who cry to Thee: Alleluia! *This kontakion we say thrice. Then:*

Ekos 1

An archangel was sent from heaven to say to the Theotokos: Rejoice! And beholding Thee, O Lord, taking bodily form, he was amazed and with his bodiless voice he stood crying to Her such things as these:

Rejoice, Thou through Whom joy will shine forth!

Rejoice, Thou through Whom the curse will cease!

Rejoice, recall of fallen Adam!

Rejoice, redemption of the tears of Eve!

Rejoice, height inaccessible to human thought!

Rejoice, depth indiscernible even for the eyes of angels!

Rejoice, for Thou art the King's throne!

Rejoice, for Thou bearest Him Who beareth all!

Rejoice, star that causest the Sun to appear!

Rejoice, womb of the Divine Incarnation!

Rejoice, Thou through Whom creation is renewed!

Rejoice, Thou through Whom we worship the Creator!

Rejoice, Thou Bride Unwedded!

Kontakion 1

To Thee, the Champion Leader, we Thy servants dedicate a feast of victory and of thanksgiving as ones rescued out of sufferings, O Theotokos;

but as Thou art one with might which is invincible, from all dangers that can be do Thou deliver us, that we may cry to Thee:

Rejoice, Thou Bride Unwedded!

Prayer to the Most Holy Theotokos:

O Most Holy Sovereign Lady Theotokos! Higher art Thou than all the angels and archangels and more honorable than all creation, a helper of the wronged art Thou, the hope of the hopeless, an intercessor for the poor, the consolation of the sorrowful, a nourisher of the hungry, a robe for the naked, healing for the sick, the salvation of sinners, the help and protection of all Christians. O All-merciful Sovereign Lady Virgin Theotokos! Through Thy mercy save and have mercy on the most holy Orthodox patriarchs, the most holy metropolitans, archbishops and bishops, and all the priestly and monastic orders, the military leaders, civic leaders and Christ-loving armed forces, and well-wishers and all Orthodox Christians do Thou defend by Thy precious omophorion and entreat, O Lady, Christ our God, Who was incarnate of Thee without seed, that He gird us with His power from on high against our enemies, visible and invisible, O All-merciful Sovereign Lady Theotokos! Raise us up out of the depths of sin, and deliver us from famine and destruction, from earthquake and flood, from fire and the sword, from invasion of aliens and civil war, and from sudden death and from noxious winds and from death-bearing plagues and from all evil. Grant, O Lady, peace and health to Thy servants, all Orthodox Christians, and enlighten their minds and the eyes of their hearts unto salvation; and vouchsafe unto us, Thy sinful servants, the kingdom of Thy Son, Christ our God: for blessed and most-glorified is His dominion, together with His unoriginate Father and His Most-holy and good and life-creating Spirit, now and ever and unto the ages of ages. Amen.

Canon of Repentance to Our Lord Jesus Christ

Sixth Tone. Ode I

Eirmos: When Israel walked on foot in the deep as on dry land, on seeing their pursuer Pharaoh drowned, they cried: Let us sing to God a song of victory.

Have mercy on me, O God, have mercy on me.

Now I, a burdened sinner, have approached Thee, my Lord and God. But I dare not raise mine eyes to heaven. I only pray, saying: Give me, O Lord, understanding, that I may weep bitterly over my deeds.

Have mercy on me, O God, have mercy on me.

O woe is me, a sinner! Wretched am I above all men. There is no repentance in me. Give me, O Lord, tears that I may weep bitterly over my deeds.

Glory to the Father and to the Son and to the Holy Spirit.

Foolish, wretched man, thou art wasting thy time in idleness! Think of thy life and turn to the Lord God, and weep bitterly over thy deeds.

Both now and ever and unto the ages of ages. Amen.

Theotokion: O Most Pure Mother of God, look upon me a sinner, and deliver me from the snares of the devil, and guide me to the way of repentance, that I may weep bitterly over my deeds.

Ode III

Eirmos: There is none holy as Thou, O Lord my God, Who hast exalted the horn of Thy faithful, O Good One, and hast established us upon the rock of Thy confession.

Have mercy on me, O God, have mercy on me.

When the thrones will be set at the dread judgment, then the deeds of all men shall be laid bare. There will be woe for sinners being sent to torment! And knowing that, my soul, repent of thine evil deeds.

Have mercy on me, O God, have mercy on me.

The righteous shall rejoice, but the sinners will weep. Then no one will be able to help us, but our deeds will condemn us. Wherefore, before the end, repent of thine evil deeds.

Glory to the Father and to the Son and to the Holy Spirit.

Alas for me, a great sinner, who have defiled myself by my deeds and thoughts. Not a teardrop do I have, because of my hardheartedness. But now, rise from the earth, my soul, and repent of thine evil deeds.

Both now and ever and unto the ages of ages. Amen.

Theotokion: Behold, Thy Son calleth, O Lady, and directeth us to what is good, yet I, a sinner, always flee from the good. But do Thou, O Merciful One, have mercy on me, that I may repent of mine evil deeds.

Lord, have mercy. *Thrice.*

Sessional Hymn, Sixth Tone:

I think of the terrible day and weep over mine evil deeds. How shall I answer the Immortal King? With what boldness shall I, a prodigal, look at the Judge? O compassionate Father, O Only-begotten Son and Holy Spirit, have mercy on me.

Glory to the Father and to the Son and to the Holy Spirit, both now and ever and unto the ages of ages. Amen.

Theotokion: Bound now with many fetters of sins and held fast by cruel passions, I flee unto Thee, my salvation, and cry aloud: Help me, O Virgin Mother of God.

Ode IV

Eirmos: Christ is my power, my God and my Lord, doth the august Church sing in godly fashion, and she doth cry out with a pure mind, keeping festival in the Lord.

Have mercy on me, O God, have mercy on me.

Broad is the way here and convenient for indulging in pleasures, but how bitter it will be on the last day when the soul is separated from the body! Beware of these things, O man, for the sake of the kingdom of God.

Have mercy on me, O God, have mercy on me.

Why dost thou wrong the poor man? Why dost thou withhold the wage of the hired servant? Why dost thou not love thy brother? Why dost thou pursue lust and pride? Therefore, abandon these things, my soul, and repent for the sake of the kingdom of God.

Glory to the Father and to the Son and to the Holy Spirit.

O mindless man! How long wilt thou busy thyself like a bee, collecting thy wealth? For it will soon perish like dust and ashes. But seek rather the kingdom of God.

Both now and ever and unto the ages of ages. Amen.

Theotokion: O Lady Theotokos, have mercy on me, a sinner, and strengthen and keep me in virtue, lest sudden death snatch me away unprepared; and lead me, O Virgin, to the kingdom of God.

Ode V

Eirmos: With Thy divine light, O Good One, illumine the souls of those who rise early to pray to Thee with love, I pray, that they may know Thee, O Word of God, as the true God, Who recalleth us from the darkness of sin.

Have mercy on me, O God, have mercy on me.

Remember, wretched man, how thou art enslaved to lies, slander, theft, infirmities and wild beasts on account of sins. O my sinful soul, is this what thou hast desired?

Have mercy on me, O God, have mercy on me.

My members tremble, for with all of them I have done wrong: with my eyes in looking, with my ears in hearing, with my tongue in speaking evil, and by surrendering the whole of myself to Gehenna. O my sinful soul, is this what thou hast desired?

Glory to the Father and to the Son and to the Holy Spirit.

Thou didst receive the prodigal and the thief who repented, O Saviour, and I alone have succumbed to sinful sloth and have become enslaved to evil deeds. O my sinful soul, is this what thou hast desired?

Both now and ever and unto the ages of ages. Amen.

Theotokion: Wonderful and speedy helper of all men, help me, O Mother of God, unworthy as I am, for my sinful soul hath desired this.

Ode VI

Eirmos: Beholding the sea of life surging with the tempest of temptations, I run to Thy calm haven and cry unto Thee: Raise up my life from corruption, O Greatly-merciful One.

Have mercy on me, O God, have mercy on me.

I have lived my life wantonly on earth and have given my soul over to darkness. But now I implore Thee, O merciful Master, free me from this work of the enemy and give me the knowledge to do Thy will.

Have mercy on me, O God, have mercy on me.

Who doeth such things as I do? For like a swine lying in the mud, so do I serve sin. But do Thou, O Lord, pull me out of this vileness and give me the heart to do Thy commandments.

Glory to the Father and to the Son and to the Holy Spirit.

Rise, wretched man, to God, and remembering thy sins, fall down before the Creator, weeping and groaning, for He is merciful and will grant thee to know His will.

Both now and ever and unto the ages of ages. Amen.

Theotokion: O Virgin Theotokos, protect me from evil visible and invisible, O Immaculate One, and accept my prayers and present them to Thy Son, that He may grant me the mind to do His will.

Lord, have mercy. *Thrice.*

Glory to the Father and to the Son and to the Holy Spirit, both now and ever and unto the ages of ages. Amen.

Kontakion:

O my soul, why dost thou become rich in sins? Why dost thou do the will of the devil? On what dost thou set thy hope? Cease from these things and turn to God with weeping and cry out: O kindhearted Lord, have mercy on me, a sinner.

Ekos: Think, my soul, of the bitter hour of death and the judgment day of thy God and Creator. For terrible angels will seize thee, my soul, and will lead thee into the eternal fire. And so, before thy death, repent and cry: O Lord, have mercy on me a sinner.

Ode VII

Eirmos: An angel made the furnace sprinkle dew on the righteous youths, but the command of God consumed the Chaldeans and prevailed upon the tyrant to cry: Blessed art Thou, O God of our fathers.

Have mercy on me, O God, have mercy on me.

Put not thy hope, my soul, in corruptible wealth and in what is unjustly collected. For thou dost not know to whom thou wilt leave it all. But cry aloud: Have mercy, O Christ God, on me, the unworthy.

Have mercy on me, O God, have mercy on me.

Trust not, my soul, in health of body and quickly-passing beauty. For thou seest that the strong and the young die. But cry aloud: Have mercy, O Christ God, on me, the unworthy.

Glory to the Father and to the Son and to the Holy Spirit.

Remember, my soul, eternal life and the heavenly kingdom prepared for the saints and the outer darkness and the wrath of God for the evil and cry: Have mercy, O Christ God, on me, the unworthy.

Both now and ever and unto the ages of ages. Amen.

Theotokion: Fall down, my soul, before the Mother of God and pray to Her; for She is the quick helper of those who repent. She entreateth the Son, Christ God, and hath mercy on me, the unworthy.

Ode VIII

Eirmos: From the flame Thou didst sprinkle dew upon the Saints and didst burn the sacrifice of a righteous man which was sprinkled with water. For Thou alone, O Christ, dost do all as Thou willest. Thee do we exalt unto all ages.

Have mercy on me, O God, have mercy on me.

How shall I not weep when I think of death? For I have seen my brother in his coffin, without glory or comeliness. What, then, do I expect? And what do I hope for? Only grant me, O Lord, repentance before the end.

Have mercy on me, O God, have mercy on me.

How shall I not weep.... *(Repeat.)*

Glory to the Father and to the Son and to the Holy Spirit.

I believe that Thou wilt come to judge the living and the dead and that all will stand in order, old and young, lords and princes, priests and virgins. Where shall I find myself? Therefore, I cry: Grant me, O Lord, repentance before the end.

Both now and ever and unto the ages of ages. Amen.

Theotokion: O Most Pure Theotokos, accept my unworthy prayer and preserve me from sudden death and grant me repentance before the end.

Ode IX

Eirmos: It is not possible for men to see God, on Whom the ranks of angels dare not gaze; but through Thee, O All-pure One, appeared to men the Word incarnate, Whom we magnify with the heavenly hosts, and we call Thee blessed.

Have mercy on me, O God, have mercy on me.

Now I flee unto you, ye angels, archangels and all the heavenly hosts who stand at the throne of God: pray to your Creator that He may deliver my soul from eternal torment.

Have mercy on me, O God, have mercy on me.

Now I turn to you with tears, holy patriarchs, kings and prophets, apostles and holy hierarchs and all the elect of Christ: Help me at the judgment, that He may save my soul from the power of the enemy.

Glory to the Father and to the Son and to the Holy Spirit.

Now I lift up my hands to you, holy martyrs, hermits, virgins, righteous ones and all the saints, who pray to the Lord for the whole world, that He may have mercy on me at the hour of my death.

Both now and ever and unto the ages of ages. Amen.

Theotokion: O Mother of God, help me who have

strong hope in Thee; implore Thy Son that He may place me, the unworthy, on His right hand when He sitteth to judge the living and the dead. Amen.

Prayer after the Canon:

O Master Christ God, Who hast healed my passions through Thy Passion and hast cured my wounds through Thy wounds: Grant me, who have sinned greatly against Thee, tears of compunction. Transform my body with the fragrance of Thy life-giving Body, and sweeten my soul with Thy precious Blood from the bitterness with which the foe hath fed me. Lift up my downcast mind to Thee, and take it out of the abyss of perdition, for I have no repentance, I have no compunction, I have no consoling tears which uplift children to their heritage. My mind hath been darkened through earthly passions; I cannot look up to Thee in pain; I cannot warm myself with tears of love for Thee. But, O Sovereign Lord Jesus Christ, Treasury of good things, give me thorough repentance and a diligent heart to seek Thee; grant me Thy grace, and renew in me the likeness of Thine image. I have forsaken Thee—do Thou not forsake me! Come out to seek me; lead me up to Thy pasturage and number me among the sheep of Thy chosen flock. Nourish me with them on the grass of Thy Holy Mysteries, through the intercessions of Thy most pure Mother and all Thy saints. Amen.

The Order of Preparation for Holy Communion

Through the prayers of our holy fathers, O Lord Jesus Christ our God, have mercy on us. Amen.

Glory to Thee, our God, glory to Thee.

O Heavenly King.... *Trisagion*.... Glory.... Both now.... O Most Holy Trinity.... Lord, have mercy, *thrice*. Glory.... Both now.... Our Father.... Lord, have mercy, *twelve*. Glory.... Both now.... O come let us worship..., *thrice. And these Psalms:*

Psalm 22

The Lord is my shepherd; therefore can I lack nothing. He maketh me to lie down in a green pasture; He leadeth me beside the still water. He hath converted my soul; He hath set me on the paths of righteousness, for His Name's sake. Yea, though I walk through the valley of the shadow of death, I will fear no evil, for Thou art with me; Thy rod and Thy staff, they have comforted me. Thou hast prepared a table before me against them that trouble me; Thou hast anointed my head with oil, and Thy cup that inebriateth me, how strong it is! And Thy mercy shall follow me all the days of my life, and I will dwell in the house of the Lord unto length of days.

Psalm 23

The earth is the Lord's, and the fullness thereof; the compass of the world, and all that dwell therein. He hath founded it upon the seas, and prepared it upon the floods. Who shall ascend into the hill of the Lord, or who shall stand in His holy place? Even he that hath clean hands, and a pure heart, who doth not take his soul in vain, nor swear falsely to his neighbor. He shall receive a blessing from the Lord, and mercy from God his Saviour. This is the generation of them that seek the Lord, even of them that seek the face of the God of Jacob. Lift up your gates, O ye princes, and be ye lift up, ye everlasting doors, and the King of glory shall come in. Who is this King of glory? It is the Lord strong and mighty, even the Lord mighty in battle. Lift up your gates, O ye princes, and be ye lift up, ye everlasting doors, and the King of glory shall come in. Who is this King of glory? Even the Lord of hosts, He is the King of glory.

Psalm 115

I believed, so I spake; but I was greatly humbled. I said in my confusion, All men are liars. What shall I render unto the Lord, for all that He hath rendered unto me? I will take the cup of salvation, and call upon the Name of the Lord. I will pay my vows unto the Lord in the presence of all His people. Precious in the sight of the Lord is the death of His saints. O Lord, I am Thy servant; I am Thy servant, and the son of Thine handmaid; Thou hast broken my bonds in sunder. I will offer unto Thee a sacrifice of thanksgiving, and will call upon the Name of the Lord. I will pay my vows unto the Lord in the presence of all His people, In the courts of the Lord's house, even in the midst of thee, O Jerusalem.

Glory to the Father and to the Son and to the Holy Spirit, both now and ever and unto the ages of ages. Amen.

Alleluia, alleluia, alleluia. Glory to Thee, O God. *Thrice.*

Lord, have mercy. *Thrice.*

Troparia, Eighth Tone: Disregard my transgressions, O Lord Who wast born of a Virgin, and purify my heart, and make it a temple for Thy spotless Body and Blood. Let me not be rejected from Thy presence, O Thou Who hast great mercy without measure.

Glory to the Father and to the Son and to the Holy Spirit.

How can I who am unworthy dare to come to the Communion of Thy Holy Things? For if I should dare to approach Thee with those who are worthy, my garment betrayeth me, for it is not a festal robe, and I shall cause the condemnation of my greatly-sinful soul. Cleanse, O Lord, the pollution from my soul, and save me, as Thou art the Lover of mankind.

Both now and ever and unto the ages of ages. Amen.

Greatly multiplied, O Theotokos, are my sins; unto Thee have I fled, O Pure One, imploring salvation. Do Thou visit mine enfeebled soul and pray to Thy Son and our God that He grant me forgiveness for the evil I have done, O Thou Only Blessed One.

During Holy and Great Lent say this:

When the glorious disciples were enlightened at the washing of the feet, then Judas the ungodly one was stricken and darkened with the love of silver. And unto the lawless judges did he deliver Thee, the Righteous Judge. Behold, O lover of money, him who for the sake thereof did hang himself; flee from that insatiable soul who dared such things against the Master. O Thou Who art good unto all, Lord, glory be to Thee.

Psalm 50

Have mercy upon me, O God, after Thy great goodness, and according to the multitude of Thy mercies do away mine offenses. Wash me thoroughly from my wickedness, and cleanse me from my sin. For I know my fault, and my sin is ever before me. Against Thee only have I sinned, and done evil before Thee, that Thou mightest be justified in Thy words, and prevail when Thou art judged. For behold, I was conceived in wickedness, and in sins did my mother bear me. For behold, Thou hast loved truth; the hidden and secret things of Thy wisdom hast Thou revealed unto me. Thou shalt sprinkle me with hyssop, and I shall be made clean; Thou shalt wash me, and I shall become whiter than snow. Thou shalt give joy and gladness to my hearing; the bones that have been humbled will rejoice. Turn Thy face from my sins, and put out all my misdeeds. Make me a clean heart, O God, and renew a right spirit within me. Cast me not away from Thy presence, and take not Thy Holy Spirit from me. O give me the comfort of Thy salvation, and stablish me with Thy governing Spirit. Then shall I teach Thy ways unto the wicked, and the ungodly shall be converted unto Thee. Deliver me from blood-guiltiness, O God, the God of my salvation, and my tongue shall rejoice in Thy righteousness. O Lord, open Thou my lips, and my mouth shall show forth Thy praise. For if Thou hadst desired sacrifice, I would have given it; but Thou delightest not in burnt offerings. The sacrifice unto God is a contrite spirit; a contrite and humble heart God shall not despise. O Lord, be favorable in Thy good will unto Zion, and let the walls of Jerusalem be builded up. Then shalt Thou be pleased with the sacrifice of righteousness, with oblation and whole-burnt offerings; then shall they offer young bullocks upon Thine altar.

And immediately:

The Canon for Holy Communion
Second Tone

Ode I

Eirmos: Come, O ye people, let us sing a hymn to Christ our God, Who divided the sea and guided the people whom He brought out of the bondage of Egypt, for He is glorified.

Refrain: *Create in me a clean heart, O God, and renew a right spirit within me.*

May Thy holy Body be unto me the Bread of life eternal, O compassionate Lord, and Thy precious Blood be also the healing of many forms of illness.

Refrain: *Cast me not away from Thy presence, and take not Thy Holy Spirit from me.*

Defiled by unseemly deeds, I, the wretched one, am unworthy, O Christ, of the communion of Thy most pure Body and divine Blood, which do Thou vouchsafe me.

Glory to the Father and to the Son and to the Holy Spirit, both now and ever and unto the ages of ages. Amen.

O Blessed Bride of God, O good soil that grew the Corn untilled and saving to the world, vouchsafe me to be saved by eating it.

Ode III

Eirmos: By establishing me on the rock of faith, Thou hast enlarged my mouth over mine enemies, for my spirit rejoiceth when I sing: There is none holy as our God and none righteous beside Thee, O Lord.

Create in me a clean heart, O God, and renew a right spirit within me.

Teardrops grant me, O Christ, to cleanse my defiled heart, that, purified and with a good conscience, I may come with faith and fear, O Master, to the communion of Thy divine Gifts.

Cast me not away from Thy presence, and take not Thy Holy Spirit from me.

May Thy most pure Body and divine Blood be unto me for remission of sins, for communion with the Holy Spirit and unto life eternal, O Lover of mankind, and to the estrangement of passions and sorrows.

Glory to the Father and to the Son and to the Holy Spirit, both now and ever and unto the ages of ages. Amen.

O Thou most holy table of the Bread of Life that for mercy's sake came down from on high, giving new life to the world, vouchsafe even me, the unworthy, to eat it with fear, and live.

Ode IV

Eirmos: From a Virgin didst Thou come, not as an ambassador nor as an angel, but the very Lord Himself incarnate and didst save me, the whole man. Wherefore, I cry to Thee: Glory to Thy power, O Lord.

Create in me a clean heart, O God, and renew a right spirit within me.

O Thou Who wast incarnate for our sake, O Most-merciful One, Thou didst will to be slain as a sheep for the sin of mankind. Wherefore, I entreat Thee to blot out my sins also.

Cast me not away from Thy presence, and take not Thy Holy Spirit from me.

Heal the wounds of my soul, O Lord, and sanctify all of me, and vouchsafe, O Master, that I, the wretched one, may partake of Thy divine Mystical Supper.

Glory to the Father and to the Son and to the Holy Spirit, both now and ever and unto the ages of ages. Amen.

Propitiate for me also Him Who came from Thy womb, O Lady, and keep me, Thy servant, undefiled and blameless, so that by obtaining the spiritual Pearl I may be sanctified.

Ode V

Eirmos: O Lord, Giver of light and Creator of the ages, guide us in the light of Thy commandments, for we know none other God beside Thee.

Create in me a clean heart, O God, and renew a right spirit within me.

As Thou didst foretell, O Christ, so let it be unto Thy wicked servant, and in me abide, as Thou didst promise; for behold, I eat Thy divine Body and drink Thy Blood.

Cast me not away from Thy presence, and take not Thy Holy Spirit from me.

O Word of God and God, may the live coal of Thy Body be unto the enlightenment of me who am in darkness and Thy Blood be unto the cleansing of my defiled soul.

Glory to the Father and to the Son and to the Holy Spirit, both now and ever and unto the ages of ages. Amen.

O Mary, Mother of God, precious tabernacle of fragrance, through Thy prayers make me a chosen vessel, that I may partake of the Sacrament of Thy Son.

Ode VI

Eirmos: Whirled about in the abyss of sin, I appeal to the unfathomable abyss of Thy compassion: From corruption raise me up, O God.

Create in me a clean heart, O God, and renew a right spirit within me.

O Saviour, sanctify my mind, my soul, my heart and my body, and vouchsafe me uncondemned, O Master, to approach the fearful Mysteries.

Cast me not away from Thy presence, and take not Thy Holy Spirit from me.

Grant that I may be rid of passions and have the assistance of Thy grace and experience strengthening of life by the communion of Thy Holy Mysteries, O Christ.

Glory to the Father and to the Son and to the Holy Spirit, both now and ever and unto the ages of ages. Amen.

O Holy Word of God and God, sanctify all of me as I now come to Thy divine Mysteries, through the prayers of Thy holy Mother.

Lord, have mercy. *Thrice.*

Glory to the Father and to the Son and to the Holy Spirit, both now and ever and unto the ages of ages. Amen.

Kontakion, Second Tone:

Count me not unworthy, O Christ, to receive now the Bread which is Thy Body and Thy divine Blood and to partake, O Master, of Thy most pure and dread Mysteries, wretched though I be. Let these not be for me unto judgment, but unto life immortal and everlasting.

Ode VII

Eirmos: The wise children did not serve the golden image, but went themselves into the flame and reviled the pagan gods. They cried in the midst of the flame, and the angel bedewed them: Already the prayer of your lips was heard.

Create in me a clean heart, O God, and renew a right spirit within me.

May the communion of Thine immortal Mysteries, the source of blessings, O Christ, be to me now light and life and dispassion and for progress and increase in the most divine virtues, O only Good One, that I may glorify Thee.

Cast me not away from Thy presence, and take not Thy Holy Spirit from me.

That I may be delivered from passions and enemies, need and every sorrow, I now draw nigh with trembling, love and reverence, O Lover of mankind, to Thine immortal and divine Mysteries. Vouchsafe me to hymn Thee: Blessed art Thou, O Lord God of our fathers.

Glory to the Father and to the Son and to the Holy Spirit, both now and ever and unto the ages of ages. Amen.

O Thou Who art full of grace, Who beyond understanding gavest birth to Christ the Saviour, I Thy servant, the impure, now entreat Thee, the pure: Cleanse me, who am now about to approach the most pure Mysteries, from all defilement of flesh and spirit.

Ode VIII

Eirmos: God, Who descended into the fiery furnace unto the Hebrew children and changed the flame into dew, praise Him as Lord, O ye works, and supremely exalt Him unto all ages.

Create in me a clean heart, O God, and renew a right spirit within me.

Of Thy heavenly and dread holy Mysteries, O Christ, and of Thy divine Mystical Supper vouchsafe now even me, the despairing one, to partake, O God my Saviour.

Cast me not away from Thy presence, and take not Thy Holy Spirit from me.

Fleeing for refuge to Thy loving-kindness, O Good One, with fear I cry unto Thee: Abide in me, O Saviour, and I, as Thou hast said, in Thee. For behold, presuming on Thy mercy, I eat Thy Body and drink Thy Blood.

Glory to the Father and to the Son and to the Holy Spirit, both now and ever and unto the ages of ages. Amen.

I tremble at taking fire, lest I be consumed as wax and grass. O fearful Mystery! O the loving-kindness of God! How is it that I, being but clay, partake of the divine Body and Blood, and am made incorruptible?

Ode IX

Eirmos: The Son of the unoriginate Father, God and Lord, hath appeared unto us incarnate of the Virgin, to enlighten those in darkness and to gather the dispersed. Wherefore, the All-hymned Theotokos do we magnify.

Create in me a clean heart, O God, and renew a right spirit within me.

Christ It is, O taste and see! The Lord for our sake made like unto us of old, once offered Himself as an offering to His Father and is ever slain, sanctifying them that partake.

Cast me not away from Thy presence, and take not Thy Holy Spirit from me.

May I be sanctified in soul and body, O Master, may I be enlightened, may I be saved, may I become Thy dwelling through the communion of Thy holy Mysteries, having Thee with the Father and the Spirit living in me, O Benefactor plenteous in mercy.

Glory to the Father and to the Son and to the Holy Spirit.

May Thy Body and Thy most precious Blood, O my Saviour, be unto me as fire and light, consuming the substance of sin and burning the thorns of passions and enlightening all of me to worship Thy Divinity.

Both now and ever and unto the ages of ages. Amen.

God took flesh of Thy pure blood; wherefore, all generations do hymn Thee, O Lady, and throngs of heavenly minds glorify Thee, for through Thee they have clearly seen Him Who ruleth all things endued with human nature.

And immediately: It is truly meet....*Trisagion.* O Most Holy Trinity....Our Father.... *And the troparion of the day, if it be the feast of the Lord's Nativity or another feast. If it be Sunday, the Sunday troparion of the tone. If not, these:*

Sixth Tone: Have mercy on us, O Lord, have mercy on us; for at a loss for any defense, this prayer do we sinners offer unto Thee as Master: Have mercy on us.

Glory to the Father and to the Son and to the Holy Spirit.

Lord, have mercy on us, for we have hoped in

Thee, be not angry with us greatly, neither remember our iniquities; but look upon us now as Thou art compassionate, and deliver us from our enemies; for Thou art our God, and we, Thy people; all are the works of Thy hands, and we call upon Thy name.

Both now and ever and unto the ages of ages. Amen.

The door of compassion open unto us, O Blessed Theotokos, for hoping in Thee, let us not perish; through Thee may we be delivered from adversities, for Thou art the salvation of the Christian race.

Then: Lord, have mercy. *Forty times.*

And reverences [bows, prostrations], as many as thou desirest.

And thereafter these lines:

If thou desirest, O man, to eat the Body of the Master,
Approach with fear, lest thou be burnt: for It is fire.
And when thou drinkest the Divine Blood unto communion,
First be reconciled to those who have grieved thee,
Then dare to eat the Mystical Food.

Other lines:

Before partaking of the awesome Sacrifice
Of the life-giving Body of the Master,
After this manner pray with trembling:

I, A Prayer of St Basil the Great:

O Master Lord Jesus Christ our God, Source of life and immortality, Creator of all things visible and invisible, the co-eternal and co-unoriginate Son of the unoriginate Father, Who out of Thy great goodness didst in the latter days clothe Thyself in flesh and wast crucified and buried for us ungrateful and evil-disposed ones and hast renewed with Thine Own Blood our nature corrupted by sin: Do Thou Thyself, O Immortal King, accept the repentance of me, a sinner, and incline Thine ear to me, and hearken unto my words. For I have sinned against heaven and before Thee, and I am not worthy to look upon the height of Thy glory; for I have angered Thy goodness by transgressing Thy commandments and by not obeying Thine injunctions. But Thou, O Lord, Who art not vengeful, but long-suffering and plenteous in mercy, hast not given me over to be destroyed with my sins, but always Thou awaitest my complete conversion. For Thou hast said, O Lover of mankind, through Thy prophet: For I desire not the death of the sinner, but that he should return and live. For Thou desirest not, O Master, to destroy the work of Thy hands, neither shalt Thou be pleased with the destruction of men, but desirest that all be saved and come to a knowledge of the truth. Wherefore, even I, although unworthy of heaven and earth and of this temporal life, having submitted my whole self to sin and made myself a slave of pleasure and having defaced Thine image, yet being Thy work and creation, wretched though I be, I despair not of my salvation and dare to approach Thine immeasurable loving-kindness. Accept then even me, O Lord, Lover of mankind, as Thou didst accept the sinful woman, the thief, the publican and the prodigal; and take away the heavy burden of my sins, Thou Who takest away the sin of the world and healest the infirmities of mankind; Who callest the weary and heavy-laden unto Thyself and givest them rest; Who camest not to call the righteous, but sinners to repentance. And do Thou cleanse me from all defilement of flesh and spirit and teach me to achieve holiness in fear of Thee; that with the pure testimony of my conscience, receiving a portion of Thy Holy Things, I may be united unto Thy holy Body and Blood and have Thee living and abiding in me with the Father and Thy Holy Spirit. Yea, O Lord Jesus Christ my God, let not the communion of Thine immaculate and life-giving Mysteries be unto me for judgment, neither unto infirmity of soul and body because of my partaking of them unworthily; but grant me until my last breath to receive without condemnation the portion of Thy Holy Things, unto communion with the Holy Spirit, as a provision for life eternal, for an acceptable defense at Thy dread judgment seat; so that I also, with all Thine elect, may become a partaker of Thine incorruptible blessings, which Thou hast prepared for those who love Thee, O Lord, in whom Thou art glorified unto the ages. Amen.

II, A Prayer of Our Father among the Saints, John Chrysostom:

O Lord my God, I know that I am not worthy nor sufficient that Thou shouldest enter beneath the roof of the temple of my soul, for all is empty and fallen, and Thou hast not in me a place worthy to lay Thy head; but as from on high Thou didst humble Thyself for our sake, do Thou now also lower Thyself to my lowliness; and as Thou didst consent to lie in a cave and in a manger of dumb beasts, so consent also to lie in the manger of mine irrational soul and to enter into my defiled body. And as Thou didst not refuse to enter and to dine with sinners in the house of Simon the Leper, so deign also to enter into the house of my lowly soul, leprous and sinful. And as Thou didst not reject the harlot and sinner like me, when she came and touched Thee, so be compassionate also with me a sinner, as I approach and touch Thee. And as Thou didst feel no loathing for the defiled and unclean lips of her who kissed Thee, do Thou also not loathe my defiled lips nor mine abominable and impure mouth and my polluted and unclean tongue. But let the fiery coal of Thy most holy Body and Thy precious Blood be unto me for sanctification and enlightenment and health for my lowly soul and body, unto the lightening of the burden of my many sins, for preservation from every act of the devil, for the expulsion and prohibition of my evil and wicked habits, unto the mortification of the passions, unto the keeping of Thy commandments, unto the application of Thy divine grace, unto the acquiring of Thy kingdom. For not with disdain do I approach Thee, O Christ God, but as one trusting in Thine ineffable goodness, and that I may not by much abstaining from Thy Communion become the prey of the spiritual wolf. Wherefore do I entreat Thee, for Thou art the only Holy One, O Master: Sanctify my soul and body, my mind and heart, my belly and inward parts, and renew me entirely. And implant Thy fear in my members, and make Thy sanctification inalienable from me, and be unto me a helper and defender, guiding my life in peace, vouchsafing me also to stand at Thy right hand with Thy saints, through the intercessions and supplications of Thy most pure Mother, of Thine immaterial ministers and immaculate hosts and of all the saints who from the ages have been pleasing unto Thee. Amen.

III, Another Prayer, of St Symeon Metaphrastes:

O Only Pure and Sinless Lord, Who through the ineffable compassion of Thy love for mankind didst take on all of our substance from the pure and virgin blood of Her Who bare Thee supernaturally through the descent of the Divine Spirit and the good will of the everlasting Father; O Christ Jesus, Wisdom of God and Peace and Power, Thou Who through the assumption of our nature didst take upon Thyself Thy life-giving and saving Passion — the cross, the nails, the spear, and death: mortify the soul-corrupting passions of my body. Thou Who by Thy burial didst lead captive the kingdom of hades, bury with good thoughts my evil schemes, and destroy the spirits of evil. Thou Who by Thy life-bearing resurrection on the third day didst raise up our fallen forefather, raise me up who have slipped down into sin, setting before me the ways of repentance. Thou Who by Thy most glorious Ascension didst deify the flesh that Thou hadst taken and didst honor it with a seat at the right hand of the Father, vouchsafe me through partaking of Thy holy Mysteries to obtain a place at Thy right hand among those who are saved. O Thou Who by the descent of Thy Spirit, the Comforter, didst make Thy holy disciples worthy vessels, show me also to be a receptacle of His coming. Thou Who art to come again to judge the world in righteousness, deign to let me also meet Thee on the clouds, my Judge and Creator, with all Thy saints; that I may endlessly glorify and praise Thee, with Thine unoriginate Father and Thy Most-holy and good and life-creating Spirit, now and ever and unto the ages of ages. Amen.

IV, Of the Divine St John of Damascus:

O Master Lord Jesus Christ our God, Who alone hast authority to remit the sins of men: Do Thou, as the Good One and Lover of mankind, overlook all mine offenses, whether committed with knowledge or in ignorance. And vouchsafe me to partake without condemnation of Thy Divine, glorious, immaculate and life-giving Mysteries; not as a burden, nor for punishment, nor for an increase of sins, but unto purification and sanctification and as a pledge of the life and kingdom to come, as a bulwark and help, and for the destruction of enemies and for the blotting out of my many transgressions. For Thou art a God of mercy and compassion and love for mankind, and unto Thee do we send up glory, with the Father and the Holy Spirit, now and ever and unto the ages of ages. Amen.

V, Of St Basil the Great:

I know, O Lord, that I partake unworthily of Thine immaculate Body and Thy precious Blood and that I am guilty and that I eat and drink damnation to myself, not discerning the Body and Blood of Thee, my Christ and God; but taking courage from Thy compassion I approach Thee Who hast said: He who eateth My Flesh and drinketh My Blood abideth in Me and I in him. Show compassion, therefore, O Lord, and do not accuse me, a sinner,

but deal with me according to Thy mercy; and let
these Holy Things be for me unto healing and purification and enlightenment and preservation and
salvation and unto sanctification of soul and body;
unto the driving away of every fantasy and evil
practice and activity of the devil working mentally
in my members; unto confidence and love toward
Thee, unto correction of life, unto steadfastness,
unto an increase of virtue and perfection, unto fulfillment of the commandments, unto communion
with the Holy Spirit, as a provision for life eternal,
as an acceptable defense at Thy dread tribunal, not
unto judgment or condemnation. Amen.

VI, A Prayer of St Symeon the New Theologian:

From sullied lips, from an abominable heart,
from a tongue impure, from a soul defiled,
accept my supplication, O my Christ, and disdain
me not, neither my words, nor my ways, nor my
shamelessness. Grant me to say boldly that which
I desire, O my Christ. Or rather, teach me what I
ought to do and say. I have sinned more than the
sinful woman who, having learned where Thou
wast lodging, bought myrrh and came daringly to
anoint Thy feet, my God, my Master and my Christ.
As Thou didst not reject her when she drew near
from her heart, neither, O Word, be Thou filled
with loathing for me, but grant me Thy feet to clasp

and kiss and with floods of tears, as with most precious myrrh, may I dare to anoint them. Wash me with my tears, and purify me with them, O Word; remit also my transgressions, and grant me pardon. Thou knowest the multitude of mine evils, Thou knowest also my sores, and Thou seest my wounds; but also Thou knowest my faith, and Thou beholdest my good intentions, and Thou hearest my sighs. Nothing is hidden from Thee, my God, my Creator, My Redeemer, neither a teardrop, nor a part of a drop. My deeds not yet done Thine eyes have seen, and in Thy book even things not yet accomplished are written by Thee. See my lowliness, see my toil, how great it is, and all my sins take from me, O God of all; that with a pure heart, a trembling mind and a contrite soul I may partake of Thy spotless and most holy Mysteries, by which all who eat and drink in purity of heart are quickened and deified. For Thou, O my Master, hast said: Everyone who eateth My Flesh and drinketh My Blood abideth in Me and I in him. True is every word of my Master and God; for whosoever partaketh of the divine and deifying grace is no more alone, but with Thee, my Christ, the three-sunned Light Who enlighteneth the world. And that I may not remain alone without Thee, the Life-giver, my Breath, my Life, my Rejoicing, the Salvation of the world, therefore have I drawn nigh unto Thee, as Thou seest, with tears and with a contrite soul. O Ransom of mine offenses, I ask Thee to receive me and that I may partake without condemnation of Thy life-giving and perfect Mysteries, that Thou mayest remain, as Thou hast said, with me, a thrice-wretched one, lest the deceiver, finding me without Thy grace, craftily seize me and having beguiled me, draw me away from Thy deifying words. Wherefore, I fall down before Thee and fervently cry unto Thee: As Thou didst receive the prodigal and the sinful woman who drew near, so receive me, the prodigal and profligate, O Compassionate One. With contrite soul I now come to Thee. I know, O Saviour, that none other hath sinned against Thee as have I, nor hath wrought the deeds that I have done. But this again I know, that neither the magnitude of mine offenses nor the multitude of my sins surpasseth the abundant long-suffering of my God and His exceeding love for mankind; but with sympathetic mercy Thou dost purify and illumine those who fervently repent and makest them partakers of the light, sharers of Thy divinity without stint. And, strange to angels and to the minds of men, Thou conversest with them oftimes, as with Thy true friends. These things make me bold, these things give me wings, O Christ. And taking courage from the wealth of Thy benefactions to us, rejoicing and trembling at once, I partake of Fire, I that am grass. And, strange wonder! I am bedewed without being consumed, as the bush of old burned without being consumed. Now with thankful mind and grateful heart, with thankfulness in my members, my soul and body, I worship and magnify and glorify Thee, my God, for blessed art Thou, both now and unto the ages of ages. Amen.

VII, Another Prayer of St John Chrysostom:

O God, loose, remit and pardon me my transgressions wherein I have sinned against Thee, whether by word, deed or thought, voluntarily or involuntarily, consciously or unconsciously; forgive me all, for Thou art good and the Lover of mankind. And through the intercessions of Thy most pure Mother, Thy noetic ministers and holy hosts, and all the saints who from the ages have been pleasing unto Thee, deign to allow me without condemnation Thy holy and immaculate Body and precious Blood, unto the healing of soul and body and unto the purification of mine evil thoughts. For Thine is the kingdom and the power and the glory, with the Father and the Holy Spirit, now and ever and unto the ages of ages. Amen.

VIII, Of the same:

I am not sufficient, O Master and Lord, that Thou shouldst enter under the roof of my soul; but as Thou dost will as the Lover of mankind to dwell in me, I dare to approach Thee. Thou commandest: I shall open the doors which Thou alone didst create, that Thou mayest enter with Thy love for mankind, as is Thy nature, that Thou mayest enter and enlighten my darkened thought. I believe that Thou wilt do this, for Thou didst not drive away the sinful woman when she came unto Thee with tears, neither didst Thou reject the publican who repented, nor didst Thou spurn the thief who acknowledged Thy kingdom, nor didst Thou leave the repentant persecutor to himself; but all of those who came unto Thee in repentance Thou didst number among Thy friends, O Thou Who alone art blessed, always, now and unto endless ages. Amen.

IX, Of the same:

O Lord Jesus Christ my God, loose, remit, cleanse and forgive me, Thy sinful and unprofitable and unworthy servant, my transgressions and offenses and fallings into sin, which I have committed against Thee from my youth until the present day and hour, whether consciously or unconsciously, whether by words or deeds or in thought or imagination, in habit and in all my senses. And through the intercessions of Her Who seedlessly gave Thee birth, the Most Pure and Ever-Virgin Mary, Thy Mother, the only hope that maketh not ashamed and my mediation and salvation, vouchsafe me without condemnation to partake of Thine immaculate, immortal, life-giving and awesome Mysteries, unto the remission of sins and for life eternal, unto sanctification and enlightenment, strength, healing and health of both soul and body and unto the consumption and complete destruction of mine evil reasonings and intentions and prejudices and nocturnal fantasies of dark and evil spirits; for Thine is the kingdom and the power and the glory and the honor and the worship, with the Father and Thy Holy Spirit, now and ever and unto the ages of ages. Amen.

X, Another Prayer of St John of Damascus:

I stand before the doors of Thy temple, yet I do not put away evil thoughts. But do Thou, O Christ God, Who didst justify the publican and didst have mercy on the woman of Canaan and didst open the doors of paradise to the thief, open unto me the abyss of Thy love for mankind, and receive me as I come and touch Thee, as Thou didst receive the woman with an issue of blood and the sinful woman. For the one received healing easily by touching the hem of Thy garment, while the other, by clasping Thy most pure feet, carried away absolution of sins. And I, a wretch, daring to receive Thy whole Body, let me not be consumed by fire; but receive me, as Thou didst receive them, and enlighten my spiritual senses, burning up my sinful errors; through the intercessions of Her Who seedlessly gave Thee birth and of the heavenly hosts, for blessed art Thou unto the ages of ages. Amen.

Another Prayer of St John Chrysostom:

I believe, O Lord, and I confess that Thou art truly the Christ, the Son of the living God, Who came into the world to save sinners, of whom I am chief. Moreover, I believe that this is truly Thy most pure Body, and this is truly Thine Own precious Blood. Wherefore, I pray Thee: Have mercy on me and forgive me my transgressions, voluntary and involuntary, whether in word or deed, in knowledge or in ignorance. And vouchsafe me to partake without condemnation of Thy most pure Mysteries, unto the remission of sins and life everlasting. Amen.

When coming to partake, say to thyself these lines of St Symeon Metaphrastes:

Behold, I approach the Divine Communion.

O Creator, let me not be burnt by communicating,

For Thou art Fire, consuming the unworthy;

But, rather, purify me of all impurity.

Then again say:

Of Thy Mystical Supper, O Son of God, receive me today as a communicant; for I will not speak of the Mystery to Thine enemies; nor will I give Thee a kiss, as did Judas, but like the thief do I confess Thee: Remember me, O Lord, in Thy kingdom.

Furthermore, these lines:

Be awe-stricken, O mortal, beholding the deifying Blood;

For It is a fire that consumeth the unworthy.
The Divine Body both deifieth and nourisheth
me.
It deifieth the spirit and wondrously
nourisheth the mind.

Then the Troparia:

Thou hast sweetened me with Thy love, O
Christ, and by Thy Divine zeal hast Thou changed
me. But do Thou consume my sins with immaterial
fire, and vouchsafe me to be filled with delight in
Thee; that, leaping for joy, O Good One, I may magnify Thy two comings.

Into the brilliant company of Thy saints how
shall I the unworthy enter? For if I dare to enter
into the bride-chamber, my garment betrayeth
me, for it is not a wedding garment, and I shall be
bound and cast out by the angels. Cleanse, O Lord,
my soul of pollution, and save me, as Thou art the
Lover of mankind.

Then the Prayer:

O Master, Lover of mankind, O Lord Jesus
Christ my God, let not these Holy Things be unto
me for judgment, through my being unworthy, but
unto the purification and sanctification of soul and
body, and as a pledge of the life and kingdom to
come. For it is good for me to cleave unto God, to
put my hope of salvation in the Lord.

And again:

Of Thy Mystical Supper, O Son of God, receive
me today as a communicant; for I will not speak of

the Mystery to Thine enemies; nor will I give Thee a kiss, as did Judas, but like the thief do I confess Thee: Remember me, O Lord, in Thy kingdom.

The Prayers after Holy Communion

When thou hast received the good Communion of the life-giving Mystical Gifts, give praise immediately, give thanks greatly, and from the soul say fervently unto God these things:

Glory to Thee, O God.
Glory to Thee, O God.
Glory to Thee, O God.
Then this:

Prayer of Thanksgiving:

I thank Thee, O Lord my God, that Thou hast not rejected me, a sinner, but hast vouchsafed me to be a communicant of Thy Holy Things. I thank Thee that Thou hast vouchsafed me, the unworthy, to partake of Thy most pure and heavenly Gifts. But, O Master, Lover of mankind, Who for our sake didst die and didst rise again and didst bestow upon us these dread and life-giving Mysteries for the well-being and sanctification of our souls and bodies, grant that these may be even unto me for the healing of both soul and body, for the averting of everything hostile, for the enlightenment of the eyes of my heart, for the peace of the powers of my soul, for faith unashamed, for love unfeigned, for the fullness of wisdom, for the keeping of Thy commandments, for an increase of Thy Divine grace and for the attainment of Thy kingdom; that being preserved by them in Thy holiness, I may always remember Thy grace and no longer live for myself, but for Thee, our Master and Benefactor; and thus when I shall have departed this life in hope of life eternal, I may attain unto everlasting rest, where the sound of those who keep festival is unceasing, and the delight is endless of those who behold the ineffable beauty of Thy countenance. For Thou art the true desire and the unutterable gladness of those who love Thee, O Christ our God, and all creation doth hymn Thee unto the ages of ages. Amen.

II, Of St Basil the Great:

O Master Christ God, King of the ages, and Creator of all things, I thank Thee for all the good things which Thou hast bestowed upon me and for the Communion of Thy most pure and life-giving Mysteries. I pray Thee, therefore, O Good One and Lover of Mankind: Keep me under Thy protection and in the shadow of Thy wings and grant me, even until my last breath, to partake worthily, with a pure conscience, of Thy Holy Things, unto the remission of sins and life eternal. For Thou art the Bread of Life, the Source of holiness, the Giver of good things; and unto Thee do we send up glory, together with the Father and the Holy Spirit, now and ever and unto the ages of ages. Amen.

III, Verses of St Symeon Metaphrastes:

O Thou who givest me willingly Thy Flesh as food, Thou Who art Fire that doth consume the unworthy, burn me not, O my Creator; but, rather, enter Thou into my members, into all my joints, my reins, my heart. Burn up the thorns of all my sins. Purify my soul, sanctify my thoughts. Strengthen my substance together with my bones. Enlighten my simple five senses. Nail down the whole of me with Thy fear. Ever protect, preserve and keep me from every soul-corrupting deed and word. Purify and cleanse and adorn me; make me comely, give me understanding and enlighten me. Show me to be the dwelling-place of Thy Spirit alone and no longer the habitation of sin; that from me as Thine abode through the entry of Communion, every evildoer, every passion may flee as from fire. As intercessors I offer unto Thee all the saints, the commanders of the bodiless hosts, Thy Forerunner, the wise apostles, and further, Thine undefiled pure Mother, whose entreaties do Thou accept, O my compassionate Christ, and make Thy servant a child of light. For Thou alone art our sanctification, O Good One, and the radiance of our souls, and unto Thee as God and Master, we all send up glory, as is meet, every day.

Another Prayer:

O Lord Jesus Christ our God, may Thy holy Body be unto me for life eternal, and Thy precious Blood for the remission of sins; and may this Eucharist be unto me for joy, health and gladness. And at Thy dread Second Coming vouchsafe me, a sinner, to stand at the right hand of Thy glory, through the intercessions of Thy most pure Mother and of all the saints.

Another Prayer, to the Most Holy Theotokos:

O Most Holy Lady Theotokos, light of my darkened soul, my hope, protection, refuge, consolation, my joy: I thank Thee that Thou hast vouchsafed me, who am unworthy, to be a partaker of the most pure Body and precious Blood of Thy Son. O Thou Who gavest birth to the True Light, do thou enlighten the spiritual eyes of my heart; Thou Who gavest birth to the Source of immortality, revive me who am dead in sin; Thou Who art the lovingly-compassionate Mother of the merciful God, have mercy on me, and grant me compunction and contrition in my heart and humility in my thoughts and the recall of my thoughts from captivity. And vouchsafe me until my last breath to receive without condemnation the sanctification of the most pure Mysteries, for the healing of both soul and body; and grant me tears of repentance and confession, that I may hymn and glorify Thee all the days of my life, for blessed and most glorious art Thou unto the ages of ages. Amen.

Then: Now lettest Thou Thy servant depart in peace, O Master, according to Thy word; for mine eyes have seen Thy salvation, which Thou hast prepared before the face of all peoples; a light of revelation for the Gentiles and the glory of Thy people Israel.

Holy God, Holy Mighty, Holy Immortal, have mercy on us. *Thrice.*

Glory to the Father and to the Son and to the Holy Spirit, both now and ever and unto the ages of ages. Amen.

O Most Holy Trinity, have mercy on us. O Lord, blot out our sins. O Master, pardon our iniquities. O Holy One, visit and heal our infirmities for Thy name's sake.

Lord, have mercy. *Thrice.*

Glory to the Father and to the Son and to the Holy Spirit, both now and ever and unto the ages of ages. Amen.

Our Father, Who art in the heavens, hallowed be Thy name. Thy kingdom come, Thy will be done, on earth as it is in heaven. Give us this day our daily bread, and forgive us our debts, as we forgive our debtors; and lead us not into temptation, but deliver us from the evil one.

Troparion to St John Chrysostom, Eighth Tone:

Grace shining forth from thy mouth like a beacon hath illumined the universe and disclosed to the world treasures of uncovetousness and shown us the heights of humility; but while instructing by thy words, O Father John Chrysostom, intercede with the Word, Christ our God, to save our souls.

Glory to the Father and to the Son and to the Holy Spirit.

Kontakion, Sixth Tone:

From the heavens hast thou received divine grace and by thy lips thou dost teach all to worship the One God in Trinity, O John Chrysostom, all-blessed righteous one. Rightly do we acclaim thee, for thou art a teacher revealing things divine.

Both now and ever and unto the ages of ages. Amen.

O protection of Christians that cannot be put to shame, O mediation unto the Creator unfailing, disdain not the suppliant voices of sinners; but be thou quick, O Good One, to help us who in faith cry unto Thee; hasten to intercession and speed Thou to make supplication, Thou Who dost ever protect, O Theotokos, those who honor Thee.

But if it be the Liturgy of St Basil, read the:

Troparion to St Basil the Great, First Tone:

Thy fame hath gone forth into all the earth, which hath received thy word. Thereby thou hast divinely taught the Faith; thou hast made manifest the nature of created things; thou hast made the moral life of men a royal priesthood. O Basil our righteous father, intercede with Christ God that our souls be saved.

Glory to the Father and to the Son and to the Holy Spirit.

Kontakion, Fourth Tone:

Thou didst prove to be an unshakable foundation of the Church, giving to all mortals an inviolate lordship, and sealing it with thy doctrines, O righteous Basil, revealer of heavenly things.

Both now ... O protection of Christians....(*page 192*).

But if it be the Liturgy of the Presanctified Gifts:

Troparion to St Gregory the Dialogist, Fourth Tone:

Thou who hast received of God divine grace from on high, O glorious Gregory, and hast been fortified by His power, thou didst will to walk according to the Gospel; wherefore, thou hast received of Christ the reward of thy labors, O all-blessed one. Entreat Him that He save our souls.

Glory to the Father and to the Son and to the Holy Spirit.

Kontakion, Third Tone:

Thou hast shown thyself to be a leader like unto the Chief Shepherd Christ, O Father Gregory, guiding flocks of monks into the heavenly sheepfold, and from whence thou didst teach the flock of Christ His commandments. And now thou dost rejoice with them and dance in the heavenly mansions.

Both now....O protection of Christians.... (*page 192*).

Lord, have mercy. *Twelve times.*

Glory ... Both now ...

More honorable than the Cherubim and beyond compare more glorious than the Seraphim, Who without corruption gavest birth to God the Word, the very Theotokos, Thee do we magnify.

And the Dismissal.

The Psalms

Psalm 1

A Psalm of David. Without superscription in the Hebrew.

BLESSED is the man that hath not walked in the counsel of the ungodly, nor stood in the way of sinners, and hath not sat in the seat of the scornful.

2 But his delight is in the Law of the Lord, and in His Law will he exercise himself day and night.

3 And he shall be like a tree planted by the water-side, that will bring forth his fruit in due season; his leaf also shall not fall, and all whatsoever he doeth, it shall prosper.

4 Not so are the ungodly, not so; but they are like the dust, which the wind scattereth away from the face of the earth.

5 Therefore the ungodly shall not rise at the judgment, neither the sinners in the council of the righteous.

6 For the Lord knoweth the way of the righteous, and the way of the ungodly shall perish.

Psalm 2

A Psalm of David.

WHY have the heathen raged, and the peoples imagined vain things?

² The kings of the earth stood up, and the rulers gathered together, against the Lord, and against His Christ:

³ Let us break their bonds asunder, and cast away their cords from us.

⁴ He that dwelleth in heaven shall laugh them to scorn; the Lord shall have them in derision.

⁵ Then shall He speak unto them in His wrath, and vex them in His sore displeasure.

⁶ Yet I am set up as King by Him upon His holy hill of Zion,

⁷ Preaching the Lord's commandment. The Lord said unto Me, Thou art My Son, this day have I begotten Thee.

⁸ Desire of Me, and I shall give Thee the nations for Thine inheritance, and the utmost parts of the earth for Thy possession.

⁹ Thou shalt herd them with a rod of iron, and break them in pieces like a potter's vessel.

¹⁰ Be wise now therefore, O ye kings; be instructed, all ye that are judges of the earth.

¹¹ Serve the Lord in fear, and rejoice unto Him with trembling.

¹² Choose chastening, lest the Lord be angry, and so ye perish from the right way, when His wrath be suddenly kindled; blessed are all they that put their trust in Him.

Psalm 3

A Psalm of David, when he fled from Absalom his son.

LORD, why are they increased that trouble me? Many are they that rise against me.

³ Many one there be that say of my soul, There is no salvation for him in his God.

⁴ But Thou, O Lord, art my helper, my glory, and the lifter up of my head.

⁵ I did call upon the Lord with my voice, and He heard me out of His holy hill.

⁶ I laid me down and slept, and rose up again, for the Lord will sustain me.

⁷ I will not be afraid for ten thousands of the people that have set themselves against me round about.

⁸ Arise, O Lord; save me, O my God, for Thou hast smitten all who without cause are mine enemy; Thou hast broken the teeth of sinners.

⁹ Salvation is of the Lord, and Thy blessing is upon Thy people.

Psalm 4

Unto the end, in verses, a Psalm of David.

WHEN I called, the God of my righteousness heard me; Thou hast set me at liberty when I was in trouble. Be gracious unto me, and hearken unto my prayer.

³ O ye sons of men, how long will ye be heavy-hearted; why do ye take such pleasure in vanity, and seek after falsehood?

⁴ Know ye also, that the Lord hath made His holy one wonderful; when I call upon Him, the Lord will hear me.

⁵ Be angry, and sin not; for what ye say in your hearts, be sorry upon your beds.

⁶ Offer the sacrifice of righteousness, and put your trust in the Lord.

⁷ There be many that say, Who will show us any good? The light of Thy countenance hath been signed upon us, O Lord.

⁸ Thou hast put gladness in my heart; from the fruit of their wheat, and wine, and oil are they increased.

⁹ I will lay me down in peace, and also take my rest, for it is Thou, Lord, only, who hast made me to dwell in hope.

Psalm 5

Unto the end, for her that obtaineth the inheritance, a Psalm of David.

HEAR my words, O Lord; consider my cry.
³ Attend unto the voice of my supplication, my King, and my God, for unto Thee will I pray, O Lord.

⁴ Early in the morning shalt Thou hear my voice; early in the morning will I stand before Thee, and Thou shalt watch over me.

⁵ For Thou art a God that hast no pleasure in wickedness; the evil-doer shall not dwell nigh Thee.

⁶ Such as be lawless shall not stand in Thy sight, for Thou hatest all them that work iniquity.

⁷ Thou shalt destroy all them that speak lies; the Lord will abhor the blood-thirsty and deceitful man.

⁸ But as for me, by the multitude of Thy mercy I will come into Thine house; in Thy fear will I worship toward Thy holy temple.

⁹ Lead me, O Lord, in Thy righteousness; because of mine enemies, make my way plain before Thee.

¹⁰ For there is no truth in their mouth; their heart is vain; their throat is an open sepulcher; they flatter with their tongue.

¹¹ Judge them, O God; let them fall through their own imaginations; cast them out according to the multitude of their ungodliness; for they have embittered Thee, O Lord.

¹² And let all them that put their trust in Thee be glad; they shall ever rejoice; and Thou shalt dwell in them and they that love Thy Name shall be joyful in Thee.

¹³ For Thou wilt bless the righteous, O Lord, for with the shield of Thy favorable kindness hast Thou crowned us.

Psalm 6

Unto the end, in verses, a Psalm of David,
among the hymns for the octave.

O LORD, rebuke me not in Thine anger, neither chasten me in Thy wrath.

³ Have mercy upon me, O Lord, for I am weak; O Lord, heal me, for my bones are vexed.

⁴ My soul also is sore troubled; but Thou, O Lord, how long?

⁵ Turn Thee, O Lord, and deliver my soul; O save me, for Thy mercy's sake.

⁶ For in death no man remembereth Thee, and who will give Thee thanks in hell?

⁷ I am worn out with my groaning; every night wash I my bed, and water my couch with my tears.

⁸ Mine eye is clouded with anger; I have grown old among all mine enemies.

⁹ Away from me, all ye that work iniquity, for the Lord hath heard the voice of my weeping.

¹⁰ The Lord hath heard my petition; the Lord will receive my prayer.

¹¹ Let all mine enemies be confounded and sore vexed; let them be turned back, and put to shame suddenly.

Psalm 7

The Psalm of David, which he sang unto the Lord,
concerning the words of Cush the Benjamite.

O LORD my God, in Thee have I put my trust;
save me from all them that persecute me, and
deliver me;

³ Lest they seize my soul like a lion, and tear it in
pieces, while there is none to deliver, nor to save.

⁴ O Lord my God, if I have done any such thing, if
there be unrighteousness in my hands;

⁵ If I have repaid evil unto him that dealt
unfriendly with me, may I then fall back empty
before my enemies.

⁶ Then let the enemy persecute my soul; yea, let
him take and trample my life into the dirt, and lay
mine honor in the dust.

⁷ Arise, O Lord, in Thy wrath, exalt Thyself in the
borders of mine enemies, and rise up, O Lord my
God, by the injunction that Thou hast enjoined,

⁸ And a congregation of the peoples shall gather
round Thee; and for their sakes return Thou on
high.

⁹ The Lord shall judge the peoples; give sentence with me, O Lord, according to my righteousness, and according to the innocency that is in me.

¹⁰ O let the wickedness of sinners come to an
end, and guide Thou the righteous, O God, who tri-
est the very hearts and reins.

¹¹ My help is from God, who saveth them that
are true of heart.

¹² God is a righteous Judge, strong, and patient, and inflicteth not vengeance every day.

¹³ Except ye be converted, He will whet His sword; He hath bent His bow, and made it ready.

¹⁴ He hath fitted it with the instruments of death; He hath forged his arrows in the fire.

¹⁵ Behold, he hath travailed with unrighteousness, he hath conceived sorrow, and brought forth iniquity.

¹⁶ He hath graven a pit, and digged it up, and is fallen himself into the hole he made,

¹⁷ For his travail shall come upon his own head, and his unrighteousness shall fall on his own pate.

¹⁸ I will give thanks unto the Lord, according to His righteousness, and I will praise the Name of the Lord Most High.

Psalm 8

Unto the end, on the presses, a Psalm of David.

O LORD, our Lord, how wonderful is Thy Name in all the world; for Thy majesty is lifted high above the heavens!

³ Out of the mouth of babes and sucklings hast Thou perfected praise, because of Thine enemies, to destroy the enemy, and the avenger.

⁴ For I will consider the heavens, even the works of Thy fingers, the moon and the stars which Thou hast ordained.

⁵ What is man, that Thou art mindful of him? Or the son of man, that Thou visitest him?

⁶ Thou hast made him little lower than the angels; Thou hast crowned him with glory and honor,

⁷ And hast set him over the works of Thy hands; Thou hast put all things in subjection under his feet;

⁸ All sheep and oxen, yea, and the beasts of the field;

⁹ The fowls of the air, and the fishes of the sea, and whatsoever walketh through the paths of the seas.

¹⁰ O Lord, our Lord, how wonderful is Thy Name in all the world!

Psalm 9

Unto the end, on the hidden things of the Son,
a Psalm of David.

I WILL give thanks unto Thee, O Lord, with my whole heart; I will speak of all Thy marvelous works.

³ I will be glad and rejoice in Thee; yea, I will sing unto Thy Name, O Thou Most Highest.

⁴ When mine enemies are driven back, they shall falter and perish at Thy presence,

⁵ For Thou hast maintained my judgment and my cause; Thou hast sat on the throne, Who rightly dividest the truth.

⁶ Thou hast rebuked the heathen, and the impious one hath perished; Thou hast wiped out his name for ever and ever.

⁷ The swords of the enemy are utterly broken, and Thou hast destroyed his cities; with a clamor is his memory wiped out,

⁸ But the Lord endureth for ever; He hath prepared His throne for judgment,

⁹ And He shall judge the whole world unto truth; He shall minister judgment unto the people in righteousness.

¹⁰ The Lord is become also a refuge for the poor, a helper in due time of trouble.

¹¹ And let them that know Thy Name put their trust in Thee, for Thou, Lord, hast never forsaken them that seek Thee.

¹² O praise the Lord which dwelleth in Zion; proclaim His doings among the nations.

¹³ As the blood-avenger doth He remember them; He forgetteth not the complaint of the poor.

¹⁴ Have mercy upon me, O Lord; see how mine enemies humiliate me, Thou that liftest me up from the gates of death,

¹⁵ That I may show all Thy praises within the gates of the daughter of Zion; we will rejoice in Thy salvation.

¹⁶ The heathen are sunk down in the ruin that they made; in the same net which they hid privily is their foot taken.

¹⁷ The Lord is known by the judgments He dealeth; the sinner is trapped in the work of his own hands.

¹⁸ Let the sinners be turned into hell, all the nations that forget God.

[19] For the lowly shall not always be forgotten; the patient abiding of the poor shall not perish for ever.

[20] Arise, O Lord, and let not man have the upper hand; let the heathen be judged before Thee.

[21] Set a law-giver over them, O Lord, that the heathen may know themselves to be but men.

[22] Why standest Thou so far off, O Lord, and disdainest us in the needful time of trouble?

[23] When the ungodly man vaunteth himself, the poor man flareth up; they are taken in the crafty wiliness that they have imagined.

[24] For in the lusts of his soul the sinner commendeth himself, and he that offendeth counteth himself blessed.

[25] The sinner hath provoked the Lord; he is so wrathful, that he careth not; God is not before him.

[26] His ways are always defiled; Thy judgments are far above out of his sight; he shall have power over all his enemies.

[27] For he hath said in his heart, I shall never be cast down; from generation unto generation shall no harm happen unto me.

[28] His mouth is full of cursing, bitterness, and deceit; under his tongue is toil and misery.

[29] With the rich he sitteth thievishly in lurking dens, to murder the innocent; his eyes are set against the poor.

[30] He lurketh in secret as a lion in his den, that he may ravish the poor; to ravish the poor, when he getteth him into his net.

³¹ He humbleth himself; he croucheth and falleth, that the poor may fall into his hands.

³² For he hath said in his heart, God hath forgotten; He hath turned away His face, that He may never see.

³³ Arise, O Lord my God, let Thy hand be lifted up; forget not Thy poor before the end.

³⁴ Wherefore hath the wicked man blasphemed God? Because he hath said in his heart, He will not look into it.

³⁵ Thou seest, for Thou beholdest misery and anger, that Thou mayest take the matter into Thy hand. The poor man is abandoned unto Thee; Thou art the helper of the orphan.

³⁶ Break Thou the arm of the sinner and the evil man; his sin shall be sought, and shall not be found.

³⁷ The Lord is King for ever, and for ever and ever; ye heathen shall perish out of His land.

³⁸ Thou hast heard the desire of the poor, O Lord; Thine ear hearkeneth unto the disposition of their hearts.

³⁹ O judge for the fatherless and humble, that no man on earth may continue to boast.

Psalm 10

Unto the end, a Psalm of David.

IN the Lord have I put my trust; how say ye then to my soul, Flee as a bird unto the hills?

² For lo, the sinners have bent their bow, they have made ready their arrows within the quiver, that they may in darkness shoot at them which are true of heart.

³ For they have cast down what Thou hast built, but what hath the righteous done? The Lord is in His holy temple.

⁴ The Lord's throne is in heaven; His eyes consider the poor, and His eye-lids try the children of men.

⁵ The Lord trieth the righteous and the ungodly, but he that delighteth in wickedness hateth his own soul.

⁶ Upon sinners He shall rain down snares; fire and brimstone, and the stormy wind, shall be the portion of their cup.

⁷ For the Lord is righteous and loveth righteousness; His countenance hath beheld just things.

Psalm 11

Unto the end, on the octave, a Psalm of David.

SAVE me, Lord, for there is not one godly man left, for truth is minished from among the children of men.

³ They have talked of vanities every one with his neighbor; they do but flatter with their lips, and dissemble in their double heart.

⁴ The Lord shall destroy all lying lips, and the tongue that speaketh proud things;

⁵ Which have said, Our tongue will we magnify, our lips are our own; who is lord over us?

⁶ For the comfortless troubles' sake of the needy, and because of the deep sighing of the poor, Now will I arise, saith the Lord; I will set myself unto salvation; I will do it for all to see.

⁷ The words of the Lord are pure words, even as the silver, which from the earth is tried, and purified seven times in the fire.

⁸ Thou shalt keep us, O Lord, and shalt preserve us from this generation and for ever.

⁹ The ungodly walk on every side; according unto Thy height hast Thou increased the children of men.

Psalm 12

Unto the end, a Psalm of David.

HOW long, O Lord, wilt Thou forget me? For ever? How long wilt Thou turn Thy face from me?

³ How long shall I seek counsel in my soul, with anguish in my heart day and night? How long shall mine enemies triumph over me?

⁴ Look upon me, hear me, O Lord my God; lighten mine eyes, that I sleep not in death.

⁵ Lest mine enemy say, I have prevailed against him.

⁶ They that trouble me will rejoice, if I be cast down.

⁷ But I have put my trust in Thy mercy. My heart shall rejoice in Thy salvation; I will sing unto the Lord Who hath dealt so lovingly with me, and I will chant unto the Name of the Lord Most High.

Psalm 13

Unto the end, a Psalm of David.

THE fool hath said in his heart, There is no God. They are corrupt, and become abominable in their doings; there is none that doeth good, no not one.

² The Lord looked down from heaven upon the children of men, to see if there were any that would understand, or seek after God.

³ They are all gone astray, they are altogether become unprofitable; there is none that doeth good, no not one.

⁴ Shall all they that are such workers of mischief never learn, that eat up my people as it were bread? They called not upon the Lord.

⁵ There did they tremble for fear, even where no fear was; for the Lord is in the generation of the righteous.

⁶ Ye have made a mock at the counsel of the poor, but the Lord is his hope.

⁷ O who shall give the salvation of Israel out of Zion?

⁸ When the Lord turneth the captivity of His people, then shall Jacob rejoice, and Israel shall be glad.

Psalm 14

A Psalm of David.

L ORD, who shall dwell in Thy tabernacle, or who shall rest upon Thy holy hill?

² Even he that walketh blameless, and doeth the thing which is right, that speaketh the truth in his heart.

³ He that hath used no deceit in his tongue, nor done evil to his neighbor, and hath not reproached his friend.

⁴ He that setteth not by the evil-doer, and maketh much of them that fear the Lord; he that sweareth unto his neighbor, and disappointeth him not.

⁵ He that hath not given his money upon usury, nor taken a bribe against the innocent; whoso doeth these things shall never fall.

Psalm 15

A pillar inscription of David.

P RESERVE me, O Lord, for in Thee have I put my trust.

² I said unto the Lord, Thou art my Lord, my goods are nothing unto Thee.

³ Unto the saints that are in His land hath the Lord made wonderful all His desires in them.

⁴ Their infirmities increased, whereupon they made haste; I will not convene their assemblies of blood, neither make mention of their names with my lips.

⁵ The Lord is the portion of mine inheritance, and of my cup; it is Thou who restorest mine inheritance unto me.

⁶ The best portions are fallen unto me; for I have a goodly inheritance.

⁷ I will bless the Lord, Who hath given me wisdom; yea, even until night have my reins corrected me.

⁸ I foresaw the Lord always before me, for He is on my right hand, that I should not be moved.

⁹ Therefore did my heart rejoice, and my tongue was glad; moreover, my flesh also shall rest in hope,

¹⁰ Because Thou shalt not leave my soul in hell, neither shalt Thou suffer Thine Holy One to see corruption.

¹¹ Thou hast made known to me the paths of life; Thou shalt make me full of gladness with Thy countenance, and beauty is in Thy right hand for evermore.

Psalm 16

A Prayer of David.

HEAR my just cause, O Lord; attend unto my supplication. Hearken unto my prayer, that goeth not out of flattering lips.

² From Thy presence shall my judgment come forth; let mine eyes look upon the things that are right.

³ Thou hast proved my heart; Thou hast visited in the night. Thou hast tried me, and unrighteousness hath not been found within me.

⁴ That my mouth shall not speak of men's works, for the sake of the words of Thy lips I have kept hard ways.

⁵ O hold Thou up my goings in Thy paths, that my footsteps slip not.

⁶ I called, for Thou hast heard me, O God; incline Thine ear to me, and hearken unto my words.

⁷ Make Thy mercies marvelous, Thou that art the Saviour of them which put their trust in Thee, from such as resist Thy right hand.

⁸ Keep me, O Lord, as the apple of Thine eye; hide me under the shelter of Thy wings,

⁹ From the presence of the ungodly that trouble me; mine enemies compass my soul round about.

¹⁰ They are enclosed in their own fat, and their mouth speaketh proud things.

¹¹ They that cast me out have now surrounded me; they have turned their eyes down to the ground,

¹² Like as a lion that is greedy of his prey, and as it were a lion's whelp, lurking in secret places.

¹³ Arise, O Lord, disappoint them, and trip them up; deliver my soul from the ungodly, Thy sword from the enemies of Thy hand.

¹⁴ O Lord, divide them in their life from the few of the earth; yea, from Thy hid treasure hath their belly been filled. They had children at their desire,

and left the rest of their substance for their babes.

¹⁵ But as for me, in righteousness shall I appear before Thy face; when Thy glory is revealed, I shall be satisfied.

Psalm 17

Unto the end, by David, the servant of the Lord, who spake
unto the Lord the words of this song in the day that the
Lord delivered him from the hand of all his enemies, and
from the hand of Saul. And he said,

I WILL love Thee, O Lord, my strength.
³ The Lord is my firm foundation, and my fortress, and my deliverer; my God is my helper, and I will trust in him, my defender, the horn also of my salvation, and my protector.

⁴ Giving praise, I will call upon the Lord, and so shall I be safe from mine enemies.

⁵ The pains of death surrounded me, and the overflowings of ungodliness made me afraid.

⁶ The pains of hell encircled me; the snares of death overtook me.

⁷ And in my trouble I called upon the Lord, and cried unto my God; so He heard my voice out of His holy temple, and my cry before Him shall enter even into His ears.

⁸ The earth trembled and quaked; the very foundations also of the hills were troubled, and shook, because God was angry with them.

⁹ There went up smoke in His wrath, and fire flared forth from His face; coals were kindled at it.

¹⁰ He bowed the heavens also, and came down, and thick darkness was under His feet.

¹¹ He mounted upon the Cherubim, and did fly; He came flying upon the wings of the wind.

¹² He made darkness His hiding-place, His tabernacle round about Him, dark water in the clouds of the air.

¹³ At the brightness that was before Him the clouds removed; hailstones and coals of fire.

¹⁴ The Lord also thundered out of heaven, and the Highest gave His voice.

¹⁵ He sent out His arrows, and scattered them; He multiplied lightnings, and troubled them.

¹⁶ And the springs of waters were seen, and the foundations of the world were uncovered, at Thy chiding, O Lord, at the blasting of the breath of Thy displeasure.

¹⁷ He sent down from on high to fetch me; He took me out of many waters.

¹⁸ He shall deliver me from my strong enemies, and from them which hate me, for they are too mighty for me.

¹⁹ They came upon me in the day of my trouble, and the Lord was my upholder.

²⁰ He brought me forth also into a place of liberty; He will deliver me, because He had a favor unto me.

²¹ The Lord also shall reward me after my righteous dealing, and according to the cleanness of my hands shall He recompense me,

²² Because I have kept the ways of the Lord, and have not forsaken my God.

²³ For all His judgments are before me, and His statutes have not departed from me,

²⁴ And I will be blameless with Him, and shall keep myself from mine own wickedness.

²⁵ And the Lord shall reward me after my righteous dealing, and according unto the cleanness of my hands in His eye-sight.

²⁶ With the holy Thou shalt be holy, and with an innocent man Thou shalt be innocent.

²⁷ With the elect Thou shalt be elect, and with the froward Thou shalt be froward.

²⁸ For Thou shalt save the humble, and shalt bring down the high looks of the proud.

²⁹ For Thou shalt light my lamp, O Lord my God; Thou shalt make my darkness to be light.

³⁰ For by Thee am I delivered from temptation, and by my God I shall leap over a wall.

³¹ As for my God, His way is undefiled; the words of the Lord also are tried in the fire; He is the defender of all them that put their trust in Him.

³² For who is God, but the Lord, or who is God, except our God?

³³ It is God that hath girded me with strength, and made my way perfect,

³⁴ That maketh my feet like harts' feet, and setteth me up on high,

³⁵ That teacheth mine hands to fight, and hath made mine arms like a bow of copper.

[36] Thou hast given me also the shield of salvation, and Thy right hand shall hold me up, and Thy chastening shall utterly correct me; and it is Thy chastening that shall teach me.

[37] Thou hast stretched my foot-steps under me, and my feet did not get tired.

[38] I will pursue mine enemies, and overtake them, neither will I turn back, until they are dead.

[39] I will smite them, and they shall not be able to stand; they shall fall under my feet.

[40] For Thou hast girded me with strength unto the battle; Thou hast crushed under me them that rose up against me.

[41] Thou hast made mine enemies also to turn their backs upon me, and Thou hast utterly destroyed them that hated me.

[42] They cried, but there was none to save them; even unto the Lord, and He did not hear them.

[43] I will grind them down as the dust before the face of the wind; I will trample them as the mud in the streets.

[44] Thou shalt deliver me from the strife of the people, and Thou shalt make me the head of the nations; a people whom I have not known have served me.

[45] As soon as they heard, they obeyed me; the strange children dissembled with me.

[46] The strange children have grown old, and tottered out of their way.

[47] The Lord liveth, and blessed be God, and praised be the God of my salvation.

⁴⁸ It is God that avengeth me, and subdueth the peoples unto me;

⁴⁹ My deliverer from my belligerent enemies, that lifteth me up above them that rise up against me; Thou shalt rid me from the wicked man.

⁵⁰ For this cause will I give thanks unto Thee among the nations, O Lord, and sing praises unto Thy Name,

⁵¹ Who extolleth the salvation of the king, and worketh mercy unto David His anointed, and unto his seed for evermore.

Psalm 18

Unto the end, a Psalm of David.

THE heavens declare the glory of God, and the firmament showeth His handy-work.

³ Day unto day uttereth speech, and night unto night showeth knowledge.

⁴ There is neither speech nor language, in which their voices are not heard.

⁵ Their sound is gone out into all the earth, and their words unto the ends of the world. He hath set His tabernacle in the sun,

⁶ And, coming forth as a bridegroom out of His chamber, He rejoiceth as a giant to run His course.

⁷ His going forth is from the uttermost part of heaven, and His circuit even unto the end of it again, and there is no one who can hide from the heat thereof.

⁸ The Law of the Lord is pure, converting the soul; the testimony of the Lord is sure, giving wisdom unto the simple.

⁹ The statutes of the Lord are right, gladdening the heart; the commandment of the Lord is bright, giving light unto the eyes.

¹⁰ The fear of the Lord is clean, enduring for ever and ever; the judgments of the Lord are true, and righteous altogether.

¹¹ More to be desired are they than gold and much precious stone; sweeter also than honey, and the honey-comb.

¹² Therefore Thy servant keepeth them, and in keeping of them there is great reward.

¹³ Who can understand his fallings into sin? O cleanse Thou me from my secret faults,

¹⁴ And from strangers spare Thy servant; if they get not the dominion over me, then shall I be undefiled, and I shall be cleansed of great sin.

¹⁵ And the words of my mouth, and the meditation of my heart shall be always acceptable before Thee, O Lord, my helper, and my deliverer.

Psalm 19

Unto the end, a Psalm of David.

THE Lord hear thee in the day of trouble; the Name of the God of Jacob defend thee;

³ Send thee help from the sanctuary, and strengthen thee out of Zion;

⁴ Remember all thy sacrifices, and make acceptable thy whole-burnt offering.

⁵ The Lord grant thee according to thy heart, and fulfill all thy counsel.

⁶ We will rejoice in thy salvation, and triumph in the Name of the Lord our God; the Lord perform all thy petitions.

⁷ Now know I, that the Lord hath saved His Christ; He will hear Him from His holy heaven; the salvation of His right hand cometh with sovereignty.

⁸ Some put their trust in chariots, and some in horses, but we will call upon the Name of the Lord our God.

⁹ They are overthrown, and fallen, but we are risen, and stand upright.

¹⁰ O Lord, save the king, and hear us in the day when we call upon Thee.

Psalm 20

Unto the end, a Psalm of David.

O LORD, the King shall be glad in Thy strength, and in Thy salvation shall he greatly rejoice.

³ Thou hast given him his heart's desire, and hast not denied him the requests of his lips.

⁴ For Thou hast gone before him with the blessings of goodness; Thou hast set a crown of precious stone upon his head.

⁵ He asked life of Thee, and Thou gavest him a long life, even for ever and ever.

⁶ Great is his glory in Thy salvation; glory and majesty shalt Thou lay upon him.

⁷ For Thou shalt give him everlasting felicity; Thou shalt make him glad with the joy of Thy countenance,

⁸ Because the King putteth his trust in the Lord, and in the mercy of the Most Highest he shall not be provoked.

⁹ Let all Thine enemies feel Thy hand; let Thy right hand find out them that hate Thee.

¹⁰ For Thou shalt make them like a fiery oven in time of Thy presence; the Lord shall trouble them in His displeasure, and the fire shall consume them.

¹¹ Their fruit shalt Thou root out of the earth, and their seed from among the children of men.

¹² For they intended mischief against Thee, and imagined such counsels as they are not able to perform.

¹³ For Thou shalt make them to turn their back; among them that are Thy remnant Thou shalt prepare their face.

¹⁴ Rise up, O Lord, by Thy power; we will chant and sing of Thy power.

Psalm 21

Unto the end, a Psalm of David,
concerning help that cometh in the morning.

O GOD, my God, hear me; why hast Thou forsaken me? Far from my salvation are the
words of my fallings into sin.

³ O my God, I cry in the day-time, and Thou hearest not; and in the night-season, and it is not foolishness unto me,

⁴ For Thou dwellest in the holy place, O Thou
praise of Israel.

⁵ Our fathers hoped in Thee; they trusted, and
Thou didst deliver them.

⁶ They called upon Thee, and were saved; they
put their trust in Thee, and were not confounded.

⁷ But as for me, I am a worm, and no man; a very
scorn of men, and the out-cast of the people.

⁸ All they that saw me laughed me to scorn; they
whispered with their lips, and wagged their heads,
saying,

⁹ He trusted in God, that He would deliver him;
let Him save him, seeing He careth for him.

¹⁰ For Thou art He that took me out of the belly;
my hope, when I hanged yet upon my mother's
breast.

¹¹ From the womb was I promised unto Thee;
Thou art my God, even from my mother's belly.

¹² O go not from me, for trouble is hard at hand,
and there is none to help me.

¹³ Many oxen are come about me; fat bulls have closed me in on every side.

¹⁴ They gape upon me with their mouths, as it were a ramping and a roaring lion.

¹⁵ I am poured out like water, and all my bones are out of joint; my heart also in the midst of my body is even like melting wax.

¹⁶ My strength is dried up like a potsherd, and my tongue hath cleaved to the back of my throat, and Thou hast brought me down into the dust of death.

¹⁷ For many dogs are come about me, and a throng of the wicked layeth siege against me; they pierced my hands and my feet.

¹⁸ They have counted all my bones; they gazed and stared upon me.

¹⁹ They parted my garments among them, and cast lots upon my vesture.

²⁰ But Thou, O Lord, withdraw not Thy help from me; attend unto my defense.

²¹ Deliver my soul from the sword, and my only-begotten from the hand of the dog.

²² Save me from the lion's mouth, and my lowliness also from the horns of the unicorns.

²³ I will declare Thy Name unto my brethren; in the midst of the church will I sing of Thee.

²⁴ O praise Him, ye that fear the Lord; glorify Him, all ye of the seed of Jacob. Let all the seed of Israel fear Him.

²⁵ For He hath not despised, nor abhorred, the

prayers of the poor; He hath not hid His face from me, and when I called unto Him, He heard me.

²⁶ My praise is of Thee; in the great church will I give thanks unto Thee; my vows will I perform in the sight of them that fear Him.

²⁷ The poor shall eat, and be satisfied, and they that seek after the Lord shall praise Him; their hearts shall live for ever and ever.

²⁸ All the ends of the world shall remember themselves, and be turned unto the Lord, and all the kindreds of the nations shall worship before Him.

²⁹ For the kingdom is the Lord's, and He is the Governor among the nations.

³⁰ All such as be fat upon earth have eaten, and worshipped; all they that go down into the dust shall kneel before Him, and my soul liveth for Him.

³¹ Yea, my seed shall serve Him; a generation to come shall tell of the Lord,

³² And they shall declare His righteousness unto a people that shall be born, whom the Lord hath made.

Psalm 22

A Psalm of David.

THE Lord is my shepherd; therefore can I lack nothing.

² He maketh me to lie down in a green pasture; He leadeth me beside the still water.

³ He hath converted my soul; He hath set me on the paths of righteousness, for His Name's sake.

⁴ Yea, though I walk through the valley of the shadow of death, I will fear no evil, for Thou art with me; Thy rod and Thy staff, they have comforted me.

⁵ Thou hast prepared a table before me against them that trouble me; Thou hast anointed my head with oil, and Thy cup that inebriateth me, how strong it is!

⁶ And Thy mercy shall follow me all the days of my life, and I will dwell in the house of the Lord unto length of days.

Psalm 23

A Psalm of David, on the first day of the week.

THE earth is the Lord's, and the fullness thereof; the compass of the world, and all that dwell therein.

² He hath founded it upon the seas, and prepared it upon the floods.

³ Who shall ascend into the hill of the Lord, or who shall stand in His holy place?

⁴ Even he that hath clean hands, and a pure heart, who doth not take his soul in vain, nor swear falsely to his neighbor.

⁵ He shall receive a blessing from the Lord, and mercy from God his Saviour.

⁶ This is the generation of them that seek the

Lord, even of them that seek the face of the God of Jacob.

⁷ Lift up your gates, O ye princes, and be ye lift up, ye everlasting doors, and the King of glory shall come in.

⁸ Who is this King of glory? It is the Lord strong and mighty, even the Lord mighty in battle.

⁹ Lift up your gates, O ye princes, and be ye lift up, ye everlasting doors, and the King of glory shall come in.

¹⁰ Who is this King of glory? Even the Lord of hosts, He is the King of glory.

Psalm 24

A Psalm of David.

Unto Thee, O Lord, have I lifted up my soul; my God, I have put my trust in Thee: O let me never be confounded, neither let mine enemies laugh me to scorn.

² For all they that wait on Thee shall not be ashamed.

³ Let them be ashamed such as transgress without a cause.

⁴ Tell me Thy ways, O Lord, and teach me Thy paths.

⁵ Lead me forth unto Thy truth, and teach me, for Thou art God my Saviour, and upon Thee have I waited all the day long.

⁶ Remember Thy loving-kindnesses, O Lord,

and Thy mercies, which are from everlasting.

⁷ O remember not the sins of my youth, and of mine ignorance; according to Thy mercy think Thou upon me, O Lord, for Thy goodness' sake.

⁸ Gracious and righteous is the Lord, therefore will He give a Law to sinners in the way.

⁹ He will guide the meek unto judgment, He shall teach the meek His ways.

¹⁰ All the paths of the Lord are mercy and truth unto such as keep His covenant, and His testimonies.

¹¹ For Thy Name's sake, O Lord, be merciful unto my sin, for it is great.

¹² What man is he, that feareth the Lord? To him shall He give a Law in the way which He hath chosen.

¹³ His soul shall dwell at ease, and his seed shall inherit the land.

¹⁴ The Lord is the strength of them that fear Him, and He will show them His covenant.

¹⁵ Mine eyes are ever toward the Lord, for He shall pluck my feet out of the net.

¹⁶ Be charitable unto me, and have mercy on me, for I am only-begotten and poor.

¹⁷ The sorrows of my heart are enlarged; O bring Thou me out of my troubles.

¹⁸ Look upon my humbleness and my hardship, and forgive all my sins.

¹⁹ Consider mine enemies, how many they are, and they bear a tyrannous hate against me.

²⁰ O keep my soul, and deliver me; let me not be confounded, for I have put my trust in Thee.

²¹ The innocent and the upright have cleaved unto me, for I waited upon Thee, O Lord.

²² Deliver Israel, O God, out of all his troubles.

Psalm 25

A Psalm of David.

BE Thou my Judge, O Lord, for I have walked innocently and, trusting in the Lord, I shall not falter.

² Examine me, O Lord, and prove me; try out my reins and my heart.

³ For Thy mercy is ever before mine eyes, and I have behaved well in Thy truth.

⁴ I have not sat with the company of the vain-glorious, neither will I have fellowship with wrong-doers.

⁵ I have hated the congregation of the wicked, and will not sit among the ungodly.

⁶ I will wash my hands in innocency, O Lord, and so will I go round about Thine altar;

⁷ That I may hear the voice of Thy praise, and tell of all Thy wondrous works.

⁸ Lord, I have loved the beauty of Thy house, and the dwelling-place of Thy glory.

⁹ O destroy not my soul with the ungodly, nor my life with the blood-thirsty;

¹⁰ In whose hand is wickedness, and their right hand is full of bribes.

¹¹ But as for me, I have walked innocently; deliver me, O Lord, and have mercy upon me.

¹² My foot hath stood on the right; I will bless Thee, O Lord, in the churches.

Psalm 26

A Psalm of David, before he was anointed.

THE Lord is my light, and my Saviour; whom then shall I fear? The Lord is the defender of my life; of whom then shall I be afraid?

² When they that had enmity against me, even mine enemies, and my foes, came nigh to eat up my flesh, they faltered and fell.

³ Though a legion were laid against me, yet shall not my heart be afraid; and though there rise up war against me, yet will I put my trust in Him.

⁴ One thing have I desired of the Lord, which I will require; even that I may dwell in the house of the Lord all the days of my life, to behold the fair beauty of the day, and to visit His holy temple.

⁵ For in the day of my trouble He hath hidden me in His tabernacle; yea, in the secret place of His dwelling did He shelter me, and set me up upon a rock.

⁶ And now, behold, He hath lifted up mine head above mine enemies; therefore have I gone round about and offered in His dwelling a sacrifice of praise and jubilation; I will sing and chant unto the Lord.

⁷ Hearken, O Lord, unto my voice, with which I have cried, Have mercy upon me, and hear me.

⁸ My heart hath said unto Thee, I will seek the Lord; my face hath sought Thee; Thy face, O Lord, will I seek.

⁹ O turn not Thou Thy face from me, nor turn away from Thy servant in displeasure; be Thou my helper; reject me not, neither forsake me, O God, my Saviour.

¹⁰ For my father and my mother have forsaken me, but the Lord taketh me up.

¹¹ Teach me a law, O Lord, in Thy way, and set me on the right path, because of mine enemies.

¹² Deliver me not over to the souls of them that afflict me, for false witnesses are risen up against me, and iniquity hath lied to itself.

¹³ I believe that I shall see the goodness of the Lord in the land of the living.

¹⁴ Wait thou on the Lord; be of good courage, and let thine heart stand firm, and wait thou on the Lord.

Psalm 27

A Psalm of David.

UNTO Thee, O Lord, will I cry; O my God, be not silent unto me, lest, if Thou keep silence unto me, I become like them that go down into the pit.

² Hear, O Lord, the voice of my humble petition when I pray unto Thee, when I hold up my hands toward Thy holy temple.

³ O pluck me not away with the sinners, neither destroy me with the wrong-doers, which speak peace to their neighbors, but imagine mischief in their hearts.

⁴ Reward them, O Lord, according to their deeds, and according to the wickedness of their own inventions; recompense them after the work of their hands; pay them that they have deserved.

⁵ For they understood not the works of the Lord, nor the operation of His hands; therefore shalt Thou break them down, and not build them up.

⁶ Blessed be the Lord, for He hath heard the voice of my humble petition.

⁷ The Lord is my helper, and my protector; my heart hath trusted in Him, and I am helped; even my flesh hath revived, and gladly will I praise Him.

⁸ The Lord is the strength of His people, and He is the defender of the salvation of His anointed.

⁹ Save Thy people, and bless Thine inheritance; and be their shepherd, and carry them for ever.

Psalm 28

A Psalm of David, of the going forth of the Tabernacle.

BRING unto the Lord, O ye sons of God, bring young rams unto the Lord; bring unto the Lord glory and honor.

² Bring unto the Lord the glory due unto His Name; worship the Lord in His holy court.

³ The voice of the Lord is upon the waters; the

God of glory hath thundered. The Lord is upon many waters.

⁴ The voice of the Lord in power; the voice of the Lord in majesty,

⁵ The voice of the Lord Who breaketh the cedar-trees; yea, the Lord will break the cedars of Lebanon.

⁶ He will break them in pieces like the calf, Lebanon, but the beloved is like a young unicorn.

⁷ The voice of the Lord Who divideth the flame of fire.

⁸ The voice of the Lord Who shaketh the wilderness; yea, the Lord will shake the wilderness of Kadesh.

⁹ The voice of the Lord Who gathereth the hinds, and discovereth the leafy glade, and in His temple doth every man speak glory.

¹⁰ The Lord dwelleth in the water-flood, and the Lord shall sit as King for ever.

¹¹ The Lord shall give strength unto His people; the Lord shall bless His people with peace.

Psalm 29

A Psalm and Song at the dedication of the house of David.

I WILL exalt Thee, O Lord, for Thou hast raised me up, and not made my foes to triumph over me.

³ O Lord my God, I cried unto Thee, and Thou hast healed me.

⁴ O Lord, Thou hast brought my soul out of hell;
Thou hast saved me from them that go down to the
pit.

⁵ Sing unto the Lord, O ye saints of His, and give
thanks at the memory of His holiness.

⁶ For there is wrath in His anger, but in His pleasure is life; tears may endure for a night, but joy
cometh in the morning.

⁷ But in my prosperity I said, I shall never be
removed.

⁸ Thou, Lord, of Thy favor hast given power to
my goodness, but Thou didst turn Thy face from
me, and I was troubled.

⁹ Unto Thee, O Lord, will I call, and I will pray
unto my God.

¹⁰ What profit is there in my blood, when I go
down to corruption? Shall the dust give thanks
unto Thee, or shall it declare Thy truth?

¹¹ The Lord heard, and had mercy upon me; the
Lord was my helper.

¹² Thou hast turned my tears into joy; Thou hast
put off my sackcloth, and girded me with gladness,

¹³ That my glory may sing unto Thee, and I shall
not be sorry; O Lord my God, I will give thanks unto
Thee for ever.

Psalm 30

Unto the end, a Psalm of David, of rapture.

I N Thee, O Lord, have I put my trust; let me never be confounded, but rescue me in Thy righteousness, and deliver me.

³ Bow down Thine ear to me; make haste to deliver me, and be Thou unto me a defending God, and a house of refuge to save me.

⁴ For Thou art my strength, and my safe haven; be Thou also my guide, and my provider, for Thy Name's sake.

⁵ Thou shalt draw me out of this net that they laid privily for me; for Thou art my protector, O Lord.

⁶ Into Thy hands will I commend my spirit, for Thou hast redeemed me, O Lord, Thou God of truth.

⁷ Thou hast hated them that hold of superstitious vanities, but my hope hath been in the Lord.

⁸ I will be glad, and rejoice in Thy mercy, for Thou hast considered my lowliness, and hast saved my soul from adversity.

⁹ And Thou hast not shut me up into the hand of the enemy, but hast set my feet in a place of liberty.

¹⁰ Have mercy upon me, O Lord, for I am in trouble; mine eye is troubled with anger; yea, my soul and my body.

¹¹ For my life hath been used up in suffering, and my years in sighing; my strength failed

me, because of my poverty, and my bones were troubled.

¹² I became a reproof among all mine enemies, but especially among my neighbors, and they of mine acquaintance were afraid of me; and they that did see me without fled from me.

¹³ I am clean forgotten, as a dead man out of mind; I am become like a broken vessel.

¹⁴ For I have heard the blasphemy of the multitude who dwell on every side, while they conspired together against me, and took their counsel to take away my life.

¹⁵ But I have put my trust in Thee, O Lord; I said, Thou art my God,

¹⁶ My lots are in Thy hand; deliver me from the hand of mine enemies, and from them that persecute me.

¹⁷ Show Thy servant the light of Thy countenance, and save me for Thy mercy's sake.

¹⁸ Let me not be confounded, O Lord, for I have called upon Thee; let the ungodly be put to confusion, and be brought down into hell.

¹⁹ Let the lying lips be put to silence which disdainfully, and scornfully, speak iniquity against the righteous.

²⁰ O Lord, how plentiful is the abundance of Thy goodness, which Thou hast laid up for them that fear Thee, and that Thou hast prepared for them that put their trust in Thee, before the sons of men!

²¹ Thou shalt hide them in the secret place of

Thy presence from the provoking of all men; Thou shalt shelter them from the strife of tongues.

²² Blessed be the Lord, for He hath marvelously showed His mercy in a strong city.

²³ But in my confusion, I said, I am cast out of the sight of Thine eyes; therefore, Thou heardest the voice of my prayer when I cried unto Thee.

²⁴ O love the Lord, all ye His saints, for the Lord requireth truth, and plenteously rewardeth the proud doer.

²⁵ Be of good courage and let your heart stand firm, all ye that put your trust in the Lord.

Psalm 31

A Psalm of David, of understanding.

BLESSED are they whose iniquities are forgiven, and whose sins are covered.

² Blessed is the man unto whom the Lord imputeth no sin, and in whose lips there is no guile.

³ Because I was silent, my bones consumed away, whereupon I called the whole day long.

⁴ For Thy hand was heavy upon me day and night; I was brought to misery by a piercing thorn.

⁵ I have acknowledged my transgression and my sin have I not hid; I said, Against myself will I confess my transgression unto the Lord, and so Thou forgavest the irreverence of my heart.

⁶ For this shall every one that is godly make his prayer unto Thee in a seasonable time; therefore

in the great water-floods the waves shall not come nigh him.

⁷ Thou art my refuge from the afflictions that overwhelm me; my Joy, deliver me from them that circle me round about.

⁸ I will teach thee, and set thee on the way wherein thou shalt go; Mine eyes shall watch over thee.

⁹ Be ye not like to horse and mule, which have no understanding, whose jaws must be bound by bit and bridle, if they be skittish unto thee.

¹⁰ Many are the wounds of the ungodly, but whoso putteth his trust in the Lord, mercy embraceth him on every side.

¹¹ Be glad in the Lord, and rejoice, O ye righteous, and sing praises, all ye that are true of heart.

Psalm 32

A Psalm of David. Without superscription in the Hebrew.

REJOICE in the Lord, O ye righteous, for praise becometh well the upright.

² Give thanks unto the Lord with harp, sing unto Him with the ten-stringed psaltery.

³ Sing unto Him a new song, sing praises lustily unto Him with jubilation.

⁴ For the word of the Lord is true, and all His works are faithful.

⁵ The Lord loveth alms-giving and justice; the earth is full of the mercy of the Lord.

⁶ By the Word of the Lord were the heavens made, and all the hosts of them by the Breath of His mouth,

⁷ Who gathereth the waters of the sea together, as it were in a wine-skin, Who layeth up the deeps, as in a treasure-house.

⁸ Let all the earth fear the Lord; be shaken of Him, all ye that dwell in the world.

⁹ For He spake, and they came to be; He commanded, and they were created.

¹⁰ The Lord bringeth the counsel of the heathen to naught, He maketh the thoughts of the people to be of none effect, and casteth out the counsels of princes.

¹¹ But the counsel of the Lord endureth for ever, and the thoughts of His heart from generation to generation.

¹² Blessed are the people, whose God is the Lord, the folk, that He hath chosen to be an inheritance unto Him.

¹³ The Lord looked down from heaven, and beheld all the children of men;

¹⁴ From His prepared habitation, He considereth all them that dwell on the earth,

¹⁵ Having made the hearts of every one of them, and understanding all their works.

¹⁶ A king is not saved by many armies, and a giant is not saved by his great strength.

¹⁷ Vain is the horse for salvation, neither shall he deliver any man by his great power.

¹⁸ Behold, the eyes of the Lord are upon them that fear Him, and upon them that put their trust in His mercy;

¹⁹ To deliver their souls from death, and to feed them in the time of dearth.

²⁰ But our soul shall patiently wait upon the Lord, for He is our helper and defender.

²¹ For our heart shall rejoice in Him, and we have hoped in His holy Name.

²² Let Thy mercy, O Lord, be upon us, according as we have put our trust in Thee.

Psalm 33

A Psalm of David, when he changed his behavior before Abimelech; who drove him away, and he departed.

I will bless the Lord at all times, His praise is ever in my mouth.

³ In the Lord shall my soul be praised; let the meek hear, and be glad.

⁴ O magnify the Lord with me, and we shall exalt His Name together.

⁵ I sought the Lord and He heard me, yea, He delivered me out of all my troubles.

⁶ Come unto Him, and be enlightened, and your faces shall not be ashamed.

⁷ This poor man cried and the Lord heard him, and saved him out of all his troubles.

⁸ The angel of the Lord tarrieth round about them that fear Him, and delivereth them.

⁹ O taste, and see, that the Lord is good; blessed is the man that trusteth in Him.

¹⁰ O fear the Lord, all ye that are His saints, for they that fear Him lack nothing.

¹¹ The rich have lacked, and suffered hunger, but they that seek the Lord shall want no manner of thing that is good.

¹² Come, ye children, and hearken unto me; I will teach you the fear of the Lord.

¹³ What man is he that lusteth to live, and would gladly see good days?

¹⁴ Keep thy tongue from evil, and thy lips, that they speak no guile.

¹⁵ Shun evil, and do good; seek peace, and pursue it.

¹⁶ The eyes of the Lord are over the righteous, and His ears are open unto their prayers.

¹⁷ But the countenance of the Lord is against them that do evil, to root out the remembrance of them from the earth.

¹⁸ The righteous cried, and the Lord heard them, and delivered them out of all their troubles.

¹⁹ The Lord is nigh unto them that are of a contrite heart, and will save such as be of an humble spirit.

²⁰ Many are the troubles of the righteous, but the Lord delivereth them out of all.

²¹ The Lord keepeth all their bones; not one of them shall be broken.

²² The death of sinners is evil, and they that hate

the righteous shall sin greatly.

²³ The Lord will deliver the souls of His servants, and all they that put their trust in Him shall do no sin.

Psalm 34
A Psalm of David.

JUDGE them, O Lord, that do me wrong; fight Thou against them that fight against me.

² Lay hold of shield and buckler, and come to my help.

³ Draw forth the sword, and stop the way against them that persecute me; say unto my soul, I am thy salvation.

⁴ Let them be confounded, and put to shame, that seek after my soul; let them be turned back, and brought to confusion, that imagine mischief for me.

⁵ Let them be as the dust before the face of the wind, and the angel of the Lord persecuting them.

⁶ Let their way be dark and slippery, and the angel of the Lord pursuing them.

⁷ For they have privily laid their net to destroy me without a cause; in vain have they reproached my soul.

⁸ Let that net come upon him unawares, and let the snare that he hath laid privily catch himself, that he may fall into his own mischief.

⁹ But my soul shall be joyful in the Lord, it shall rejoice in His salvation.

¹⁰ All my bones shall say, Lord, O Lord, who is like unto Thee, who deliverest the poor from him that is too strong for him, and the poor man, and the needy, from him that despoileth him?

¹¹ False witnesses did rise up against me, they laid to my charge things that I knew not.

¹² They repaid me evil for good, and barrenness to my soul.

¹³ But when they troubled me, I put on sackcloth, and humbled my soul with fasting, and my prayer shall turn into mine own bosom.

¹⁴ As to a neighbor, as to our brother, so I behaved friendly; as one weeping and mourning, so I humbled myself.

¹⁵ But they rejoiced, and gathered themselves together against me; they plotted harm against me, and I was unawares; they were beside themselves and had no mercy.

¹⁶ They tempted me, they mocked at me with busy mockery, they gnashed upon me with their teeth.

¹⁷ Lord, when wilt Thou see? O rescue my soul from their evil-doing, my only-begotten from the lions.

¹⁸ I will give Thee thanks in the great congregation; I will praise thee among much people.

¹⁹ O let not them triumph over me that are mine enemies unjustly, that hate me without a cause and wink with their eyes.

²⁰ For while they spake peaceably unto me, in

their anger they imagined lies.

²¹ They gaped upon me with their mouths, and said, Well, well, our eyes have seen.

²² Thou hast seen, O Lord; hold not Thy tongue. O Lord, forsake me not.

²³ Rise up, O Lord, and attend unto my judgment, O my God; even, O my Lord, unto my cause.

²⁴ Judge me, O Lord, according to Thy righteousness, and let them not triumph over me, O Lord my God.

²⁵ Let them not say in their hearts, Good! It doeth our hearts good! Neither let them say, We have swallowed him up.

²⁶ Let them be put to confusion and shame together, that rejoice at my trouble; let them be clothed with rebuke and dishonor, that boast themselves against me.

²⁷ Let them be glad and rejoice, that favor my righteous dealing; and let them say always, The Lord be praised, who hath pleasure in the peace of His servant.

²⁸ And my tongue shall teach of Thy righteousness, and of Thy praise all day.

Psalm 35

Unto the end, a Psalm of David, the servant of the Lord.

THE sinner, that he may sin, saith within himself, There is no fear of God before his eyes.

³ For he hath dissembled before Him, that he

may find his wickedness, and learn to hate.

⁴ The words of his mouth are iniquity and deceit; he hath not wished to understand how to do good.

⁵ He hath imagined mischief upon his bed; he hath set himself in no good way, neither doth he abhor any thing that is evil.

⁶ Thy mercy, O Lord, is unto the heavens, and Thy truth unto the clouds.

⁷ Thy justice is as the mountains of God, Thy judgments are as the bottomless deep; man and beast shalt Thou save, O Lord.

⁸ O how hast Thou multiplied Thy mercy, O God; so shall the children of men put their trust in the shelter of Thy wings.

⁹ They shall be drunk from the plenteousness of Thy house, and Thou shalt give them drink of Thy pleasure, as out of a river.

¹⁰ For with Thee is the fountain of life; in Thy light shall we see light.

¹¹ O continue Thy mercy unto them that know Thee, and Thy righteousness unto them that are true of heart.

¹² O let not the foot of pride come against me, and let not the hand of the ungodly provoke me.

¹³ There are they fallen, all them that work wickedness; they are cast down, and shall not be able to stand.

Psalm 36

A Psalm of David.

Fret not thyself because of the wicked, neither be thou envious against them that do unlawfulness,

² For they shall soon wither like the grass, and quickly fall away even as the green herb.

³ Put thou thy trust in the Lord, and be doing good, and dwell in the land, and thou shalt graze on the riches thereof.

⁴ Delight thou in the Lord, and He shall give thee thy heart's desire.

⁵ Open thy way unto the Lord, and put thy trust in Him, and He shall bring it to pass,

⁶ And He shall make thy righteousness as plain as the light, and thy judgment as the noonday.

⁷ Give thyself up to the Lord, and pray unto Him; fret not thyself at him whose way doth prosper, at the man that doeth after evil counsels.

⁸ Leave off from wrath, and let go displeasure; fret not thyself, else thou do evil,

⁹ For the wicked doers shall be utterly consumed, but they that patiently abide the Lord, those shall inherit the land.

¹⁰ Yet a little while, and the sinner shall be clean gone; yea, thou shalt seek after his place, and wilt not find it,

¹¹ But the meek shall inherit the earth, and shall be refreshed in the multitude of peace.

¹² The sinner shall watch over the just man, and gnash upon him with his teeth,

¹³ But the Lord shall laugh him to scorn, for He seeth that his day is coming.

¹⁴ The sinners have drawn out the sword, they have bent their bow, to cast down the poor and needy, to slay such as are true of heart.

¹⁵ Let their sword pierce their own hearts, and let their bows be broken.

¹⁶ A small thing that the righteous hath, is better than great riches of the ungodly,

¹⁷ For the arms of the sinner shall be broken, but the Lord upholdeth the righteous.

¹⁸ The Lord knoweth the ways of the blameless, and their inheritance shall endure for ever.

¹⁹ They shall not be confounded in the perilous time, and in the days of dearth they shall have enough; as for the sinners, they shall perish.

²⁰ But the enemies of the Lord, as soon as they are honored and exalted, shall vanish away; even as smoke, shall they vanish.

²¹ The sinner borroweth, and payeth not again, but the righteous is merciful, and giveth,

²² For such as bless him shall possess the land, but such as curse him shall be rooted out.

²³ By the Lord are a man's steps directed, and he shall well like His way.

²⁴ Though he fall, he shall not be harmed, for the Lord upholdeth him with His hand.

²⁵ I have been young, and now am old, and yet

saw I never the righteous forsaken, nor his seed begging their bread.

²⁶ The righteous is merciful all day, and lendeth, and his seed shall be blessed.

²⁷ Shun evil, and do good, and dwell for evermore,

²⁸ For the Lord loveth justice, and will not forsake His saints; they shall be kept forever, but the unrighteous will be driven out, and the seed of the ungodly shall be utterly consumed.

²⁹ And the righteous shall inherit the land, and dwell therein for ever.

³⁰ The mouth of the righteous is exercised in wisdom, and his tongue will be talking of judgment.

³¹ The Law of his God is in his heart, and his footsteps shall not slide.

³² The sinner seeth the righteous, and seeketh occasion to slay him,

³³ But the Lord will not leave him in his hand, nor condemn him when He judgeth him.

³⁴ Wait thou on the Lord, and keep His way, and He shall promote thee, that thou shalt possess the land; when the sinners perish, thou shalt see it.

³⁵ I have seen the ungodly in great power, and flourishing like the cedars of Lebanon,

³⁶ Then I went by, and lo, he was gone; yea, I sought him, but his place could nowhere be found.

³⁷ Keep innocency, and heed the right, for that shall bring a man peace at the last,

³⁸ But the transgressors shall perish together,

and the ungodly shall be rooted out to the last one.

³⁹ But the salvation of the righteous is from the Lord, and He is their defender in time of trouble,

⁴⁰ And the Lord shall help them, and deliver them; He shall rescue them from the sinner, and shall save them, because they put their trust in Him.

Psalm 37

A Psalm of David, for a remembrance of the Sabbath.

O LORD, rebuke me not in Thine anger, neither chasten me in Thy wrath:

³ For Thine arrows are stuck fast in me, and Thy hand presseth me sore.

⁴ There is no health in my flesh, because of Thy displeasure; neither is there any rest in my bones, by reason of my sin.

⁵ For my wickednesses are gone over my head; like a sore burden have they become too heavy for me.

⁶ My wounds stink, and are corrupt, because of my foolishness.

⁷ I am brought into great torment and misery; I go mourning all the day long.

⁸ For my loins are filled with sores, and there is no healing in my flesh.

⁹ I was bitter, and utterly humbled; I roared for the very groaning of my heart.

¹⁰ Lord, all my desire is before Thee, and my lamentation is not hid from Thee.

¹¹ My heart is troubled; my strength hath failed me, and the light of mine eyes, even that is gone from me.

¹² My friends and my neighbors came right up to me and confronted me,

¹³ While my kinsmen stood afar off, and they that sought my soul clamored for it; and they that wished me evil spake vanity, and imagined deceit all the day long.

¹⁴ But I was like a deaf man, and heard not, and as one that is dumb, who doth not open his mouth.

¹⁵ And I became as a man that heareth not, and in whose mouth are no reproofs.

¹⁶ For in Thee, O Lord, have I put my trust; Thou wilt hear me, O Lord my God.

¹⁷ For I said, Let never mine enemies triumph over me; for when my foot slipped, they boasted against me.

¹⁸ For I am ready for scourges, and my pain is ever before me.

¹⁹ For I will confess my wickedness, and be sorry for my sin.

²⁰ But mine enemies live, and are stronger than I, and they are become many that hate me wrongfully.

²¹ They also that reward me evil for good have slandered me, because I follow the thing that good is.

²² Forsake me not, O Lord my God, be not far from me.

²³ Attend unto my help, O Lord of my salvation.

Psalm 38

Unto the end, even to Jeduthun, a Song of David.

I SAID, I will take heed to my ways, that I sin not with my tongue; I kept my mouth as it were with a bridle, when the sinner stood up against me.

³ I was mute and held my peace; I kept silent, even from good words, and my sorrow was renewed.

⁴ My heart grew hot within me, and while I was thus musing, the fire kindled; I spake with my tongue,

⁵ O Lord, tell me mine end, and the number of my days, what it is, that I may know what is wanting to me.

⁶ Behold, Thou hast made my days as it were a span long, and my existence is as nothing before Thee; verily, every man living is altogether vanity.

⁷ Therefore man walketh as a shadow, and disquieteth himself in vain; he heapeth up riches, and knoweth not for whom he gathereth them.

⁸ And now, who is my patient endurance? Is it not the Lord? Even my existence is from Thee.

⁹ From all mine offenses deliver me; Thou hast made me a rebuke unto the foolish.

¹⁰ I became dumb, and opened not my mouth, for it was Thy doing.

¹¹ Take Thy scourges from me, for I have fainted from the vehemence of Thy hand.

¹² With rebukes hast Thou chastened man for sin, and hast brushed his life away like a spider's web; yea, every man is but vanity.

¹³ Hear my prayer, O Lord, and give ear unto my petition; hold not Thy peace at my tears. For I am a sojourner with Thee, and a pilgrim, as all my fathers were.

¹⁴ O spare me, that I may recover my strength, before I go hence, and be no more.

Psalm 39

To the chief Musician, a Psalm of David.

WITH hope did I wait for the Lord, and He heard me, and heeded my prayer.

³ And He brought me up out of the horrible pit, and out of the miry clay, and set my feet upon the rock, and ordered my steps.

⁴ And He hath put a new song in my mouth, even a hymn unto our God. Many shall see it, and fear, and shall put their trust in the Lord.

⁵ Blessed is the man whose hope is in the Name of the Lord, and hath not had regard unto vanities and lying follies.

⁶ O Lord my God, many are the wondrous works which Thou hast done, and in Thy thoughts there is none that compareth unto Thee. I declared and spake, They are multiplied beyond number.

⁷ Sacrifice and offering Thou wouldest not, but a body hast Thou made for me; whole-burnt offerings, and sin offerings, hast Thou not required.

⁸ Then said I, Lo, I come; in the heading of the book it is written of me,

⁹ That I should long to do Thy will, O my God; yea, Thy Law is within my heart.

¹⁰ I have preached righteousness in the great church; lo, I will not refrain my lips; O Lord, Thou knowest.

¹¹ I have not hid Thy righteousness within my heart; I have declared Thy truth and Thy salvation; I have not kept back Thy mercy and truth from the great assembly.

¹² And Thou, O Lord, withdraw not Thy loving-kindness from me; let Thy mercy and Thy truth always preserve me.

¹³ For innumerable troubles are come about me; my sins have taken such hold upon me, that I am not able to look up; yea, they are more in number than the hairs of my head, and my heart hath failed me.

¹⁴ O Lord, let it be Thy pleasure to deliver me; O Lord, attend unto my help.

¹⁵ Let them be ashamed, and confounded together, that seek after my soul to destroy it; let them be driven backward, and put to rebuke, that wish me evil.

¹⁶ Let them quickly receive shame for their reward, that say unto me, Well, well.

¹⁷ Let all them that seek Thee be joyful and glad in Thee, O Lord, and let such as love Thy salvation say always, The Lord be praised.

¹⁸ As for me, I am poor and needy, but the Lord will care for me; My helper and my defender art Thou, O my God, make no long tarrying.

Psalm 40

Unto the end, a Psalm of David.

BLESSED is he that considereth the poor and needy; the Lord shall deliver him on the evil day.

³ The Lord preserve him, and keep him alive, and bless him upon the earth, and deliver him not into the hands of his enemies.

⁴ The Lord comfort him on his sick-bed; Thou hast turned all his bed in his sickness.

⁵ I said, Lord, have mercy on me; heal my soul, for I have sinned against Thee.

⁶ Mine enemies spake evil of me, When shall he die, and his name perish?

⁷ And if he came to see me, he spake vanity in his heart, he gathered iniquity to himself; he went forth and spake in like manner.

⁸ All mine enemies whispered against me; even against me did they imagine this evil.

⁹ They spread a slanderous word against me, Now that he sleepeth, he shall not rise up again.

¹⁰ Yea, even mine own familiar friend, in whom I trusted, who did eat of my bread, hath lifted up his heel against me.

¹¹ But Thou, O Lord, have mercy upon me, and raise me up, and I shall pay them back.

¹² By this I know Thou favorest me, that mine enemy doth not triumph against me.

¹³ But Thou hast taken my side by reason of my innocence, and hast established me before Thee for ever.

¹⁴ Blessed be the Lord God of Israel from everlasting to everlasting. So be it. So be it.

Psalm 41

Unto the end, for instruction, of the sons of Korah,
a Psalm of David.

LIKE as the hart panteth after the water-brooks, so longeth my soul after Thee, O God.

³ My soul hath thirsted for the mighty living God; when shall I come and appear before God's face?

⁴ My tears have been my bread day and night, while they daily said unto me, Where is now thy God?

⁵ I thought upon these things, and poured out my soul within me, for I shall go over into the place of the wonderful tabernacle, even unto the house of God, with a voice of rejoicing and thanksgiving, the noise of such as keep holy-day.

⁶ Why art thou so full of sadness, O my soul? And why dost thou trouble me? Put thy trust in God, for I will yet give Him thanks, the salvation of my countenance, and my God.

⁷ My soul is vexed within me; therefore will I

remember Thee from the land of Jordan and Hermon, from the little hill.

⁸ Deep unto deep calleth at the voice of Thy water-floods; all Thy billows and Thy waves are gone over me.

⁹ The Lord hath commanded His mercy by day, and His song from me by night, a prayer unto the God of my life.

¹⁰ I will say unto God, Thou art my helper, why hast Thou forgotten me? Why go I thus mournfully, while the enemy oppresseth me?

¹¹ While my bones were broken, mine enemies reproached me, whilst they said daily unto me, Where is now thy God?

¹² Why art thou so full of sadness, O my soul? And why dost thou trouble me? Put thy trust in God, for I will yet give Him thanks, the salvation of my countenance, and my God.

Psalm 42

A Psalm of David. Without superscription in the Hebrew.

JUDGE me, O God, and defend my cause; from an unholy nation, from the unjust and crafty man, deliver me.

² For Thou, O God, art my strength; why hast Thou rejected me? And why go I so heavily, while the enemy oppresseth me?

³ O send out Thy light and Thy truth; they have led me, and brought me unto Thy holy hill, and to Thy dwellings.

⁴ And I will go in unto the altar of God, even unto the God who giveth joy to my youth; upon the harp will I give thanks unto Thee, O God, my God.

⁵ Why art thou so full of sadness, O my soul? And why dost thou trouble me? Put thy trust in God, for I will yet give Him thanks, the salvation of my countenance, and my God.

Psalm 43

Unto the end, of the sons of Korah, for instruction.

O GOD, we have heard with our ears, and our fathers have told us, the work which Thou hast done in their days, in the days of old;

³ How Thou hast driven out the heathen with Thy hand, and planted them in; how Thou didst afflict the people, and cast them out.

⁴ For they gat not the land in possession through their own sword, neither was it their own arm that saved them; but Thy right hand, and Thine arm, and the light of Thy countenance, because Thou hadst a favor unto them.

⁵ Thou art Thyself my King and my God, Who dost command the salvation of Jacob.

⁶ Through Thee will we gore our enemies as with horns, and in Thy Name will we wipe out them that rise up against us.

⁷ For I will not trust in my bow, and my sword shall not save me;

⁸ For Thou hast saved us from them that afflict us, and hast put them to shame that hate us.

⁹ We make our boast of God all day long, and in Thy Name we will give thanks for ever.

¹⁰ But now Thou hast rejected us and put us to shame, and goest not forth, O God, with our armies.

¹¹ Thou hast turned us back before our enemies, and they which hate us have plundered our goods.

¹² Thou hast given us to be eaten like sheep, and hast scattered us among the heathen.

¹³ Thou didst sell Thy people for naught, and there were not many at our auction.

¹⁴ Thou hast made us the rebuke of our neighbors, a scoff and derision of them that are round about us.

¹⁵ Thou hast made us to be a by-word among the nations, and that the peoples shake their heads at us.

¹⁶ All day long my confusion is before me, and my face is covered with shame,

¹⁷ At the voice of the slanderer and blasphemer, at the face of the enemy and avenger.

¹⁸ All this hath come upon us, yet have we not forgotten Thee, neither behaved ourselves frowardly in Thy covenant,

¹⁹ And our heart hath not turned back, but Thou hast turned aside our paths from Thy ways.

²⁰ For Thou hast humbled us in a place of affliction, and covered us with the shadow of death.

²¹ If we have forgotten the Name of our God, and if we have holden up our hands to any strange god,

²² Shall not God search it out? For He knoweth

the very secrets of the heart.

²³ For Thy sake we are killed all the day long; we are accounted as sheep for the slaughter.

²⁴ Up, Lord, why sleepest Thou? Arise, and reject us not before the end.

²⁵ Wherefore hidest Thou Thy face? Dost Thou forget our poverty and our affliction?

²⁶ For our soul is humbled down into the dust; our belly cleaveth unto the ground.

²⁷ Arise, O Lord; help us, and deliver us for Thy Name's sake.

Psalm 44

Unto the end, concerning the verses that are to be
alternated, of the sons of Korah, for instruction,
a Song of the Beloved.

MY heart hath poured forth a good Word; I speak of my works unto the King. My tongue is the pen of a ready writer.

³ Thou art fairer than the sons of men; full of grace are Thy lips, therefore hath God blessed Thee for ever.

⁴ Gird Thy sword upon Thy thigh, O Thou most Mighty, according to Thy splendor and Thy beauty,

⁵ And bend Thy bow, and prosper, and reign, for the sake of truth, and meekness, and righteousness; and Thy right hand shall guide Thee wonderfully.

⁶ Thy arrows are very sharp, O Thou most

Mighty, in the hearts of the king's enemies; the peoples shall fall under Thee.

⁷ Thy throne, O God, is for ever and ever; the scepter of Thy kingdom is a rod of justice.

⁸ Thou hast loved righteousness, and hated iniquity, wherefore God, even Thy God, hath anointed Thee with the oil of gladness above Thy fellows.

⁹ Thy garments smell of myrrh, frankincense, and cassia from the ivory palaces, from where they have made Thee glad.

¹⁰ Kings' daughters are among Thy honorable women. Upon Thy right hand did stand the queen; in garments of gold is she vested, wrought about with divers colors.

¹¹ Hearken, O daughter, and see, and incline thine ear, and forget thy people, and thy father's house.

¹² And the King shall greatly desire thy beauty; for He is thy Lord, and thou shalt worship Him,

¹³ And the daughters of Tyre with gifts; the rich among the people shall entreat thy countenance.

¹⁴ All the glory of the King's daughter is within; with gold fringes is she adorned, and needle-work of many colors.

¹⁵ The virgins in her train shall be brought unto the King; her companions shall be brought unto Thee.

¹⁶ With joy and gladness shall they be brought in; they shall be brought into the King's house.

¹⁷ In the place of thy fathers will be thy sons;

thou shalt make them princes over all the earth.

¹⁸ I will remember thy name in every generation and generation; therefore shall the peoples
give thanks unto thee for ever, and for ever and
ever.

Psalm 45

Unto the end, of the sons of Korah,
concerning hidden things.

GOD is our refuge and strength, a very present
helper in the troubles which greatly afflict us.

³ Therefore will we not fear, when the earth be
shaken, and the hills be cast into the midst of the
sea.

⁴ The waters thereof did rage and swell, and the
mountains shook at His power.

⁵ The rushings of the river gladden the city of
God; the Most High hath sanctified His tabernacle.

⁶ God is in the midst of her, and she shall not be
moved; God shall help her in the morning, and that
right early.

⁷ The nations were troubled; kingdoms toppled;
the Most High lifted up His voice; the earth quaked.

⁸ The Lord of hosts is with us; the God of Jacob
is our protector.

⁹ O come hither, and behold the works of the
Lord, what wonders He hath wrought on earth.

¹⁰ Making wars to cease in all the world, He
breaketh the bow, and knappeth the spear in sunder, and burneth the shields in the fire.

¹¹ Be still, and know that I am God; I will be exalted among the nations, and I will be lifted up on the earth.

¹² The Lord of hosts is with us; the God of Jacob is our protector.

Psalm 46

Unto the end, of the sons of Korah, a Psalm.

ALL ye peoples, clap your hands; O shout unto God with a voice of rejoicing.

³ For the Lord Most High is terrible, a great King over all the earth.

⁴ He hath subdued the peoples unto us, and the nations under our feet.

⁵ He hath chosen out His inheritance for us, even the goodness of Jacob, whom He loved.

⁶ God is gone up with a merry noise, the Lord with the sound of the trump.

⁷ O sing unto our God, sing ye; O sing unto our King, sing ye.

⁸ For God is the King of all the earth, sing ye with understanding.

⁹ God reigneth over the nations; God sitteth upon His holy throne.

¹⁰ The princes of the peoples are gathered together, even with the God of Abraham; for God's mighty in the land are very high exalted.

Psalm 47

A Psalm and Song of the sons of Korah,
on the second day of the week.

GREAT is the Lord, and highly to be praised, in
the city of our God, even upon His holy hill,

³ The well-situated joy of the whole world. The
hills of Zion are the northern sides; the city of the
great King.

⁴ God is known in her towers, when He cometh
to her help.

⁵ For lo, the kings of the earth did gather, and
come together.

⁶ They marveled to see her thus; they were troubled; they were shaken.

⁷ Fear came upon them; there was pain, as upon
a woman in her travail.

⁸ With a stormy wind shalt Thou break the ships
of Tarshish.

⁹ Like as we have heard, so have we seen in the
city of the Lord of hosts, in the city of our God; God
hath established her for ever.

¹⁰ We have received Thy mercy, O God, in the
midst of Thy temple.

¹¹ According to Thy Name, O God, even so is Thy
praise unto the ends of the earth; Thy right hand is
full of righteousness.

¹² Let Mount Zion rejoice, and let the daughters of Judah be glad, because of Thy judgments,
O Lord.

¹³ Walk about Zion, and go round about her, and tell the towers thereof.

¹⁴ Set your hearts on her strength, and consider her houses, that ye may tell it to another generation.

¹⁵ For He is our God for ever, even for ever and ever; He shall be our shepherd for evermore.

Psalm 48

Unto the end, of the sons of Korah, a Psalm.

O HEAR this, all ye nations; take heed, all ye that dwell in the world;

³ High and low, rich and poor, one with another.

⁴ My mouth shall speak wisdom, and the meditation of my heart shall be of understanding.

⁵ I will incline mine ear to the parable, and show my dark speech upon the harp.

⁶ Wherefore should I fear in the evil day, when the wickedness at my heels shall compass me round about?

⁷ There be some that put their trust in their own strength, and boast themselves in the multitude of their riches.

⁸ A brother doth not redeem; shall a man redeem? He cannot give ransom to God even for himself,

⁹ Nor the price of redemption of his own soul, though he hath labored long,

¹⁰ And shall live until the end, and not see corruption,

¹¹ When he will see the wise also dying; together with the ignorant and foolish shall they perish, and leave their riches for other.

¹² And their graves shall be their houses for ever; their dwelling-places from one generation to another; they named the land after their names.

¹³ But man, being in honor, understood it not; he shall be compared unto the brute beasts, and is become like unto them.

¹⁴ This way of theirs is a stumbling-block unto them, yet afterwards they wish well with their mouths.

¹⁵ They are driven to hell like sheep; death shall be their shepherd, and the righteous shall have dominion over them in the morning, and their help shall rot in hell; they have been cast out from their glory.

¹⁶ But God will deliver my soul from the hand of hell, when He receiveth me.

¹⁷ Be not thou afraid, though a man be made rich, or though the glory of his house be increased;

¹⁸ For when he dieth, he shall carry nothing away, neither shall his pomp follow him.

¹⁹ For while he liveth, he counteth himself a happy man; he will speak well of Thee, so long as Thou doest good unto him.

²⁰ He shall go in even to the generation of his fathers; he shall never see the light.

²¹ But man, being in honor, understood it not; he shall be compared unto the brute beasts, and is become like unto them.

Psalm 49

A Psalm for Asaph.

T HE God of gods, even the Lord, hath spoken, and summoned the earth, from the rising up of the sun, unto the going down thereof.

² Out of Zion is the splendor of His perfect beauty.

³ God shall plainly come, even our God, and He shall not keep silence; there shall burn before Him a consuming fire, and a mighty tempest is round about Him.

⁴ He shall summon the heavens from above, and the earth, that He may judge His people.

⁵ Gather His saints together unto Him, those that have made a covenant with Him for sacrifice,

⁶ And the heavens shall declare His righteousness, for God is Judge.

⁷ Hear, O my people, and I will speak unto you, and I will testify against thee, O Israel; I am God, even thy God.

⁸ I will not reprove thee because of thy sacrifices, for thy whole-burnt offerings are always before Me.

⁹ I will take no bullock out of thine house, nor he-goat out of thy folds.

¹⁰ For all the beasts of the forest are Mine, and so are the cattle upon a thousand hills, and the oxen.

¹¹ I know all the fowls of the heavens, and the beauty of the field is with Me.

¹² If I be hungry, I will not tell thee; for the whole world is Mine, and the fullness thereof.

¹³ Shall I eat bulls' flesh? Or drink the blood of goats?

¹⁴ Offer unto God a sacrifice of praise, and pay thy vows unto the Most High.

¹⁵ And call upon Me in the day of thy trouble, and I will deliver thee, and thou shalt glorify Me.

¹⁶ But unto the sinners God said, Why dost thou preach My statutes, and takest My covenant in thy mouth?

¹⁷ For thou hast hated correction, and hast cast My words behind thee.

¹⁸ If thou sawest a thief, thou didst run with him, and hast been partaker with the adulterer.

¹⁹ Thy mouth hath embroidered evil, and thy tongue hath woven lies.

²⁰ Sitting, thou didst slander thy brother, and hast laid temptation on thine own mother's son.

²¹ These things hast thou done, and I held My tongue; thou thoughtest wickedly, that I could be even such a one as thyself; I will reprove thee, and set thy sins before thy face.

²² Therefore consider this, ye that forget God, lest He pluck you away, and there be none to deliver.

²³ The sacrifice of praise shall glorify Me; and there is the way, by which I will show him My salvation.

Psalm 50

Unto the end, a Psalm of instruction by David, when
Nathan the prophet came unto him, after he had gone
in to Bathsheba, the wife of Uriah.

HAVE mercy upon me, O God, after Thy great
goodness, and according to the multitude of
Thy mercies do away mine offenses.

4 Wash me thoroughly from my wickedness, and
cleanse me from my sin.

5 For I know my fault, and my sin is ever before
me.

6 Against Thee only have I sinned, and done evil
before Thee, that Thou mightest be justified in Thy
words, and prevail when Thou art judged.

7 For behold, I was conceived in wickedness,
and in sins did my mother bear me.

8 For behold, Thou hast loved truth; the hidden and secret things of Thy wisdom hast Thou
revealed unto me.

9 Thou shalt sprinkle me with hyssop, and I
shall be made clean; Thou shalt wash me, and I
shall become whiter than snow.

10 Thou shalt give joy and gladness to my hearing; the bones that have been humbled will rejoice.

11 Turn Thy face from my sins, and put out all
my misdeeds.

12 Make me a clean heart, O God, and renew a
right spirit within me.

13 Cast me not away from Thy presence, and
take not Thy Holy Spirit from me.

¹⁴ O give me the comfort of Thy salvation, and stablish me with Thy governing Spirit.

¹⁵ Then shall I teach Thy ways unto the wicked, and the ungodly shall be converted unto Thee.

¹⁶ Deliver me from blood-guiltiness, O God, the God of my salvation, and my tongue shall rejoice in Thy righteousness.

¹⁷ O Lord, open Thou my lips, and my mouth shall show forth Thy praise.

¹⁸ For if Thou hadst desired sacrifice, I would have given it; but Thou delightest not in burnt offerings.

¹⁹ The sacrifice unto God is a contrite spirit; a contrite and humble heart God shall not despise.

²⁰ O Lord, be favorable in Thy good will unto Zion, and let the walls of Jerusalem be builded up.

²¹ Then shalt Thou be pleased with the sacrifice of righteousness, with oblation and whole-burnt offerings; then shall they offer young bullocks upon Thine altar.

Psalm 51

Unto the end, a Psalm of David, for instruction, when Doeg the Edomite came and told Saul, and said unto him, David is come to the house of Abimelech.

WHY boastest thou thyself in evil, thou tyrant, and in mischief all day?

⁴ Thy tongue imagineth wickedness; thou hast stropped lies like a sharp razor.

⁵ Thou hast loved evil more than goodness; falsehood, more than to speak the truth.

⁶ Thou hast loved all words that may do hurt, O thou false tongue.

⁷ Therefore shall God destroy thee utterly; He shall pluck thee out, and tear thee from thy dwelling, and thy root from the land of the living.

⁸ The righteous shall see, and be afraid, and shall laugh at him, and say,

⁹ Behold the man that took not God for his helper, but trusted unto the multitude of his riches, and puffed up his vanity.

¹⁰ But I am like a fruitful olive-tree in the house of God; I have trusted in God's mercy for ever, and for ever and ever.

¹¹ I will always give thanks unto Thee for that Thou hast done, and I will wait upon Thy Name, for it is good before Thy saints.

Psalm 52

Unto the end, concerning Mahalath,
an instruction of David.

THE fool hath said in his heart, There is no God. Corrupt are they, and become abominable in their wickedness, there is none that doeth good.

³ God looked down from heaven upon the children of men, to see if there were any that did understand, or seek after God.

⁴ They are all gone astray; they are altogether

become unprofitable; there is none that doeth good, no not one.

⁵ Will they never understand, all that work wickedness, who eat up my people as they would eat bread? They have not called upon the Lord.

⁶ There were they afraid, where no fear was; for God hath scattered the bones of the man-pleasers; they were put to confusion, because God hath despised them.

⁷ Oh, who will give the salvation of Israel out of Zion? When God shall turn back the captivity of His people, Jacob shall rejoice, and Israel shall be right glad.

Psalm 53

Unto the end, among the songs of instruction by David,
when the Ziphites came and said to Saul, Lo,
is not David hid with us?

O GOD, in Thy Name save me, and judge me by Thy power.

⁴ Hear my prayer, O God; hearken unto the words of my mouth.

⁵ For strangers are risen up against me, and mighty men have sought after my soul, which have not set God before them.

⁶ For behold, God helpeth me, and the Lord is the defender of my soul.

⁷ He shall repay mine enemies for their evil; destroy Thou them by Thy truth.

⁸ Willingly shall I sacrifice unto Thee; I will praise Thy Name, O Lord, for it is good.

⁹ For Thou hast delivered me out of every trouble, and mine eye hath looked upon mine enemies.

Psalm 54

Unto the end, among the songs of instruction for Asaph, a Psalm.

HEAR my prayer, O God, and despise not my petition.

³ Take heed unto me, and hear me; I mourned in my grief, and was vexed

⁴ By the voice of the enemy, and by the oppression of the sinner, for they minded to do me mischief; and have wrathfully set themselves against me.

⁵ My heart is disquieted within me, and the fear of death is fallen upon me.

⁶ Fearfulness and trembling are come upon me, and darkness hath covered me.

⁷ And I said, Who will give me wings like a dove's? And I will fly away, and be at rest.

⁸ Lo, I ran away far off, and dwelt in the wilderness.

⁹ I waited for God, Who saveth me from faint-heartedness and from tempest.

¹⁰ Drown their voices, O Lord, and divide their tongues, for I have seen mischief and strife in the city.

¹¹ Day and night they go about the walls thereof; mischief also and hardship are in the midst of it, and injustice,

¹² And neither usury nor fraud go out of its streets.

¹³ For if an enemy had reviled me, I could have borne it; or if he that hateth me had blustered against me, then I would have hid myself from him.

¹⁴ But it was even thou, a man of like mind, my guide, and my own familiar friend,

¹⁵ Who took sweet counsel with me at table; we walked in the house of God in concord.

¹⁶ Let death come upon them, and let them go down alive into hell; for wickedness is in their dwellings, and in their midst.

¹⁷ As for me, I called upon God, and the Lord heard me.

¹⁸ Evening, and morning, and noon-day will I call out, and cry aloud, and He shall hear my voice.

¹⁹ He will deliver my soul in peace from them that draw nigh against me, for they were with me in crowds.

²⁰ God will hear, and He that is before the ages shall humble them; there is no change with them, for they have not feared God.

²¹ He hath stretched forth His hand for retribution; they have defiled His covenant.

²² They were divided at the wrath of His countenance, and their hearts drew nigh; their words were smoother than oil, and yet are they arrows.

²³ O cast thy care upon the Lord, and He shall nourish thee; He shall never suffer the righteous to stumble.

²⁴ But Thou, O God, shalt bring them into the pit of destruction; the blood-thirsty and deceitful men shall not live out half their days, but I shall trust in Thee, O Lord.

Psalm 55

Unto the end, concerning the people that were removed from the sanctuary, a pillar inscription of David, when the Philistines took him in Gath.

HAVE mercy upon me, O God, for man hath trodden me down; fighting all day, he hath pressed me sore.

³ Mine enemies have trodden on me all day long, for there be many that fight against me from on high.

⁴ I will not be afraid by day, for I will trust in Thee.

⁵ My words shall speak praise concerning God; I have put my trust in God, I will not fear what flesh can do unto me.

⁶ They had a loathing unto my words all day; all their thoughts were for evil against me.

⁷ They linger and lurk, they dog my heels, because they are lying in wait for my soul.

⁸ By no means shalt Thou save them, Thou wilt cast down peoples in displeasure.

⁹ O God, I have made known my life unto Thee; Thou hast put my tears before Thee, even as in Thy promise.

¹⁰ Let my enemies turn back on the very day that I call upon Thee; Lo, I have come to know that Thou art my God.

¹¹ My talk shall be of God's praise; my speech shall be in praise of the Lord.

¹² In God have I put my trust; I will not fear what man can do unto me.

¹³ In me, O God, are vows, which I will pay in Thy praise.

¹⁴ For Thou hast delivered my soul from death, mine eyes from tears, and my feet from slipping, that I may be acceptable before God in the light of the living.

Psalm 56

Unto the end, destroy not: by David, for a pillar inscription, when he fled from the presence of Saul into the cave.

HAVE mercy upon me, O God, have mercy upon me, for in Thee hath my soul trusted, and in the shadow of Thy wings shall I hope, until wickedness be over-past.

³ I will call unto the most high God, even unto the God that doeth good things for me.

⁴ He sent from heaven and saved me, He hath given over to reproof them that trod me down; God hath sent forth His mercy, and His truth.

⁵ And He hath delivered my soul from the midst of the lions' whelps; troubled, I slept my sleep. As for the children of men, their teeth are spears and arrows, and their tongue is a sharp sword.

⁶ Be Thou exalted above the heavens, O God, and Thy glory above all the earth.

⁷ They have laid a net for my feet, and pressed down my soul; they have digged a pit before me, and are fallen into it themselves.

⁸ My heart is ready, O God, my heart is ready; I will chant and sing in my glory.

⁹ Awake up, my glory; awake, psaltery and harp; I myself will awake right early.

¹⁰ I will give thanks unto Thee among the peoples, O Lord; I will sing unto Thee among the nations.

¹¹ For the greatness of Thy mercy reacheth unto the heavens, and Thy truth even unto the clouds.

¹² Be Thou exalted above the heavens, O God, and Thy glory above all the earth.

Psalm 57

Unto the end, destroy not: a pillar inscription of David.

IF ye indeed speak the truth, judge righteously, O ye sons of men.

³ For ye imagine mischief in your heart upon the earth, and your hands weave wickedness.

⁴ Sinners are froward from the womb, even from the belly have they gone astray, and spoken lies.

⁵ Their venom is like that of a serpent, even like the deaf adder, that stoppeth her ears;

⁶ Which refuseth to hear the voice of the charmer, charm he never so wisely.

⁷ God will break their teeth in their mouths; the Lord hath crushed the jaw-bones of the lions.

⁸ They shall go down like water that runneth out; He shall bend his bow until they falter.

⁹ Like melting wax shall they vanish away; fire hath fallen on them, and they shall not see the sun.

¹⁰ Before your briars can feel the thorn, He shall swallow them up alive in His wrath.

¹¹ The righteous man shall rejoice when he seeth the vengeance; he shall wash his hands in the blood of the sinner.

¹² And a man shall say, If indeed there is a reward for the righteous, then verily there is a God that judgeth them on earth.

Psalm 58

Unto the end, destroy not: a pillar inscription of David, when Saul sent, and they watched the house to kill him.

RESCUE me from mine enemies, O God, and deliver me from them that rise up against me.

³ O deliver me from the wicked-doers, and save me from the blood-thirsty men.

⁴ For lo, they have seized my soul, the mighty men have fallen upon me; neither is it my wrong-doing, nor my fault, O Lord.

⁵ Without misdemeanor have I run and directed my steps; rise up to meet me and see.

⁶ And Thou, O Lord God of hosts, the God of Israel, be attentive to visit all the heathen, and be not merciful unto them that do wickedness.

⁷ They shall go to and fro in the evening, and scavenge like a dog, and run about through the city.

⁸ Behold, they speak with their mouth, and a sword is in their lips, for who hath heard?

⁹ But Thou, O Lord, shalt have them in derision; Thou shalt humble all the heathen.

¹⁰ I will save my strength for Thee, for Thou, O God, art my defender.

¹¹ My God, His mercy shall go before me; my God, He will flaunt me over mine enemies.

¹² Slay them not, that they may never forget Thy Law, but scatter them abroad by Thy power, and bring them down, O Lord, my defender,

¹³ For the sin of their mouth, and for the words of their lips; let them be taken in their pride, and they shall be notorious for their cursing and lies in the end.

¹⁴ Wrath is the end of them, and they shall be no more, and they shall know that God ruleth Jacob, and the ends of the world.

¹⁵ They shall go to and fro in the evening, and scavenge like a dog, and run about through the city.

¹⁶ They will run here and there for food, and grudge if they be not satisfied.

¹⁷ As for me, I will sing of Thy power, and will

rejoice in Thy mercy betimes in the morning, for Thou hast been my defender and my refuge in the day of my trouble.

¹⁸ Thou art my helper; unto Thee will I sing, for Thou, O God, art my defender, and my merciful God.

Psalm 59

Unto the end, concerning the verses to be alternated,
a pillar inscription of David, for instruction, when he had
burned Mesopotamian Syria and Syria Zobah,
when Joab returned, and smote of Edom
in the Valley of Salt twelve thousand.

O GOD, Thou hast cast us out, and overthrown us; Thou hast been displeased with us and hast been merciful unto us.

⁴ Thou hast shaken the earth, and troubled it; heal the distress thereof, for it hath been stirred up.

⁵ Thou hast showed Thy people hard things; Thou hast made us drink the wine of contrition.

⁶ Thou hast given a sign unto such as fear Thee, that they may flee from before the bow.

⁷ That Thy beloved may be delivered, help me with Thy right hand, and hear me.

⁸ God hath spoken in His holiness, I will rejoice, and divide Shechem, and measure out the valley of Succoth.

⁹ Gilead is mine, and Manasseh is mine;

Ephraim also is the strength of my head; Judah is my scepter.

¹⁰ Moab is the laver of my hope; over Edom will I stretch forth my shoe; the Philistines have submitted themselves unto me.

¹¹ Who will lead me into the strong city, or who will bring me into Edom?

¹² Wilt not Thou, O God, Who hast cast us out? And wilt not Thou, O God, go out with our hosts?

¹³ O give us help from affliction, for vain is the salvation of man.

¹⁴ Through God will we do mightily, and He shall wipe out them that afflict us.

Psalm 60

Unto the end, among the Hymns of David.

HEAR my petition, O God; heed my prayer.
³ From the ends of the earth have I called upon Thee, when my heart was in heaviness, and Thou didst lift me up and set me upon a rock.

⁴ For Thou hast been my hope, and a tower of strength against the face of the enemy.

⁵ I will dwell in Thy tabernacle for ever; I will hide myself under the shelter of Thy wings.

⁶ For Thou, O God, hast heard my prayers, and hast given an inheritance unto those that fear Thy Name.

⁷ Thou shalt grant the King a long life, that his years may endure throughout all generations.

⁸ He shall abide before God for ever. Who can search out His mercy and truth?

⁹ So will I always sing praise unto Thy Name, that I may daily perform my vows.

Psalm 61

Unto the end, for Jeduthun, a Psalm of David.

DOTH not my soul wait still upon God? For of Him cometh my salvation.

³ Yea, He is my God, and my Saviour, He is my defender; I shall no more be moved.

⁴ How long will ye threaten a man? Ye kill, all of you; yea, as ye might push over a leaning wall, or a broken rampart.

⁵ Moreover, they took counsel to impugn my honor; they ran in greed; they spake good words with their mouth, but cursed with their heart.

⁶ O my soul, wait thou still upon God, for from Him is my patient endurance.

⁷ Yea, He is my God, and my Saviour, He is my defender; I shall no more be moved.

⁸ In God is my salvation, and my glory; He is the God of my help, and in God is my trust.

⁹ O put your trust in Him, all ye congregation of people; pour out your hearts before Him, for God is our helper.

¹⁰ But the children of men are vain; the children of men are deceitful upon the weights, that they may deal crookedly; they are altogether vanity.

¹¹ O trust not in wrong and do not imagine robbery; if riches increase, set not your heart upon them.

¹² God spake once, and twice I have heard the same, that power belongeth unto God,

¹³ And Thine, O Lord, is the mercy; for Thou rewardest every man according to his work.

Psalm 62

A Psalm of David, when he was in the wilderness of Judah.

O GOD, my God, early will I seek Thee. My soul hath thirsted for Thee, and how my flesh also hath longed after Thee in a barren and empty land where no water is.

³ Thus have I looked for Thee in the sanctuary, that I might behold Thy power and Thy glory.

⁴ For Thy mercy is better than life itself; my lips shall praise Thee.

⁵ I will bless Thee in my life on this manner: I will lift up my hands in Thy Name.

⁶ For my soul shall be satisfied, even as it were with marrow and fatness, and my mouth shall praise Thee with joyful lips.

⁷ If I remembered Thee upon my bed, in the morning I would take comfort in Thee,

⁸ Because Thou hast been my helper, and in the shelter of Thy wings will I rejoice.

⁹ My soul hath hanged upon Thee; Thy right hand hath upholden me.

¹⁰ These also that in vain seek my soul shall go under the earth.

¹¹ They shall be given over to the hand of the sword; they shall be a portion for foxes.

¹² But the King shall rejoice in God; every one that sweareth by Him shall be commended, for the mouth of them that speak lies hath been stopped.

Psalm 63

Unto the end, a Psalm of David.

HEAR my voice, O God, when I pray unto Thee; deliver my soul from fear of the enemy.

³ Hide me from the gathering together of the froward; and from the mob of wicked doers,

⁴ Who have whet their tongues like a sword; they have bent their bow, a bitter thing,

⁵ That they may privily shoot at the innocent man. Suddenly will they shoot at him, and fear not.

⁶ They have set themselves up by a deceitful word, and have communed among themselves how they may lay snares; they said, Who shall see them?

⁷ They have searched out wickedness, they have grown weary in their seeking of it; a man shall come, and a deep heart,

⁸ And God shall rise up; their wounds were as if made by the arrows of babes.

⁹ Yea, their tongues were weakened against them; all who saw them were troubled.

¹⁰ And every man was afraid; and they proclaimed the works of God, and understood His creation.

¹¹ The righteous man shall rejoice in the Lord, and shall put his trust in Him, and all they that are true of heart shall be praised.

Psalm 64

Unto the end, a Psalm and Song of David,
sung by Jeremiah and Ezekiel and the people,
when they were about to be led captive away.

UNTO Thee, O God, belongeth praise in Zion, and unto Thee shall the vow be performed in Jerusalem.

³ Hear my prayer; unto Thee shall all flesh come.

⁴ The words of the ungodly have overpowered us, but Thou shalt wash away our impiety.

⁵ Blessed is the man whom Thou hast chosen and taken unto Thyself; he shall dwell in Thy courts. We shall be satisfied with the pleasures of Thy house; Thy temple is holy,

⁶ Wonderful in truth; hear us, O God of our salvation, the hope of all the ends of the earth, and of them that be afar off at sea.

⁷ Raising up the mountains by His strength, He is girded with power;

⁸ Stirring up the depths of the sea, who can abide the noise of its waves? The heathen shall be brought to confusion.

⁹ They also that dwell in the uttermost parts of the earth shall be afraid at Thy signs; Thou dost embellish the outgoings of the morning and evening.

¹⁰ Thou didst visit the earth, and water it, Thou hast greatly enriched it; the river of God is full of water. Thou hast prepared food for them, for such is Thy providence.

¹¹ Water her furrows; increase her crops; the shoots shall rejoice in her showers.

¹² Thou shalt bless the crown of the year with Thy goodness, and Thy fields shall be full of plenty.

¹³ The beauty of the wilderness shall grow lush, and the little hills shall be girded with rejoicing on every side.

¹⁴ The sheep will be clothed with wool, and the valleys also shall stand so thick with wheat, that they shall laugh and sing.

Psalm 65

Unto the end, a Song or Psalm of Resurrection.

O MAKE a joyful noise unto the Lord, all the earth, and sing unto His Name; make His praise to be glorious.

³ Say unto God, O how wonderful are Thy works! In the greatness of Thy power shall Thine enemies bow down unto Thee.

⁴ Let all the world worship Thee, and sing unto Thee; let it also praise Thy Name, O Most High.

⁵ O come hither, and behold the works of God, how wonderful He is in His counsels more than the children of men.

⁶ Who turneth the sea into dry land, so that they go through the river on foot; there shall we rejoice in Him,

⁷ Who by His power ruleth for ever; His eyes watch over the nations, let those who grieve Him be not exalted in themselves.

⁸ O bless our God, ye peoples, and make the voice of His praise to be heard;

⁹ Who hath set my soul unto life, and hath not suffered my feet to slip.

¹⁰ For Thou hast proved us, O God; Thou hast tried us, like as silver is tried.

¹¹ Thou broughtest us into the snare, and laidest trouble upon our back.

¹² Thou sufferedst men to ride over our heads; we went through fire and water, and Thou broughtest us out into refreshment.

¹³ I will go into Thine house with a whole-burnt offering, and will pay Thee my vows,

¹⁴ Which I promised with my lips, and spake with my mouth, when I was in trouble.

¹⁵ I will offer unto Thee fat whole-burnt sacrifices with incense, and rams; I will bring bullocks and goats unto Thee.

¹⁶ O come hither and hearken, all ye that fear God, and I will tell you what He hath done for my soul.

¹⁷ I called unto Him with my mouth, and gave Him praises with my tongue.

¹⁸ If I regarded falsehood in mine heart, may the Lord not hear me.

¹⁹ Wherefore God hath heard me, and considered the voice of my prayer.

²⁰ Blessed be God, who hath not set aside my prayer, nor His mercy from me.

Psalm 66

Unto the end, in verses, a Psalm or Song of David.

O GOD, be merciful unto us, and bless us; shine the light of Thy countenance upon us, and have mercy upon us,

³ That Thy way may be known upon earth, Thy salvation among all nations.

⁴ Let the peoples give thanks unto Thee, O God; let all the peoples give thanks unto Thee.

⁵ O let the nations rejoice and be glad, for Thou shalt judge the folk with justice, and govern the nations upon earth.

⁶ Let the peoples give thanks unto Thee, O God; let all the peoples give thanks unto Thee.

⁷ The earth hath brought forth her increase; bless us, O God, our God.

⁸ Bless us, O God, and let all the ends of the world fear Him.

Psalm 67

Unto the end, a Psalm or Song of David.

L ET God arise, and let His enemies be scattered, and let them that hate Him flee from before His face.

³ Like as smoke vanisheth, so let them vanish; like as wax melteth at the presence of fire, so let sinners perish at the presence of God,

⁴ But let the righteous be glad, and let them rejoice before God; let them take pleasure in gladness.

⁵ O sing unto God, sing unto His Name; prepare ye the way for Him that rideth upon the setting of the sun, LORD is His Name, and rejoice before Him.

⁶ Let them be troubled at the presence of Him, the Father of the fatherless, and the defender of the widow, even God in His holy habitation.

⁷ He is the God that maketh men to be of one mind in an house, leading forth the fettered with courage, and likewise the distressed living in the sepulchers.

⁸ O God, when Thou wentest forth before Thy people, when Thou wentest through the wilderness,

⁹ The earth quaked; indeed, the heavens dropped rain at the presence of the God of Sinai, at the presence of the God of Israel.

¹⁰ Thou dost withhold the bountiful rain, O God,

from Thine inheritance, and it fainted, but Thou
didst restore it.

¹¹ Thy creatures dwell therein; Thou hast prepared good things for the poor, O God.

¹² The Lord shall give speech with great power
to them that preach the good tidings.

¹³ The king of the hosts of the Beloved shall
divide the spoils for the beauty of the house.

¹⁴ If ye sleep within the boundary, ye shall be
as a dove with silver wings, and her feathers like
gleaming gold.

¹⁵ When the Heavenly One shall separate out
kings over her, they shall be covered with snow in
Zalmon.

¹⁶ God's hill is a rich mountain, a mountain of
plenty, a rich mountain.

¹⁷ Why do ye ponder over mountains of plenty?
This is the hill wherein it pleaseth God to dwell;
yea, the Lord will abide in it for ever.

¹⁸ The chariots of God are ten thousand more
than the thousand of those living in prosperity; the
Lord is among them at Sinai, in the holy place.

¹⁹ Thou art gone up on high, Thou hast led captivity captive; Thou hast received gifts among men,
even the disobedient, that Thou mightest settle
Thyself in.

²⁰ The Lord God is blessed. Blessed be the Lord
day by day; the God of our salvation shall speed us
on our way.

²¹ Our God is the God that saveth, and of the

Lord's Lord is the escape from death.

²² But God shall crush the heads of His enemies, and the hairy scalp of such a one as goeth on still in his wickedness.

²³ The Lord said, I will turn from Bashan; I will turn in the depths of the sea,

²⁴ That thy foot may be drenched in the blood of thine enemies, and that the tongue of thy dogs may be red from it.

²⁵ Thy goings were seen, O God, the processions of God my King in the sanctuary.

²⁶ The princes go before, the singers follow after, in the midst of damsels playing the timbrels.

²⁷ In churches bless ye God, the Lord from the fountains of Israel.

²⁸ There is Benjamin the younger in ecstasy, and the princes of Judah their rulers, the princes of Zebulun, and the princes of Naphtali;

²⁹ Declare Thyself, O God, by Thy might; stablish the thing, O God, which Thou hast wrought in us,

³⁰ For Thy temple's sake at Jerusalem shall kings bring presents unto Thee.

³¹ Drive off the wild beasts with reeds, the herd of bulls among the kine of the people, to shut away those tempted by silver; scatter the nations that take pleasure in the field of battle.

³² Ambassadors shall come out of Egypt; Ethiopia shall hasten to stretch out her hands unto God.

³³ Sing unto God, O ye kingdoms of the earth, sing praises unto the Lord,

³⁴ Unto Him Who hath gone into the heaven of heavens in the east; lo, He shall give to His voice the voice of power.

³⁵ Give ye glory to God; His majesty is upon Israel, and His power is upon the clouds.

³⁶ Wonderful is God in His saints, the God of Israel; He will give power and might unto His people. Blessed be God.

Psalm 68

Unto the end, concerning those that shall be changed,
a Psalm of David.

SAVE me, O God, for the waters are come in, even unto my soul.

³ I was stuck fast in the deep mire, where no ground is; I am come into deep waters, and a tempest hath run over me.

⁴ I am weary of crying, my throat is become hoarse; my sight hath failed me, because I have been waiting so long upon my God.

⁵ They that hate me without a cause are become more than the hairs of my head; mine enemies, which persecute me unjustly, are become mighty. I paid them, then, for things I never took.

⁶ God, Thou knowest my foolishness, and my faults are not hid from Thee.

⁷ Let not them that wait upon Thee, O Lord, Lord of hosts, be ashamed because of me; let not those that seek Thee be confounded through me, O God of Israel.

⁸ For Thy sake have I suffered reproof; shame hath covered my face.

⁹ I am become a stranger unto my brethren, even an alien unto my mother's children.

¹⁰ For the zeal of Thine house hath eaten me up, and the rebukes of them that rebuked Thee are fallen upon me.

¹¹ I chastened my soul with fasting, and that was turned to my reproof.

¹² I put on sackcloth also, and they jested upon me.

¹³ They that sit in the gate amused themselves against me, and the drunkards made songs upon me.

¹⁴ But I make my prayer unto Thee, O God, at the acceptable time; O God, in the multitude of Thy mercy, hear me, even in the truth of Thy salvation.

¹⁵ Save me out of the mire, that I sink not; O let me be delivered from them that hate me, and out of the deep waters.

¹⁶ Let not the water-flood drown me, neither let the deep swallow me up, and let not the pit shut her mouth upon me.

¹⁷ Hear me, O Lord, for Thy mercy is gracious; turn Thee unto me according to the multitude of Thy loving-kindness.

¹⁸ Turn not Thy face from Thy servant, for I am in trouble; O quickly hearken unto me.

¹⁹ Draw nigh unto my soul, and deliver it; O deliver me, because of mine enemies.

²⁰ For Thou knowest my reproof, and my shame, and my dishonor; mine adversaries are all before Thee.

²¹ My soul was expecting rebuke, and misery; so I looked for some to have pity on me, but there was no one, neither found I any to comfort me.

²² They gave me also gall to eat, and when I was thirsty they gave me vinegar to drink.

²³ Let their table be made a snare to take themselves withal, and for a recompense, and an occasion of falling.

²⁴ Let their eyes be darkened, that they see not, and their backs be always bent.

²⁵ Pour out Thine indignation upon them, and let Thy wrathful displeasure take hold of them.

²⁶ Let their habitation be desolate, and no man to dwell in their tents.

²⁷ For they persecuted him whom Thou hast smitten, and have added to the pain of my wounds.

²⁸ Add iniquity unto their wickedness, and let them not come into Thy righteousness.

²⁹ Let them be blotted out of the book of the living, and not be written among the righteous.

³⁰ I am poor and in heaviness; let Thy salvation, O God, lift me up.

³¹ I will praise the Name of my God with a song; and I will magnify Him with praise.

³² And this shall please the Lord, better than a bullock that hath horns and hoofs.

³³ Let the humble consider this, and be glad;

seek ye after God, and your soul shall live.

³⁴ For the Lord hath heard the poor and hath not despised His prisoners.

³⁵ Let heaven and earth praise Him, the sea, and all that liveth therein.

³⁶ For God will save Zion, and build the cities of Judah, and they shall dwell there, and have it in possession.

³⁷ The posterity also of Thy servants shall inherit it, and they that love Thy Name shall dwell therein.

Psalm 69

Unto the end, by David for remembrance,
that the Lord may save me.

O GOD, make speed to save me; O Lord, make haste to help me.

³ Let them be ashamed and confounded that seek after my soul. Let them be turned backward and be ashamed that wish me evil.

⁴ Let them for their reward be soon brought to shame that say over me, Well, well.

⁵ Let all those that seek Thee be joyful and glad in Thee, O God, and let all such as delight in Thy salvation say always, The Lord be praised.

⁶ But I am poor and needy, O God; help me! Thou art my helper and my redeemer, O Lord; make no long tarrying.

Psalm 70

David's, a Psalm of the sons of Jonadab and of the first to be taken captive. Without superscription in the Hebrew.

IN Thee, O Lord, have I put my trust, let me never be confounded.

2 Rescue me in Thy righteousness, and deliver me; incline Thine ear unto me, and save me.

3 Be Thou unto me a defending God, and a strong-hold to save me, for Thou art my buttress and my safe haven.

4 O my God, deliver me out of the hands of the sinner, out of the hands of the law-breaker and the offender.

5 For Thou art the thing that I long for, O Lord; O Lord, Thou art my hope, even from my youth.

6 Through Thee have I been holden up from the womb, from my mother's belly art Thou my protector; my praise shall be always of Thee.

7 I am become as it were a spectacle unto many, but Thou art my strong helper.

8 O let my mouth be filled with Thy praise, that I may sing unto Thy glory, and all day unto Thy majesty.

9 Cast me not away in the time of old age; forsake me not when my strength faileth me.

10 For mine enemies spake against me, and they that lay wait for my soul took their counsel together.

11 They said, God hath forsaken him; persecute him, and take him, for there is none to deliver him.

¹² O my God, go not far from me; my God, haste Thee to help me.

¹³ Let them be confounded and wiped out that are against my soul; let them be covered with shame and confusion that seek to do me evil.

¹⁴ But I shall always hope in Thee, and will set myself to praise Thee more and more.

¹⁵ My mouth shall speak of Thy righteousness, and all day of Thy salvation, because I have not learned the art of writing.

¹⁶ I will go forth in the strength of the Lord; O Lord, I will remember Thy righteousness only.

¹⁷ O my God, which hath taught me from my youth up even until now, I will declare Thy wondrous works,

¹⁸ Yea, forsake me not, O my God, even unto mine old age, when I am gray-headed, until I have made known Thy strength unto every generation that is yet to come.

¹⁹ Thy power and Thy righteousness, O God, are very high, for Thou hast done great things for me. O God, who is like unto Thee?

²⁰ O what great troubles and adversities hast Thou showed me! And yet didst Thou turn and revive me, and broughtest me up from the depths of the earth.

²¹ Thou hast heaped Thy majesty upon me, and Thou hast returned to comfort me, and broughtest me up again from the depths of the earth.

²² Therefore will I confess Thy truth to Thee

among the people, O Lord, upon instruments of psalmody; I will sing unto Thee upon the harp, O God, Thou Holy One of Israel.

²³ My lips will be glad when I sing unto Thee, and so will my soul whom Thou hast delivered.

²⁴ My tongue also shall be occupied in Thy righteousness all the day long, when they are confounded and brought unto shame that seek to do me evil.

Psalm 71

Concerning Solomon, a Psalm of David.

GIVE the King Thy judgment, O God, and Thy righteousness unto the King's son,

² To judge Thy people according unto justice, and Thy poor with judgment.

³ Let the mountains stand witness for peace unto the people, and the little hills for justice.

⁴ He shall judge the simple folk, and shall save the children of the poor, and humble the slanderer.

⁵ Even as long as the sun shall He endure, and before the moon, from one generation to another.

⁶ He shall come down like the rain upon a fleece of wool, even as the drops that water the earth.

⁷ In His days shall righteousness flourish, and abundance of peace, so long as the moon endureth.

⁸ He shall have dominion also from sea to sea, and from the rivers unto the world's end.

⁹ The Ethiopians shall kneel before Him, and His enemies shall lick the dust.

¹⁰ The kings of Tarshish and of the isles shall give presents, the kings of Arabia and Sheba shall bring gifts.

¹¹ Yea, all the kings of the earth shall fall down before Him, all nations shall do Him service.

¹² For He hath delivered the poor from the mighty, and the needy, that had no helper.

¹³ He shall spare the simple and needy, and shall save the souls of the poor.

¹⁴ He shall deliver their souls from usury and from injustice, and His Name shall be precious in their sight.

¹⁵ And He shall live, and unto Him shall be given of the gold of Arabia, and they shall ever pray concerning Him; they shall bless Him the day long.

¹⁶ There shall be a firmament on the earth upon the tops of the mountains; above Lebanon shall the fruit thereof be exalted, and they of the city shall flourish like the grass of the earth.

¹⁷ His Name shall be blessed for ever; His Name shall abide before the sun; and all the tribes of the earth shall be blessed in Him; all the nations shall bless Him.

¹⁸ Blessed be the Lord God of Israel, Who alone worketh wonders,

¹⁹ And blessed be the Name of His glory for ever, and for ever and ever, and all the earth shall be filled with His glory. So be it. So be it.

Psalm 72

A Psalm for Asaph.

H OW good is God unto Israel, unto them of an upright heart!

² Nevertheless, my feet were almost moved; my steps had well-nigh slipped,

³ For I was envious of the wicked, seeing the peace of sinners,

⁴ For there is no fear in their death, and they are steadfast under the knout.

⁵ They are not in the labor of other folk, neither are they plagued like other men.

⁶ Therefore hath their pride mastered them utterly; they have clothed themselves in their unrighteousness and impiety.

⁷ Their injustice swelleth out like fat; they have surpassed even the lust of their heart.

⁸ They have thought and spoken in craftiness; they have spoken injustice in the high place.

⁹ They set their mouth against the heavens, and their tongue goeth throughout the world.

¹⁰ Therefore shall my people turn hither; and full days shall come to them.

¹¹ And they said, How should God see it? and, Is there knowledge in the Most High?

¹² Lo, these are the sinners and the prosperous of this age, and they have riches in possession.

¹³ And I said, Then in vain have I cleansed my heart and washed mine hands in innocency.

¹⁴ For I have been scourged all day, and chastened every morning.

¹⁵ If I said, I will speak thus, lo, I would have been faithless to the generation of Thy children.

¹⁶ And I sought to understand, but it was too hard for me,

¹⁷ Until I went into the sanctuary of God; then understood I their end,

¹⁸ Namely, that Thou hast laid evil upon them for their fraud; Thou didst cast them down, when they vaunted themselves.

¹⁹ Oh, such was their desolation! They were suddenly wiped out; they perished because of their lawlessness.

²⁰ Like as a dream when one awaketh, O Lord, so didst Thou make their image to vanish out of Thy city.

²¹ For my heart was kindled, and my insides were changed.

²² And I was humbled, and did not understand; I became as a beast before Thee.

²³ Nevertheless, I am always with Thee, for Thou hast holden me by my right hand,

²⁴ And hast guided me by Thy counsel, and with glory hast Thou received me.

²⁵ For what have I in heaven, and what have I desired upon earth from Thee?

²⁶ My flesh and my heart have failed, O God of my heart, but Thou art my portion, O God, for ever.

²⁷ For lo, they that go far from Thee shall perish;

Thou hast destroyed all them that are unfaithful against Thee.

²⁸ But it is good for me to cleave unto God, to put my trust in the Lord, that I may declare all Thy praises in the gates of the daughter of Zion.

Psalm 73
Of instruction, for Asaph.

O GOD, why hast Thou so utterly rejected us? Why hath Thy wrath been so hot against the sheep of Thy pasture?

² O remember Thy congregation, which Thou hast purchased of old; by Thy staff hast Thou delivered Thine inheritance, this holy hill of Zion, wherein Thou hast dwelt.

³ Lift up Thy hands against their overweening pride, all that the enemy hath done wickedly in Thy sanctuary.

⁴ Even they that hate Thee have boasted in the midst of Thy holy-day; they set up their banners; banners, though they knew it not,

⁵ As in the going-forth on high. Like as in the oak forest the tree hath been hewn down by the axe,

⁶ So with the doors thereof; with axes and hammers they demolished it.

⁷ They burned with fire Thy sanctuary on earth; they defiled the dwelling-place of Thy Name.

⁸ They said in their hearts, the brood of them together, Come, and let us abolish all the festivals of God from the earth.

⁹ We have not seen our signs, there is no more any prophet, nor will he any more acknowledge us.

¹⁰ How long, O God, shall the enemy carry on? Shall the adversary blaspheme Thy Name for ever?

¹¹ Why dost Thou utterly withdraw Thy hand and Thy right hand out of the midst of Thy bosom?

¹² But God is our King before the ages; He hath wrought salvation in the midst of the earth.

¹³ Thou didst establish the sea through Thy power; Thou brakest the heads of the dragons in the waters.

¹⁴ Thou smotest the heads of Leviathan in pieces; Thou gavest him as food for the people of Ethiopia.

¹⁵ Thou hast disrupted the springs and streams; Thou hast dried up the rivers of Etham.

¹⁶ Thine is the day, and Thine is the night; Thou hast perfected the light and the sun.

¹⁷ Thou hast fixed all the borders of the earth; the harvest and the spring, Thou hast established them.

¹⁸ Remember this, the enemy hath reviled the Lord, and a foolish people hath blasphemed Thy Name.

¹⁹ O deliver not the soul that confesseth Thee unto the wild beasts; forget not the souls of the poor for ever.

²⁰ Give refuge unto Thy covenant, for the dark places of the earth are filled with houses of iniquity.

²¹ O let not the meek be turned away ashamed;

the poor and needy shall praise Thy Name.

²² Arise, O God, defend Thine own cause; remember the blasphemy against Thee, which is from the foolish man all day.

²³ Forget not the voice of Thy suppliants; the arrogance of them that hate Thee increaseth ever more and more.

Psalm 74

Unto the end, destroy not, a Psalm or Song for Asaph.

WE will give thanks unto Thee, O God; we will give thanks unto Thee, and call upon Thy Name; we will declare all Thy wondrous works.

³ In a time of my reckoning, I shall judge according unto right.

⁴ The earth is growing weak, and all who live on it; I have shored up the pillars thereof.

⁵ I said unto the lawless, Deal not so lawlessly, and to the sinners, Lift not up the horn.

⁶ Set not up your horn on high, and speak not injustice against God;

⁷ For justice cometh neither from the coming forth of the sun, nor from the west, nor yet from the barren hills,

⁸ For God is judge; He putteth down one, and setteth up another.

⁹ For the cup in the hand of the Lord is wine unmingled, full to overflowing, and He hath swirled it to and fro, but the dregs thereof did not

settle out; all the sinners of the earth shall drink them up.

¹⁰ But I shall rejoice for ever; I shall sing unto the God of Jacob.

¹¹ And I will break all the horns of sinners, but the horn of the righteous shall be exalted.

Psalm 75

Unto the end, among the songs, a Psalm for Asaph,
a Song concerning the Assyrian.

IN Judah is God known; His Name is great in Israel.

³ And His place hath been at Salem, and His tabernacle in Zion.

⁴ There brake He the power of the bow, the shield and the sword, and the battle.

⁵ Thou dost shine wondrously from the everlasting hills.

⁶ All the simple-hearted were troubled, they slept their sleep, and all the men of wealth found nothing in their hands.

⁷ At Thy rebuke, O God of Jacob, all those mounted on horse-back slumbered.

⁸ Thou art terrible, and who may stand against Thee? From that time is Thy wrath.

⁹ Thou didst cause judgment to be heard from heaven; the earth trembled in fear, and was still,

¹⁰ When God arose to judgment, to save all the meek of the earth.

¹¹ For the thought of man shall turn unto Thee in thanksgiving, and the remainder of the thought shall keep festival unto Thee.

¹² Make a vow unto the Lord our God, and keep it; all that are round about Him shall bring presents,

¹³ Unto Him that is terrible and taketh away the spirits of princes, unto Him that is to be feared among the kings of the earth.

Psalm 76

Unto the end, concerning Jeduthun, a Psalm for Asaph.

WITH my voice I cried unto the Lord, even unto God with my voice, and He heard me.

³ In the day of my trouble I reached out to God with my hands by night before Him, and I was not deceived; my soul refused to be comforted.

⁴ I remembered God, and I was glad; I mused, and my spirit faltered.

⁵ Mine eyes anticipated the morning watches; I was troubled and spake not.

⁶ I considered the days of old, and remembered the years of ages past, and I pondered.

⁷ By night I communed with mine own heart, and searched my soul.

⁸ Will the Lord be contemptuous for ever, and will He be no more favorably disposed?

⁹ Or will He cut off His mercy for ever, His word from generation to generation?

¹⁰ Will God forget to be gracious, or will He withhold His loving-kindness in His displeasure?

¹¹ And I said, Now have I begun; this change is of the right hand of the Most High.

¹² I remembered the works of the Lord, for I will be mindful of Thy wonders from the beginning.

¹³ And I will ponder all Thy works, and muse upon Thy undertakings.

¹⁴ Thy way, O God, is in the sanctuary; who is so great a god as our God?

¹⁵ Thou art the God that doest wonders; Thou hast declared Thy power among the peoples.

¹⁶ With Thine arm hast Thou delivered Thy people, even the sons of Jacob and Joseph.

¹⁷ The waters saw Thee, O God, the waters saw Thee, and were afraid; the depths were troubled.

¹⁸ Great was the noise of the waters; the clouds gave voice, for Thine arrows shall pass.

¹⁹ The voice of Thy thunder is in the wheel, Thy lightnings lit up the whole world; the earth trembled and shook.

²⁰ Thy ways are in the sea, and Thy paths in many waters, and Thy footsteps shall not be known.

²¹ Thou leddest Thy people like sheep, by the hand of Moses and Aaron.

Psalm 77

A Psalm of instruction, for Asaph.

HEED my Law, O my people; incline your ears unto the words of my mouth.

² I will open my mouth in parables; I will declare hard sayings of old;

³ Which we have heard, and known, and our fathers have told us;

⁴ They were not hidden from their children in another generation, declaring the praises of the Lord, and His mighty deeds, and the wonderful works that He hath done.

⁵ He made a covenant with Jacob, and gave Israel a Law, which He commanded our fathers to teach their children;

⁶ That another generation might know it, children as yet unborn, and they shall grow up and show their children the same;

⁷ That they might put their trust in God, and not forget the works of God, but search after His commandments.

⁸ Let them not be as their fathers, a perverse and vexing generation, a generation that amended not their heart, and whose spirit was not faithful unto God;

⁹ Like as the sons of Ephraim, bending and shooting the bow, who turned back in the day of battle;

¹⁰ They kept not the covenant of God and would not walk in His Law.

¹¹ And they forgat His good deeds, and the wonderful works that He had showed for them;

¹² Marvelous things did He in the sight of their fathers, in the land of Egypt, even in the field of Tanis.

¹³ He divided the sea, and led them through; He held up the waters as in a wine-skin.

¹⁴ In the daytime also He led them with a cloud, and all the night through with a light of fire.

¹⁵ He clave a hard rock in the wilderness, and gave them drink, as it had been out of the great deep.

¹⁶ And He brought water out of the stony rock, and made the waters run down like rivers.

¹⁷ Yet they sinned still more against Him; they provoked the Most High in the desert.

¹⁸ And they tempted God in their hearts, asking for food for their souls.

¹⁹ They spake against God also, and said, Shall God be able to prepare a table in the wilderness?

²⁰ He smote the stony rock indeed, and the waters gushed out, and the streams overflowed; but can He give food also, or set a table for His people?

²¹ Wherefore the Lord heard and was wroth, and a fire was kindled in Jacob, and there came up heavy displeasure against Israel;

²² Because they believed not in God, nor trusted in His salvation.

²³ Yet He commanded the clouds above, and

opened the doors of heaven;

²⁴ He rained down manna also upon them for to eat, and gave them bread of heaven.

²⁵ Angel's bread did man eat; He sent them their fill of food.

²⁶ He revoked the south wind from heaven, and by His power He brought in the south-west wind;

²⁷ And He rained flesh upon them as thick as dust, and feathered fowls like as the sand of the sea.

²⁸ And they fell in the midst of their camp, even round about their habitations.

²⁹ So did they eat, and were well filled, and their wish was brought unto them.

³⁰ They were not deprived of their desire. The food was still in their mouths,

³¹ And the heavy wrath of God came upon them, and slew the fattest of them, and the chosen of Israel He put in bonds.

³² In all this they sinned yet more, and believed not His wondrous works;

³³ And their days melted away in vanity, and their years in striving.

³⁴ When He slew them, they sought Him, and repented and performed their morning prayer unto God.

³⁵ And they remembered that God was their helper, and the most high God was their redeemer.

³⁶ Yet they did but flatter Him with their mouth, and dissembled unto Him with their tongue.

³⁷ For their heart was not whole with Him, neither continued they steadfast in His covenant.

³⁸ But He is merciful, and will cleanse their sins, and destroy them not; yea, many a time will He turn His wrath away, and will not kindle all His displeasure.

³⁹ For I will remember that they are but flesh, with a spirit that goeth forth, and returneth not again.

⁴⁰ How often did they provoke Him in the wilderness, and anger Him in the desert?

⁴¹ They both turned back, and tempted God, and provoked the Holy One of Israel.

⁴² And they remembered not His hand in the day when He delivered them from the hand of the tyrant;

⁴³ How He laid down His signs in Egypt, and His wonders in the field of Tanis,

⁴⁴ And turned into blood their rivers and their springs, that they might not drink.

⁴⁵ He sent swarms of flies against them, and they devoured them up, and frogs, and they corrupted them.

⁴⁶ And He gave their fruits to the caterpillar, and their labors to the locust.

⁴⁷ He killed their grapevines with hailstones, and their mulberry trees with frost.

⁴⁸ He gave over their cattle also to the hail, and their possessions to the fire.

⁴⁹ He sent down upon them the furiousness of

His wrath: anger, and displeasure, and grief, the message of fierce angels.

⁵⁰ He laid the path for His indignation, and spared not their souls from death; their cattle also ended in death.

⁵¹ And He smote every first-born in the land of Egypt, the first-fruits of all their labor in the dwellings of Ham.

⁵² But His own people He drove like sheep, and led them forth into the wilderness like a flock.

⁵³ And He set them up unto faith, and they were not afraid, and the sea covered their enemies.

⁵⁴ And He brought them to the mountain of His holiness, even to the mountain which His right hand had purchased.

⁵⁵ He cast out the heathen also before them, and gave them the land by lot with a line of division, and settled the tribes of Israel in their tents.

⁵⁶ Yet they tempted and displeased the most high God, and kept not His testimonies;

⁵⁷ But turned backward, and fell away like their fathers, becoming like a sprung bow.

⁵⁸ And they angered Him in their hill places, and vexed Him with their idols.

⁵⁹ God heard and turned away, and greatly disparaged Israel.

⁶⁰ And He forsook the tabernacle in Shiloh, even the tent that He had pitched among men.

⁶¹ And delivered their power into captivity, and their beauty into the hands of the enemy.

⁶² He consigned His people also unto the sword, and disregarded His inheritance.

⁶³ Fire consumed their young men, and their maidens were not tearful.

⁶⁴ Their priests fell by the sword, and their widows will not be mournful.

⁶⁵ And the Lord rose up as one out of sleep, like one strong and rowdy from wine.

⁶⁶ And He smote His enemies backwards; He put them to perpetual shame.

⁶⁷ And He refused the tabernacle of Joseph, and chose not the tribe of Ephraim;

⁶⁸ But chose the tribe of Judah, even the hill of Zion, which He loved.

⁶⁹ And like a unicorn He set up His sanctuary on earth; He established it for ever.

⁷⁰ He chose David also His servant, and took him away from the sheepfolds.

⁷¹ From the freshening ewes He took him, that he might tend Jacob His servant, and Israel His inheritance.

⁷² And he tended them in the innocence of his heart, and guided them by the skillfulness of his hands.

Psalm 78

A Psalm for Asaph.

O GOD, the heathen are come into Thine inheritance; they have defiled Thy holy temple.

² They have made Jerusalem as a root cellar; the dead bodies of Thy servants have they given to be meat unto the fowls of the air, and the flesh of Thy saints unto the beasts of the land.

³ Their blood have they poured out like water on every side of Jerusalem, and there was none to bury them.

⁴ We are become an open shame to our neighbors, a very scorn and derision unto them that are round about us.

⁵ How long, O Lord, wilt Thou be angry? For ever? Will Thy jealousy kindle like a fire?

⁶ Pour out Thine indignation upon the nations that have not known Thee, and upon the kingdoms that have not called upon Thy Name.

⁷ For they have devoured Jacob, and laid waste his dwelling-place.

⁸ O remember not our old sins; but let Thy mercy overtake us, for we are come to great poverty.

⁹ Help us, O God our Saviour, for the glory of Thy Name; O Lord, deliver us, and wash away our sins, for Thy Name's sake,

¹⁰ Lest the nations say, Where is now their God? And let the vengeance of Thy servants' blood that hath been shed be openly showed upon the nations in our eyesight.

¹¹ O let the sorrowful sighing of the prisoners come before Thee; according to the greatness of Thy power, preserve Thou the sons of the slain.

¹² Reward Thou unto our neighbors seven-fold

into their bosom for their blasphemy, wherewith they have blasphemed Thee, O Lord.

¹³ For we are Thy people, and the sheep of Thy pasture. We shall give Thee thanks, O God, for ever; from generation to generation will we show forth Thy praise.

Psalm 79

Unto the end, concerning the antiphons, a testimony for Asaph, a Psalm concerning the Assyrian.

HEAR, O Thou Shepherd of Israel, Thou that leadest Joseph like a sheep; show Thyself, Thou that sittest upon the Cherubim.

³ Before Ephraim, and Benjamin, and Manasseh stir up Thy strength, and come to save us.

⁴ Convert us, O God; show the light of Thy countenance, and we shall be saved.

⁵ O Lord God of hosts, how long wilt Thou be angry over the prayer of Thy servants?

⁶ Thou feedest us with the bread of sorrow, and givest us tears to drink in full measure.

⁷ Thou hast made us a very strife unto our neighbors, and our enemies laugh us to scorn.

⁸ O Lord God of hosts, convert us; show the light of Thy countenance, and we shall be saved.

⁹ Thou hast brought a vine out of Egypt; Thou hast cast out the heathen, and planted it.

¹⁰ Thou didst lay the way before it, and hast planted the roots thereof, and it filled the land.

¹¹ The shadow thereof covered the hills, and its boughs God's cedar-trees.

¹² She stretched out her runners unto the sea, and her shoots even unto the river.

¹³ Why hast Thou then broken down her fence, and all they that go by pluck off her grapes?

¹⁴ The wild boar out of the wood hath rooted it up, and the shy beast of the forest hath devoured it.

¹⁵ O God of hosts, turn Thee again, and look down from heaven, and see, and visit this vine,

¹⁶ And perfect that which Thy right hand hath planted, and upon the son of man, whom Thou hast strengthened for Thyself.

¹⁷ Burnt with fire, and digged up, at the rebuke of Thy countenance shall they perish.

¹⁸ Let Thy hand be upon the man of Thy right hand, and upon the son of man, whom Thou hast strengthened for Thyself.

¹⁹ And we shall not depart from Thee; Thou shalt quicken us, and we shall call upon Thy Name.

²⁰ O Lord God of hosts, convert us; show the light of Thy countenance, and we shall be saved.

Psalm 80

Unto the end, a Psalm for Asaph,
concerning the wine-presses.

REJOICE unto God our helper; make a joyful noise unto the God of Jacob.

³ Take the psalm, bring hither the timbrel, the merry harp with the psaltery.

⁴ Blow the trumpet in the new-moon, on the appointed day of our solemn feast.

⁵ For this is a statute for Israel, and a judgment to the God of Jacob.

⁶ This He ordained in Joseph for a testimony, when he came out unto Him from the land of Egypt; he heard a language which he knew not.

⁷ He eased his back of the burden; his hands had labored at the straw.

⁸ Thou calledst upon Me in troubles, and I delivered thee, I heard thee in the thick darkness, I tested thee also at the waters of Meribah.

⁹ Hear, O My people, and I will testify unto thee, O Israel, if thou wilt hearken unto Me,

¹⁰ There shall not be another god in thee, neither shalt thou worship any strange god.

¹¹ For I am the Lord Thy God, who brought thee out of the land of Egypt; open thy mouth wide, and I shall fill it.

¹² But My people would not hear My voice, and Israel would not heed Me.

¹³ So I gave them up unto their hearts' lusts; they shall walk in their own imaginations.

¹⁴ O that My people would have hearkened unto Me, for if Israel had walked in My ways,

¹⁵ I should soon have put down their enemies, and laid My hand upon their adversaries.

¹⁶ The enemies of the Lord have lied to Him, and their time shall be for ever.

¹⁷ He fed them also with wheaten flour, and with honey out of the stony rock did He satisfy them.

Psalm 81

A Psalm for Asaph.

GOD standeth in the gathering of the gods, for in the midst of the gods He shall judge.

² How long will ye judge unjustly, and accept the persons of sinners?

³ Judge for the fatherless and the poor, do right unto such as are humble and needy.

⁴ Rescue the needy and the poor, out of the hand of the sinner deliver him.

⁵ They have not known, nor understood. They walk in darkness; let all the foundations of the earth be shaken.

⁶ I said, Ye are gods, and ye are all children of the Most High.

⁷ But ye shall die like men, and like one of the princes shall ye fall.

⁸ Arise, O God; judge the earth, for Thou shalt be heir in all nations.

Psalm 82

A Song or Psalm for Asaph.

O GOD, who is like unto Thee? Keep not still silence, neither refrain Thyself, O God.

³ For lo, Thine enemies have made a murmuring, and they that hate Thee have lift up their head.

⁴ They have taken craftily against Thy people, and taken counsel against Thy saints.

⁵ They have said, Come, and let us root them out from among the nations, and that the name of Israel may be no more in remembrance.

⁶ For they have put their heads together with one consent, and made a covenant against Thee;

⁷ The tabernacles of the Edomites, and the Ishmaelites, the Moabites, and Hagarenes;

⁸ Gebal, and Ammon, and Amalek, and the Philistines, with them that dwell at Tyre.

⁹ For Assur also is come with them, they have been a defense for the children of Lot.

¹⁰ Do Thou to them as unto the Midianites and unto Sisera, as unto Jabin at the brook of Kishon.

¹¹ They perished at Endor, they became as dung for the earth.

¹² Make their princes like Oreb and Zeeb, and Zebah and Zalmunna, all their princes;

¹³ Who said, Let us take to ourselves God's sanctuary for an inheritance.

¹⁴ O my God, make them like unto a wheel, as stubble before the face of the wind,

¹⁵ Like as a fire burning the forest, as a flame burning up the mountains.

¹⁶ So shalt Thou persecute them with Thy tempest, and trouble them with Thy wrath.

¹⁷ Make their faces ashamed, O Lord, and they shall seek Thy Name.

¹⁸ Let them be confounded and vexed for ever

and ever; let them be put to shame, and perish.

¹⁹ And let them know that Thy Name is LORD;
Thou only art the Most High over all the earth.

Psalm 83

Unto the end, concerning the wine-presses,
of the sons of Korah, a Psalm.

HOW amiable are Thy dwellings, O Lord of
hosts!

³ My soul desireth and longeth for the courts of
the Lord; my heart and my flesh have rejoiced in
the living God.

⁴ Yea, the sparrow hath found her an house, and
the dove a nest where she may lay her young, even
Thy altars, O Lord of hosts, my King and my God.

⁵ Blessed are they that dwell in Thy house, for
ever and ever will they praise Thee.

⁶ Blessed is the man whose help is from Thee, in
his heart he hath proposed ascents

⁷ Into the valley of tears, unto the place which
he hath appointed, for the lawgiver shall give the
blessing.

⁸ They will go from strength to strength; the God
of gods shall appear in Zion.

⁹ O Lord God of hosts, hear my prayer; hearken,
O God of Jacob.

¹⁰ Behold, O God, our defender, and look upon
the face of Thy Christ.

¹¹ For one day in Thy courts is better than a
thousand; I have preferred to be a doorkeeper in

the house of my God, than to dwell in the tents of sinners.

¹² For the Lord loveth mercy and truth, God will give grace and glory; the Lord shall withhold no good thing from them that walk innocently.

¹³ O Lord God of hosts, blessed is the man that putteth his trust in Thee.

Psalm 84

Unto the end, of the sons of Korah, a Psalm.

THOU hast been gracious, O Lord, unto Thy land, Thou hast turned back the captivity of Jacob.

³ Thou hast forgiven the offenses of Thy people; Thou hast covered all their sins.

⁴ Thou hast curtailed all Thy displeasure; Thou hast relented from the wrath of Thine indignation.

⁵ Convert us, then, O God of our salvation, and let Thine anger cease from us.

⁶ Wilt Thou be displeased at us for ever? Or wilt Thou stretch out Thy wrath from one generation to another?

⁷ O God, Thou shalt stay Thyself; Thou shalt revive us, and Thy people shall rejoice in Thee.

⁸ Show us, O Lord, Thy mercy, and grant us Thy salvation.

⁹ I will hear what the Lord God will say concerning me; for He shall speak peace unto His people, and to His saints, and to them that turn their hearts unto Him.

¹⁰ Surely His salvation is nigh them that fear Him, that glory may dwell in our land.

¹¹ Mercy and truth are met together, justice and peace have kissed each other.

¹² Truth hath flourished out of the earth, and justice hath looked down from heaven.

¹³ For the Lord shall show loving-kindness, and our land shall give her increase.

¹⁴ Justice shall go before Him, and shall set His steps in the way.

Psalm 85
A Prayer of David.

BOW down Thine ear, O Lord, and hear me, for I am poor and in misery.

² Preserve Thou my soul, for I am holy; save Thy servant, O my God, that putteth his trust in Thee.

³ Have mercy upon me, O Lord, for I will call upon Thee all day.

⁴ Give joy to the soul of Thy servant, for unto Thee have I lifted up my soul.

⁵ For Thou, Lord, art good and gentle, and of great mercy unto all them that call upon Thee.

⁶ Give ear, Lord, unto my prayer, and heed the voice of my supplication.

⁷ In the day of my trouble I called upon Thee, for Thou hast heard me.

⁸ Among the gods there is none like unto Thee, O Lord, nor are there any deeds according unto Thy deeds.

⁹ All nations whom Thou hast made shall come and bow down before Thee, O Lord, and shall glorify Thy Name.

¹⁰ For Thou art great, and doest wondrous things; Thou art God alone.

¹¹ Guide me, O Lord, in Thy way, and I will walk in Thy truth; O let my heart rejoice to fear Thy Name.

¹² I will thank Thee, O Lord my God, with all my heart, and I will praise Thy Name for evermore.

¹³ For great is Thy mercy toward me, and Thou hast delivered my soul from the nethermost hell.

¹⁴ O God, the wicked are risen against me, and the congregations of the mighty have sought after my soul, and have not set Thee before them.

¹⁵ But Thou, O Lord my God, art compassionate and merciful, long-suffering, and greatly charitable and true.

¹⁶ O look upon me, and have mercy upon me, give Thy strength unto Thy servant, and help the son of Thine handmaid.

¹⁷ Work some sign upon me for good, that they who hate me may see, and be ashamed, because Thou, Lord, hast holpen me, and comforted me.

Psalm 86

A Psalm and Song of the sons of Korah.

HER foundations are upon the holy hills; the Lord loveth the gates of Zion more than all the dwellings of Jacob.

³ Very glorious things are spoken of thee, O city of God.

⁴ I will speak of Rahab and Babylon with them that know me; behold, the Philistines also, and Tyre, with the Ethiopians, such were there.

⁵ Mother Zion, shall a man say, and the man was born in her, and the Most High Himself hath founded her.

⁶ The Lord shall tell in writing of the peoples and the princes that were in her,

⁷ How joyful are all they whose habitation is in thee!

Psalm 87

A Song and Psalm by the sons of Korah, unto the end,
for the Mahalath to respond, of instruction
to Heman the Ezrahite.

O LORD God of my salvation, by day have I cried, and by night before Thee.

³ O let my prayer come in before Thee; incline Thine ear unto my calling.

⁴ For my soul is full of trouble, and my life hath drawn nigh unto hell.

⁵ I have been counted as one of them that go down into the pit; I have become even as a man without help,

⁶ Free among the dead; like the wounded sleeping in the grave, whom Thou rememberest no more, and which have been cast away from Thy hand.

⁷ They laid me in the lowest pit, in the darkness and shadow of death.

⁸ Upon me hath Thine anger fixed itself, and all Thy waves hast Thou aimed at me.

⁹ Thou hast put away mine acquaintances far from me, they have made me to be an abomination unto them; I was betrayed, and did not go forth.

¹⁰ Mine eyes are grown weak from poverty. I called upon Thee, O Lord, all day; I stretched forth my hands unto Thee.

¹¹ Shalt Thou indeed work wonders with the dead? Or shall physicians revive them, and they shall praise Thee?

¹² Shall any in the grave declare Thy mercy and Thy truth in perdition?

¹³ Shall Thy wondrous works be known in the dark, and Thy righteousness in the Land of Oblivion?

¹⁴ But unto Thee have I cried, O Lord, and in the morning shall my prayer come before Thee.

¹⁵ Lord, why abhorrest Thou my soul? Why turnest Thou Thy face from me?

¹⁶ I am poor, and in hardship from my youth; having risen up, I have humbled myself and become utterly worn down.

¹⁷ Thy wrathful displeasure goeth over me; Thy terrors have undone me.

¹⁸ They came round about me like water; all day they compassed me about together.

¹⁹ Friend and neighbor hast Thou put away

from me, and mine acquaintances, because of sufferings.

Psalm 88

Of instruction, by Ethan the Ezrahite.

I SHALL sing of Thy mercy, O Lord, for ever; from one generation to another I will proclaim Thy truth with my mouth.

³ For Thou hast said, Mercy shall be set up for ever; Thy truth shall be stablished in the heavens.

⁴ I have made a covenant with My chosen; I have sworn unto David My servant,

⁵ Thy seed will I stablish for ever, and set up thy throne from one generation to another.

⁶ The heavens shall declare Thy wondrous works, O Lord, even Thy truth in the church of the saints.

⁷ For who among the clouds shall be compared unto the Lord? Who among the sons of the gods shall be like unto the Lord?

⁸ We shall glorify God in the council of the saints; great and terrible is He over all them that are round about Him.

⁹ O Lord God of hosts, who is like unto Thee? Thou art strong, O Lord, and Thy truth is round about Thee.

¹⁰ Thou rulest the power of the sea; Thou stillest the raging of its waves.

¹¹ Thou hast humbled the arrogant, as one

wounded; Thou hast scattered Thine enemies with the might of Thy strength.

¹² The heavens are Thine, the earth also is Thine; Thou hast laid the foundation of the whole world, and all that therein is.

¹³ Thou hast made the north and the sea; Tabor and Hermon shall rejoice in Thy Name.

¹⁴ Thy arm is mighty; let Thy hand be strengthened, and Thy right hand be lifted up.

¹⁵ Justice and judgment are the pedestal of Thy throne; mercy and truth shall go before Thy face.

¹⁶ Blessed is the people that know jubilation; O Lord, they shall walk in the light of Thy countenance,

¹⁷ And in Thy Name shall they rejoice all day, and by Thy righteousness shall they be exalted.

¹⁸ For Thou art the glory of their strength, and in Thy good pleasure shall our horn be lifted up.

¹⁹ For defense is of the Lord, and of the Holy One of Israel, our King.

²⁰ Then spakest Thou in a vision unto Thy sons, and saidst, I have laid help upon one that is mighty; I have raised up the chosen one of My people.

²¹ I have found David My servant; with My holy oil have I anointed him.

²² For My hand shall hold him up, and My arm shall strengthen him.

²³ The enemy shall be able to do nothing against him, and the son of iniquity shall not be able to hurt him.

²⁴ And I will smite down his foes before his face, and vanquish them that hate him.

²⁵ My truth also and My mercy are with him, and in My Name shall his horn be exalted.

²⁶ I will set his hand also upon the seas, and his right hand in the rivers.

²⁷ He shall call Me, Thou art my Father, my God, and the defender of my salvation.

²⁸ And I will make him My first-born, higher than the kings of the earth.

²⁹ My mercy will I keep for him for evermore, and My covenant shall be true to him.

³⁰ His seed also will I stablish for ever and ever, and his throne as the days of heaven.

³¹ But if his children forsake My Law, and walk not in My judgments;

³² If they profane My statutes, and keep not My commandments,

³³ I will visit their offenses with the rod, and their sin with scourges.

³⁴ Nevertheless, My mercy will I not unbind from them, nor act harmfully in My truth,

³⁵ Neither will I profane my covenant, nor alter the thing that is gone out of My lips.

³⁶ I have sworn once by My holiness, that I will not lie unto David.

³⁷ His seed shall endure for ever, and his throne shall be like as the sun before Me,

³⁸ And as the moon, perfect for ever, and a faithful witness in heaven.

³⁹ But Thou hast rejected and humiliated, Thou hast been indignant with Thine anointed.

⁴⁰ Thou hast annulled the covenant of Thy servant; Thou hast profaned his sanctuary on earth.

⁴¹ Thou hast overthrown all his bulwarks; Thou hast put fear in his strong-holds.

⁴² All they that pass by on the way have despoiled him; he is become a shame to his neighbors.

⁴³ Thou hast raised the right hand of them that oppress him; Thou hast gladdened all his enemies.

⁴⁴ Thou hast turned away the help of his sword, and took not up for him in battle.

⁴⁵ Thou hast made an end of his purification; Thou hast cast his throne down to the ground.

⁴⁶ Thou hast shortened the span of his days; Thou hast drenched him with shame.

⁴⁷ How long, O Lord, wilt Thou turn Thyself away? For ever? Shall Thy wrath kindle like fire?

⁴⁸ O remember what my substance is, for hast Thou made all the children of men for naught?

⁴⁹ What man is he that liveth, and shall not see death? Shall he deliver his soul from the hand of hell?

⁵⁰ Where are Thy mercies of old, O Lord, which Thou swarest unto David in Thy truth?

⁵¹ Remember, Lord, the rebuke that Thy servants have, which I have borne in my bosom from many nations,

⁵² Wherewith Thine enemies have blasphemed, O Lord, wherewith they have slandered the change

of Thine anointed.

⁵³ Blessed be the Lord for evermore. So be it. So be it.

Psalm 89

A Prayer of Moses the man of God.

LORD, Thou hast been our refuge from generation to generation.

³ Before ever the mountains were formed, or the earth and the world were created, even from age to age Thou art.

⁴ Turn not man away unto humiliation; yea, Thou hast said, Be converted, ye children of men.

⁵ For a thousand years before Thine eyes, O Lord, are but as yesterday when it is past, and as a watch in the night.

⁶ Fleeting shall their years be; he shall go by in the morning like the grass; in the morning it shall flourish, and grow up, but in the evening it shall fall away, and dry up, and wither.

⁷ For we consumed away in Thy displeasure, and were troubled at Thy wrathful indignation.

⁸ Thou hast set our misdeeds before Thee, our years are in the light of Thy countenance.

⁹ For all our days are spent, and we have disappeared in Thy wrath;

¹⁰ Our years are spun out like a spider's web. The days of our age are threescore years and ten, or if we be so strong, fourscore years, and more

than these is but labor and sorrow; for frailty shall come upon us, and we shall be chastened.

¹¹ Who knoweth the power of Thy wrath, and from fear of Thee, who can recount Thine anger?

¹² So make Thy right hand known to me, and to them that are bound by the heart in wisdom.

¹³ Turn Thee again, O Lord; how long? And be gracious unto Thy servants.

¹⁴ We were satisfied with Thy mercy in the morning, O Lord, and we rejoiced and were glad;

¹⁵ We were glad all our days; for the days wherein Thou didst humble us, the years wherein we saw adversity.

¹⁶ And look upon Thy servants, and upon Thy works, and guide their children,

¹⁷ And let the brightness of the Lord our God be upon us, and prosper Thou the work of our hands upon us; yea, prosper Thou our handy-work.

Psalm 90

A Praise-song of David.
Without superscription in the Hebrew.

WHOSO dwelleth in the help of the Most High shall abide in the shelter of the God of heaven.

² He will say unto the Lord, Thou art my defender, and my refuge, my God, and I will trust in Him.

³ For He shall deliver thee from the snare of the hunter, and from every mutinous word.

⁴ With His wings will He overshadow thee, and thou shalt be safe under His feathers; His truth shall compass thee round about like a shield.

⁵ Thou shalt not be afraid for any terror by night, nor for the arrow that flieth by day;

⁶ For the thing that walketh in darkness, for sickness, or the demon of noon-day.

⁷ A thousand shall fall beside thee, and ten thousand at thy right hand, but unto thee it shall not come nigh.

⁸ But thou shalt behold with thine eyes, and see the reward of sinners.

⁹ For Thou, Lord, art my hope; thou hast made the Most High thy refuge.

¹⁰ There shall no evil happen unto thee, neither shall any plague come nigh thy dwelling.

¹¹ For He shall give His angels charge over thee, to keep thee in all thy ways.

¹² They shall bear thee in their hands, that thou hurt not thy foot against a stone.

¹³ Thou shalt step upon the asp and basilisk; the lion and the serpent shalt thou tread under thy feet.

¹⁴ Because he hath set his hope upon Me, therefore will I deliver him; I will shelter him, because he hath known My Name.

¹⁵ He shall call upon Me, and I will hear him; yea, I am with him in trouble, I will deliver him, and bring him to glory.

¹⁶ With long life will I satisfy him, and show him My salvation.

Psalm 91

A Psalm and Song for the Sabbath day.

I T is a good thing to give thanks unto the Lord, and to sing unto Thy Name, O Most High;

³ To tell of Thy mercy in the morning, and of Thy truth every night,

⁴ Upon the ten-stringed psaltery, and with a song upon the harp.

⁵ For Thou hast made me glad, O Lord, by Thy works, and in the operations of Thy hands will I rejoice.

⁶ How glorious are Thy works, O Lord; Thy thoughts are very deep.

⁷ These things an unwise man perceiveth not, and a fool doth not understand.

⁸ When sinners spring up as the grass, and when all the workers of wickedness do flourish, it is so they may be consumed for ever and ever.

⁹ But Thou art the Most High for evermore, O Lord.

¹⁰ For lo, Thine enemies, O Lord, for lo, Thine enemies shall perish, and all the workers of wickedness shall be driven off,

¹¹ But my horn shall be exalted like the horn of a unicorn, and my old age in plentiful oil.

¹² Mine eye also hath looked upon mine enemies, and mine ear shall hear the malignant that arise up against me.

¹³ The righteous shall flourish like a palm-tree, and shall spread abroad like a cedar in Lebanon.

¹⁴ Such as are planted in the house of the Lord, shall flourish in the courts of our God.

¹⁵ They shall bring forth fruit in ripe old age, and shall be well-acceptable,

¹⁶ That they may show how true the Lord our God is, and that there is no unrighteousness in Him.

Psalm 92

For the Sabbath day eve, when the earth was first inhabited, a Praise-song of David.

Without superscription in the Hebrew.

THE Lord is King, He is clothed with majesty; the Lord is clothed in strength, and hath girt Himself, for He hath made the whole world so sure, that it shall not be moved.

² From the beginning is Thy throne prepared; Thou art from everlasting.

³ The rivers are risen, O Lord, the rivers have lift up their voices.

⁴ The rivers shall stir up their havoc; from the voices of many waters,

⁵ Wonderful are the heights of the sea; wonderful is the Lord on high.

⁶ Thy testimonies are very sure; holiness becometh Thine house, O Lord, unto length of days.

Psalm 93

A Psalm of David, for the fourth day of the week.
Without superscription in the Hebrew.

G OD is an avenging Lord; the God of vengeance
hath acted freely.

2 Arise, Thou Judge of the world, and reward the proud after their deserving.

3 Lord, how long shall sinners, how long shall sinners boast?

4 Shall they utter and speak untruth? Shall all speak that work iniquity?

5 They have humbled Thy peoples, O Lord, and embittered Thine inheritance.

6 They murder the widow, and the orphan, and put the pilgrim to death.

7 And they said, The Lord shall not see, neither shall the God of Jacob comprehend.

8 Take heed, ye thoughtless among the people, and ye fools, when will ye be wise?

9 He that planted the ear, shall He not hear? Or He that made the eye, shall He not see?

10 He that chasteneth the heathen, shall He not rebuke, He that teacheth man knowledge?

11 The Lord knoweth the thoughts of man, that they are but vain.

12 Blessed is the man whom Thou chastenest, O Lord, and teachest him out of Thy Law;

13 That Thou mayest give him relief from cruel days, until the pit be digged up for the sinner.

¹⁴ For the Lord will not reject His people, neither will He forsake His inheritance,

¹⁵ Until righteousness turn again unto judgment, and all such as are true in heart shall follow it.

¹⁶ Who will rise up for me against the evildoers? Or who will stand up for me against the workers of iniquity?

¹⁷ If the Lord had not helped me, my soul had almost dwelt in hell.

¹⁸ If I said, My foot hath slipped, Thy mercy, O Lord, helped me.

¹⁹ According to the multitude of sorrows in my heart have Thy comforts refreshed my soul.

²⁰ Let not the throne of wickedness abide with Thee, which maketh trouble on command.

²¹ They shall seize upon the soul of the righteous, and condemn innocent blood.

²² But the Lord is become a refuge for me, and my God the help of my hope.

²³ And the Lord shall recompense them their wickedness, and according unto their own malice shall the Lord God destroy them.

Psalm 94

A Praise-song of David.

Without superscription in the Hebrew.

O COME, let us rejoice unto the Lord; let us make a joyful noise unto God our Saviour.

² Let us come before His presence with thanksgiving, and rejoice unto Him in psalms.

³ For the Lord is a great God, and a great King over all the earth.

⁴ For in His hand are all the corners of the earth, and the heights of the hills are His also.

⁵ For the sea is His, and He made it, and His hands formed the dry land.

⁶ O come, let us worship and fall down before Him, and weep before the Lord that made us.

⁷ For He is our God, and we are the people of His pasture, and the sheep of His hand. Today if ye will hear His voice,

⁸ Harden not your hearts, as in the provocation, and as in the day of temptation in the wilderness;

⁹ When your fathers tempted Me, proved Me, and saw My works.

¹⁰ Forty years long was I grieved with that generation, and said, They do always err in their hearts, for they have not known My ways;

¹¹ So I swore in My wrath, that they should not enter into My rest.

Psalm 95

A Praise-song of David, when the house was built after the Captivity. Without superscription in the Hebrew.

O SING unto the Lord a new song; sing unto the Lord, all the earth;

² Sing unto the Lord; bless His Name; be telling of His salvation from day to day.

³ Declare among the nations His glory, among all peoples His wonders.

⁴ For the Lord is great, and highly to be praised; He is more to be feared than all gods.

⁵ For all the gods of the heathen are demons, but the Lord made the heavens.

⁶ Thanksgiving and beauty are before Him; holiness and majesty are in His sanctuary.

⁷ Bring unto the Lord, O ye kindreds of the nations, bring unto the Lord glory and honor.

⁸ Bring unto the Lord the glory due unto His Name; take up sacrifices, and enter into His courts.

⁹ O worship the Lord in His holy court; let the whole earth be shaken at His presence.

¹⁰ Tell it out among the heathen that the Lord is King, for He hath made the whole world, which shall not be moved; He shall judge the peoples with equity.

¹¹ Let the heavens be glad, and let the earth rejoice; let the sea be moved, and all that therein is.

¹² Let the fields be joyful, and all that are in them; then shall all the trees of the wood rejoice

¹³ At the presence of the Lord, for He cometh, for He cometh to judge the earth; to judge the whole world with righteousness, and the peoples with His truth.

Psalm 96

A Psalm of David, when the land was restored to him.
Without superscription in the Hebrew.

THE Lord is King, let the earth rejoice; let the many isles be glad.

² Clouds and darkness are round about Him; righteousness and judgment are the restoration of His throne.

³ There shall go a fire before Him, and burn up His enemies on every side.

⁴ His lightnings shone forth upon the whole world; the earth saw, and trembled.

⁵ The hills melted like wax at the presence of the Lord, at the presence of the Lord of the whole earth.

⁶ The heavens have declared His righteousness, and all the people have seen His glory.

⁷ Confounded be all they that worship carved images, that boast of their idols; worship Him, all ye His angels.

⁸ Zion heard, and was glad, and the daughters of Judah rejoiced, because of Thy judgments, O Lord.

⁹ For Thou art the Lord Most High over all the earth; Thou art exalted far above all gods.

¹⁰ O ye that love the Lord, hate the thing which is evil. The Lord preserveth the souls of His saints; He shall deliver them from the hand of the sinner.

¹¹ There is sprung up a light for the righteous, and gladness for such as are true-hearted.

¹² Be glad in the Lord, ye righteous, and give thanks at the memory of His holiness.

Psalm 97

A Psalm of David.

O SING unto the Lord a new song, for the Lord hath done marvelous things; His own right hand hath saved Him, and His holy arm.

² The Lord hath declared His salvation; His righteousness hath He openly showed in the sight of the heathen.

³ He hath remembered His mercy to Jacob, and His truth to the house of Israel; all the ends of the earth have seen the salvation of our God.

⁴ Shout with jubilation unto God, all ye lands; chant ye, and be joyful; O sing ye.

⁵ Sing unto the Lord upon the harp, upon the harp with the voice of a psalm,

⁶ On forged trumpets and with the sound of a ram's horn; blow the horn before the Lord the King.

⁷ Let the sea be moved, and all that therein is, the whole world, and all they that dwell therein.

⁸ The rivers shall clap their hands together, and the hills shall be joyful

⁹ At the presence of the Lord, for He draweth nigh, yea, He cometh to judge the earth; to judge the whole world in righteousness, and the peoples with equity.

Psalm 98

A Psalm of David. Without superscription in the Hebrew.

THE Lord is King, be the peoples never so impatient; He that sitteth upon the Cherubim, be the earth never so unquiet.

² The Lord is great in Zion, and high above all peoples.

³ Let them give thanks unto Thy great Name, for it is terrible and holy,

⁴ And the King's honor loveth judgment; Thou hast prepared justice, Thou hast executed judgment and righteousness in Jacob.

⁵ O magnify the Lord our God, and fall down at the footstool of His feet, for He is holy.

⁶ Moses and Aaron among His priests, and Samuel among such as call upon His Name; these called upon the Lord, and He heard them.

⁷ He spake unto them out of the cloudy pillar, for they kept His testimonies, and the ordinances that He gave them.

⁸ O Lord our God, Thou heardest them; O God, Thou wast merciful unto them, and vengeful unto all their provocations.

⁹ O magnify the Lord our God, and worship at His holy hill, for the Lord our God is holy.

Psalm 99

A Psalm of David, of thanksgiving.

O BE joyful unto God, all the earth;
² Serve the Lord with gladness, and come in before Him with joy.

³ Know ye, that the Lord, He is our God; it is He that hath made us, and not we ourselves, for we are His people, and the sheep of His pasture.

⁴ Enter into His gates with thanksgiving, and into His courts with praise; be thankful unto Him, and praise His Name.

⁵ For the Lord is gracious; His mercy is everlasting, and His truth even from generation to generation.

Psalm 100

A Psalm of David.

M ERCY and judgment shall be my song unto Thee, O Lord;
² I sing and understand in a blameless way; when wilt Thou come unto me? I have walked in the innocency of my heart in the midst of my house.

³ I have set no unlawful thing before mine eyes; I have hated the workers of iniquity.

⁴ A forward heart hath not cleaved unto me; I did not know the crafty man that turned away from me.

⁵ Whoso privily slandereth his neighbor, him did I drive out; whoso hath a proud look and

a greedy stomach, with such I did not eat.

⁶ Mine eyes look upon such as are faithful in the land, that they may dwell with me; whoso leadeth a godly life, he shall be my servant.

⁷ The proud doer hath not dwelt in the midst of my house; he that speaketh unjustly shall have no place in my sight.

⁸ In the morning I slew all the sinners of the land, to consume all the workers of lawlessness from the city of the Lord.

Psalm 101

A Prayer of the poor man, when he is downcast, and poureth out his complaint before the Lord.

O LORD, hear my prayer, and let my cry come unto Thee.

³ Turn not Thy face from me; in the day of my trouble, incline Thine ear unto me; in the day when I call upon Thee, quickly hearken unto me.

⁴ For my days have disappeared like smoke, and my bones are burnt up like kindling.

⁵ I have been smitten down like grass, and my heart is withered, for I forgot to eat my bread.

⁶ From the voice of my groaning hath my bone cleaved unto my flesh.

⁷ I am become like a pelican in the wilderness, I was like an owl in the ruins.

⁸ I have watched, and was even as it were a sparrow, that sitteth alone upon the house-top.

⁹ Mine enemies reviled me all the day long, and they that praised me swore at me.

¹⁰ For I have eaten ashes as it were bread, and mingled my drink with tears,

¹¹ Because of the face of Thine indignation and Thy wrath, for, having taken me up, Thou hast cast me down.

¹² My days are gone like a shadow, and I am withered like grass.

¹³ But, Thou, O Lord, shalt endure for ever, and Thy remembrance is unto generation and generation.

¹⁴ Thou shalt arise, and have mercy upon Zion, for it is time that Thou have mercy upon her, yea, the time is come.

¹⁵ For Thy servants have been well pleased by the stones thereof, and they shall be merciful unto her dust.

¹⁶ And the nations shall fear the Name of the Lord, and all the kings of the earth Thy glory.

¹⁷ For the Lord shall build up Zion, and reveal Himself in His glory.

¹⁸ He hath regarded the prayer of the humble, and hath not despised their petition.

¹⁹ Let this be written for another generation, and a people yet to be born shall praise the Lord;

²⁰ For He hath looked down from the height of His sanctuary; out of heaven did the Lord behold the earth,

²¹ To hear the moaning of such as are in shackles, to free the sons of the slain,

²² To declare the Name of the Lord in Zion, and His praise in Jerusalem,

²³ When the peoples are gathered together, and the kings also, to serve the Lord.

²⁴ He answered Him in the way of his strength; the fewness of my days shalt Thou make known unto me.

²⁵ O take me not away in the midst of my days; as for Thy years, they endure throughout all generations.

²⁶ In the beginning, O Lord, hast Thou laid the foundation of the earth, and the heavens are the work of Thy hands.

²⁷ They shall perish, but Thou shalt endure; yea, they all shall wax old as doth a garment, and as a vesture shalt Thou change them, and they shall be changed.

²⁸ But Thou art the same, and Thy years shall not fail.

²⁹ The sons of Thy servants shall abide, and their seed shall prosper for ever.

Psalm 102

A Psalm of David.

B LESS the Lord, O my soul, and all that is within me bless His holy Name.

² Bless the Lord, O my soul, and forget not all His benefits;

³ Who forgiveth all thine iniquities, and healeth all thy diseases;

⁴ Who redeemeth thy life from corruption, and crowneth thee with mercy and compassion;

⁵ Who satisfieth thy desire with good things; thy youth shall be renewed like the eagle's.

⁶ The Lord performeth deeds of mercy, and judgment for all them that are wronged.

⁷ He made known His ways unto Moses, His will unto the children of Israel.

⁸ The Lord is compassionate and merciful, long-suffering, and of great kindness.

⁹ He will not always be chiding, neither keepeth He His anger for ever.

¹⁰ He hath not dealt with us after our sins, nor rewarded us according to our wickednesses.

¹¹ For as high as the heaven is in comparison of the earth, so great is the Lord's mercy also toward them that fear Him.

¹² As wide as the east is from the west, so far hath He set our iniquity from us.

¹³ Like as a father pitieth his own children, even so hath the Lord been merciful unto them that fear Him.

¹⁴ For He knoweth whereof we are made; He remembereth that we are but dust.

¹⁵ As for man, his days are as the grass; for he flourisheth as a flower of the field.

¹⁶ For as soon as the wind goeth over it, it is gone; and it shall no more know the place thereof.

¹⁷ But the mercy of the Lord is from everlasting to everlasting upon them that fear Him,

¹⁸ And His righteousness upon sons of sons for such as keep His covenant, and remember His commandments to do them.

¹⁹ The Lord hath prepared His throne in heaven, and His kingdom ruleth over all.

²⁰ O bless the Lord, all ye His angels, ye that excel in strength, ye that fulfill His commandment, to hearken unto the voice of His words.

²¹ O bless the Lord, all ye His hosts, ye servants of His that do His will.

²² O bless the Lord, all ye works of His, in every place of His dominion; bless the Lord, O my soul.

Psalm 103

A Psalm of David, concerning the Genesis of the World.

BLESS the Lord, O my soul. O Lord my God, Thou art become exceeding glorious; in honor and majesty hast Thou clothed Thyself,

² Wrapping Thyself with light as it were with a garment, and spreading out the heavens like a curtain,

³ Who covereth the beams of His chambers by the waters, Who appointeth the clouds for His going forth, Who walketh upon the wings of the wind,

⁴ Who maketh His angels spirits, and His ministers a flaming fire,

⁵ Whoso layeth the earth on its foundations, that it shall never be moved.

⁶ The deep like a garment is its clothing; the waters stand above the hills.

⁷ At Thy rebuke they shall flee; at the voice of Thy thunder they shall be afraid.

⁸ The hills shall go up and the plains shall go down, even unto the place which Thou hast appointed for them.

⁹ Thou hast set a boundary which they shall not pass, neither return again to cover the earth,

¹⁰ Who sendeth the springs into the valleys; the waters will run between the hills.

¹¹ All beasts of the field shall drink thereof, and the wild asses quench their thirst.

¹² Beside them shall the fowls of the air have their habitation; they shall sing among the rocks.

¹³ He watereth the hills from His heights; the earth shall be well-fed by the fruit of Thy works,

¹⁴ Who bringeth forth grass for the cattle, and green herb for the service of men, to bring forth bread from the earth,

¹⁵ And wine maketh a man's heart glad; to anoint the face with oil, and bread strengtheneth man's heart.

¹⁶ The trees of the plain shall be full of sap, the cedars of Lebanon which He hath planted;

¹⁷ In them the birds shall make their nests; the home of the stork is chief among them.

¹⁸ The high hills are for the deer, and the stony

rocks are a refuge for the conies.

¹⁹ He made the moon to mark the seasons; the sun knoweth his going down.

²⁰ Thou didst ordain darkness, and there was night, wherein all the beasts of the forest do move,

²¹ Young lions roaring after their prey and seeking their meat from God.

²² The sun arose, and they gathered together, and shall lie down in their dens.

²³ Man shall go forth to his work, and to his labor, until the evening.

²⁴ How great are Thy works, O Lord! In wisdom hast Thou made them all; the earth is filled with Thy handiwork.

²⁵ So is the great and wide sea also, wherein are things creeping innumerable, both small and great beasts.

²⁶ There go the ships, and that Leviathan, whom Thou hast made to take his pastime therein.

²⁷ These wait all upon Thee, that Thou mayest give them food in due season.

²⁸ When Thou givest it them, they shall gather it; when Thou openest Thy hand, all things shall be filled with good,

²⁹ But when Thou hidest Thy face, they shall be troubled; Thou shalt take away their spirit, and they shall pass away, and return again to their dust.

³⁰ Thou shalt send forth Thy Spirit, and they shall be made, and Thou shalt renew the face of the earth.

³¹ O let the glory of the Lord endure for ever; the Lord shall rejoice in His works,

³² Who looketh upon the earth, and it trembleth; Who toucheth the hills, and they smoke.

³³ I will sing unto the Lord as long as I live; I will praise my God while I have my being.

³⁴ Let my conversation be pleasing unto Him, for I shall be glad in the Lord.

³⁵ O that sinners should cease from the earth, and the ungodly, that they should be no more! Bless the Lord, O my soul.

Psalm 104
Alleluia.

O GIVE thanks unto the Lord, and call upon His Name; proclaim among the nations His deeds.

² O sing unto Him, and praise Him with psalms; tell of all His wondrous works.

³ Glory in His holy Name; let the heart of them be glad that seek the Lord.

⁴ Seek the Lord and be strengthened; seek His face always.

⁵ Remember the marvelous works that He hath done, His wonders, and the judgments of His mouth,

⁶ O ye seed of Abraham, His servants; ye children of Jacob, His chosen.

⁷ He is the Lord our God; His judgments are in all the world.

⁸ He hath been always mindful of His covenant, the promise that He made to a thousand generations;

⁹ That He made with Abraham, and His oath unto Isaac;

¹⁰ And appointed the same unto Jacob for an ordinance, and to Israel for an everlasting testament,

¹¹ Saying, Unto thee will I give the land of Canaan, the lot of your inheritance,

¹² When they were yet but few in number, of little consequence, and strangers therein.

¹³ And they went from one nation to another, from one kingdom to another people.

¹⁴ He suffered no man to do them wrong, and reproved even kings for their sakes, saying,

¹⁵ Touch not Mine anointed, and do My prophets no harm.

¹⁶ Moreover, He called for a famine upon the land, and destroyed all the provision of bread.

¹⁷ He sent a man before them, even Joseph, who was sold to be a slave.

¹⁸ They humbled his feet with fetters; he passed his life in irons,

¹⁹ Until his word came to pass; the word of the Lord tried him.

²⁰ The king sent, and released him, even the prince of the people, and let him go free.

²¹ He made him lord of his house, and ruler of all his substance;

²² To instruct his princes after his will, and teach his senators wisdom.

²³ Israel also came into Egypt, and Jacob was a stranger in the land of Ham.

²⁴ And He increased His people exceedingly, and made them stronger than their enemies;

²⁵ He turned their heart to hate His people; to deal craftily with His servants.

²⁶ He sent Moses His servant, and Aaron whom He had chosen.

²⁷ To them He committed the words of His signs and of His wonders in the land of Ham.

²⁸ He sent darkness, and it was dark, for they were galled by His words.

²⁹ He turned their waters into blood, and slew their fish.

³⁰ Their land was overrun with frogs, even in the storerooms of their kings.

³¹ He spake, and there came swarms of flies, and lice in all their quarters.

³² He gave them hail-stones for rain, and grievous fire in their land.

³³ He smote their vines also and their fig-trees, and brake every tree that was in their coasts.

³⁴ He spake, and the locusts came, and caterpillars innumerable,

³⁵ And did eat up all the grass in their land, and devoured all the fruit of their ground.

³⁶ He smote also all the first-born in their land, the first-fruit of all their labor.

³⁷ He brought them forth also with silver and gold, and there was not one feeble person among their tribes.

³⁸ Egypt was glad at their departing, for a fear of them had fallen upon her.

³⁹ He spread out a cloud to be a covering for them, and fire to give light unto them by night.

⁴⁰ They asked, and quails came, and He filled them with the bread of heaven.

⁴¹ He clave the rock of stone, and the waters flowed out, so that rivers ran in the dry places.

⁴² For He remembered His holy word, which He had given unto Abraham His servant.

⁴³ And He brought forth His people with joy, and His chosen with gladness.

⁴⁴ And gave them the lands of the heathen, and they took the labors of the peoples in possession;

⁴⁵ That they might keep His statutes, and seek out His Law.

Psalm 105

Alleluia.

O GIVE thanks unto the Lord, for He is good; for His mercy endureth for ever.

² Who shall speak of the mighty acts of the Lord? Who shall make all His praise to be heard?

³ Blessed are they that keep judgment, and do righteousness always.

⁴ Remember us, O Lord, according to the favor

that Thou bearest unto Thy people; O visit us with Thy salvation,

⁵ That we may see the goodness of Thy chosen, and be glad in the gladness of Thy nation, and glory with Thine inheritance.

⁶ We have sinned with our fathers; we have done amiss, and dealt wickedly.

⁷ Our fathers considered not Thy wonders in Egypt, neither kept they Thy great mercy in remembrance, but were disobedient when they went up to the Red Sea.

⁸ Nevertheless, He helped them for His Name's sake, that He might make His power to be known.

⁹ He rebuked the Red Sea also, and it was dried up, and He led them through the deep, as through a wilderness.

¹⁰ And He saved them from the hand of the adversaries, and delivered them from the hand of the enemy.

¹¹ The waters overwhelmed them that troubled them; there was not one of them left.

¹² Then believed they His words, and sang praise unto Him.

¹³ But within a while they forgat His works; they waited not for His counsel,

¹⁴ But they lusted with desire in the wilderness, and they tempted God in the desert.

¹⁵ And He gave them their desire, and sent satiety into their soul.

¹⁶ They angered Moses also in the camp, and

Aaron the holy one of the Lord.

¹⁷ So the earth opened, and swallowed up Dathan, and covered the congregation of Abiram.

¹⁸ And a fire was kindled in their company; the flame burnt up the sinners.

¹⁹ They made a calf also in Horeb, and worshipped a graven image.

²⁰ Thus they turned His glory into the similitude of a calf that eateth hay.

²¹ And they forgat the God Who had saved them, Who had done so great things in Egypt;

²² Wondrous works in the land of Ham, and fearful things by the Red Sea.

²³ And He said He would have destroyed them, had not Moses His chosen stood before Him in the breach, to turn away His wrathful indignation, lest He should destroy them.

²⁴ Yea, they thought scorn of that longed-for land; they gave no credence unto His word,

²⁵ But murmured in their tents; they hearkened not unto the voice of the Lord.

²⁶ Therefore lifted He up His hand against them, to cast them down in the wilderness;

²⁷ To cast out their seed among the nations, and to scatter them in the lands.

²⁸ Then were they joined unto Baal-peor, and ate the sacrifices of the dead.

²⁹ And they provoked Him to anger with their undertakings, and the plague was great among them.

³⁰ Then stood up Phineas and made propitiation, and so the plague ceased.

³¹ And that was counted unto him for righteousness, from generation to generation for evermore.

³² They angered Him also at the waters of Meribah, and it went ill with Moses for their sakes;

³³ Because they provoked his spirit, and he spake unadvisedly with his lips.

³⁴ Neither destroyed they the heathen, as the Lord commanded them,

³⁵ But were mingled among the heathen, and learned their works,

³⁶ And they worshipped their graven images, and it became a stumbling-block unto them.

³⁷ Yea, they sacrificed their sons and their daughters unto demons,

³⁸ And shed innocent blood, even the blood of their sons and of their daughters, whom they sacrificed unto the graven images of Canaan, and the land was putrid with their blood.

³⁹ Thus was it defiled by their works; moreover, they played the whore in their doings.

⁴⁰ Therefore was the wrath of the Lord kindled against His people, and He abhorred His own inheritance.

⁴¹ And He gave them over into the hand of the enemy, and they that hated them were lords over them.

⁴² Their enemies oppressed them also, and had them in subjection under their hands.

⁴³ Many a time did He deliver them, but they vexed Him by their obstinacy, and wallowed in their wickedness.

⁴⁴ But the Lord took notice, when they were being afflicted, when He heard their entreaty.

⁴⁵ And He remembered His covenant, and repented, according unto the abundance of His mercy;

⁴⁶ Yea, He caused them to be pitied in the sight of all those that led them away captive.

⁴⁷ Save us, O Lord our God, and gather us from among the nations, that we may give thanks unto Thy holy Name, and make our boast of Thy praise.

⁴⁸ Blessed be the Lord God of Israel from everlasting to everlasting, and all the people shall say, Amen. So be it.

Psalm 106

Alleluia.

O GIVE thanks unto the Lord, for He is good; for His mercy endureth for ever.

² So let them say, whom the Lord hath redeemed, whom He hath delivered from the hand of the enemy,

³ And gathered them out of the lands, from the east, and the west, and the north, and the sea.

⁴ They wandered in the waterless wilderness; they found no city to dwell in.

⁵ Hungry and thirsty, their soul fainted within them.

⁶ So they cried unto the Lord in their trouble, and He delivered them from their distress.

⁷ And He led them forth by the right way, that they might go to a habitable city.

⁸ O let them give thanks unto the Lord for His mercy, and for His wonderful works to the children of men!

⁹ For He hath filled the empty soul, and satisfied the hungry soul with goodness,

¹⁰ Such as sit in darkness, and in the shadow of death, fast bound in penury and iron,

¹¹ Because they rebelled against the words of God, and spurned the counsel of the Most High.

¹² He also brought down their heart through hard labor; they were used up, and there was none to help them.

¹³ So they cried unto the Lord in their trouble, and He saved them out of their distress,

¹⁴ And He brought them out of darkness, and the shadow of death, and brake their bonds in sunder.

¹⁵ O let them give thanks unto the Lord for His mercy, and for His wonderful works to the children of men!

¹⁶ For He hath shattered the gates of brass, and broken the bars of iron.

¹⁷ He took them from their path of wickedness, for because of their wickedness were they brought low.

¹⁸ Their soul abhorred all manner of food, and they were hard at death's door.

¹⁹ So they cried unto the Lord in their affliction, and He saved them out of their distress.

²⁰ He sent His Word, and healed them, and delivered them from their destruction.

²¹ O let them give thanks unto the Lord for His mercy, and for His wonderful works to the children of men!

²² And let them offer unto Him a sacrifice of praise, and proclaim His works with rejoicing!

²³ They that go down to the sea in ships, that do business in great waters;

²⁴ These men have seen the works of the Lord, and His wonders in the deep.

²⁵ He spake, and there stood up a stormy wind, and lifted up the waves thereof.

²⁶ They go up as high as the heavens, and they go down as far as the deep; their soul melted away because of the peril.

²⁷ They were tossed to and fro; they staggered like a drunken man, and were at their wit's end.

²⁸ So they cried unto the Lord in their trouble, and He delivered them out of their distress.

²⁹ And He commanded the storm, and it stood down into a calm, and the waves thereof grew still.

³⁰ Then were they glad, because they were at rest, and He guided them unto the haven of His will.

³¹ O let them give thanks unto the Lord for His mercy, and for His wonderful works to the children of men!

³² Let them exalt Him in the congregation of the people, and praise Him in the seat of the elders!

³³ He hath turned rivers into a desert, and springs of water into dry ground,

³⁴ A fruitful land into a salt marsh, because of the wickedness of them that dwell therein.

³⁵ He turned a desert into pools of water, and a parched land into springs of water.

³⁶ And there He settled in the hungry, and they built cities to dwell in;

³⁷ And they sowed the fields, and planted vineyards, and made a plentiful harvest.

³⁸ And He blessed them, and they multiplied exceedingly, and He suffered not their cattle to decrease.

³⁹ And again, they were minished, and brought low, through affliction, calamity, and suffering.

⁴⁰ Contempt was poured out upon their princes, and He caused them to wander out of the way in the wilderness.

⁴¹ Yet helped He the poor out of misery, and made His households like a flock of sheep.

⁴² The righteous will consider this, and be glad, and the mouth of all wickedness shall be stopped.

⁴³ Who is wise, and will keep these things? And will they understand the mercies of the Lord?

Psalm 107

A Song or Psalm of David.

MY heart is ready, O God, my heart is ready; I will chant and sing in my glory.

³ Awake, my glory; awake, psaltery and harp; I myself will awake right early.

⁴ I will give thanks unto Thee among the peoples, O Lord; I will sing praises unto Thee among the nations.

⁵ For Thy mercy is greater than the heavens, and Thy truth reacheth unto the clouds.

⁶ Be Thou exalted above the heavens, O God, and Thy glory over all the earth.

⁷ So that Thy beloved may be delivered, do Thou save with Thy right hand, and hear me.

⁸ God hath spoken in His holiness; I will be exalted therefore, and divide Shechem, and measure out the valley of Succoth.

⁹ Gilead is mine, and Manasseh is mine; Ephraim also is my helmet; Judah is my king.

¹⁰ Moab is the laver of my hope; over Edom will I stretch forth my shoe; the Philistines have submitted themselves unto me.

¹¹ Who will lead me into the strong city, and who will bring me into Edom?

¹² Wilt not Thou, O God, who hast forsaken us? And wilt not Thou, O God, go forth with our hosts?

¹³ O give us help from affliction, for vain is the help of man.

¹⁴ Through God we shall do great deeds, and it is He that shall wipe out our enemies.

Psalm 108

Unto the end, a Psalm of David.

O GOD, be not silent of my praise,
² For the mouth of the ungodly, yea, the mouth of the deceitful is opened upon me, and they have spoken against me with a false tongue;

³ They compassed me about also with words of hatred, and fought against me without a cause.

⁴ Instead of the love that I had unto them, they would defame me, but I gave myself unto prayer.

⁵ And they rewarded me evil for good, and hatred for my love.

⁶ Set Thou a sinner to be ruler over him, and let the Devil stand at his right hand.

⁷ When sentence is given upon him, let him be condemned, and let his prayer be turned into sin.

⁸ Let his days be few, and let another take his office.

⁹ Let his children be fatherless, and his wife a widow.

¹⁰ Let his children be homeless wanderers, and beg their bread; let them be driven out of their homes.

¹¹ Let the usurer consume all that he hath, and let the stranger plunder his labor.

¹² Let there be no man to defend him, nor to have compassion upon his fatherless children.

¹³ Let his offspring be destroyed; in a single generation let his name be clean wiped out.

¹⁴ Let the wickedness of his fathers be had in remembrance in the sight of the Lord, and let not the sin of his mother be done away;

¹⁵ Let them always be before the Lord, and let the memory of them be rooted out from off the earth;

¹⁶ Because he remembered not to do mercy, but persecuted to death the poor helpless man, and him that was vexed at heart.

¹⁷ He loved cursing also, and it shall happen unto him, and he loved not blessing, therefore shall it be far from him.

¹⁸ And he clothed himself with cursing, like as with a raiment, and it came into his bowels like water, and like oil into his bones.

¹⁹ Let it be unto him as the cloak that he hath upon him, and as the girdle that he is always girded withal.

²⁰ This is the dealing from the Lord unto them that slander me, and to those that speak evil against my soul.

²¹ But do Thou, Lord, O Lord, deal with me according unto Thy Name, for sweet is Thy mercy.

²² O deliver me, for I am poor and in misery, and my heart is wounded within me.

²³ I go hence like a shadow that departeth; I am driven away as the locust.

²⁴ My knees are weak from fasting; my flesh is

dried up for want of oil.

²⁵ I became also a reproach unto them; they that looked upon me shaked their heads.

²⁶ Help me, O Lord my God, and save me according to Thy mercy;

²⁷ And let them know, how that this is Thy hand, and that Thou, Lord, hast done it.

²⁸ They shall curse, yet Thou shalt bless; let them be confounded that rise up against me, but Thy servant shall be glad.

²⁹ Let those who slander me be clothed with shame, and let them cover themselves with their own confusion, as with a cloak.

³⁰ I will give great thanks unto the Lord with my mouth, and praise Him among the multitude;

³¹ For He stood at the right hand of the poor, to save my soul from the persecutors.

Psalm 109

A Psalm of David.

THE Lord said unto my Lord, Sit Thou at my right hand, until I make Thine enemies the footstool of Thy feet.

² The Lord shall send the scepter of power unto Thee out of Zion; be Thou ruler, even in the midst of Thine enemies.

³ With Thee is dominion in the day of Thy power, in the splendor of Thy saints; from the womb before the morning star have I begotten Thee.

⁴ The Lord hath sworn, and will not repent, Thou art a Priest for ever, after the order of Melchizedek.

⁵ The Lord at Thy right hand hath broken kings in the day of His wrath.

⁶ He shall judge among the nations, He shall wreak havoc, He shall smite in sunder the heads of many on earth.

⁷ He shall drink of the brook in the way; therefore shall He lift up His head.

Psalm 110

Alleluia.

I will give thanks unto Thee, O Lord, with my whole heart, in the council of the righteous, and in the congregation.

² Great are the works of the Lord, sought out according unto all His will.

³ His work is praise and splendor, and His righteousness endureth for ever and ever.

⁴ He hath made His marvelous works to be remembered; the Lord is merciful and compassionate.

⁵ He hath given food unto them that fear Him; He shall ever be mindful of His covenant.

⁶ He hath showed His people the power of His works, that He may give them the inheritance of the nations.

⁷ The works of His hands are truth and judgment; all His commandments are faithful,

⁸ Confirmed for ever and ever, done in truth and equity.

⁹ He hath sent redemption unto His people, He hath established His covenant for ever; holy and terrible is His Name.

¹⁰ The fear of the Lord is the beginning of wisdom, a good understanding have all they that do thereafter; His praise endureth for ever and ever.

Psalm 111

Alleluia.

Blessed is the man that feareth the Lord, in His commandments shall he greatly delight.

² His seed shall be mighty upon earth, the generation of the righteous shall be blessed.

³ Glory and riches are in his house, and his righteousness endureth for ever and ever.

⁴ Unto the godly hath dawned a Light in the darkness; He is merciful, and compassionate, and righteous.

⁵ A good man showeth compassion, and giveth, he will guide his words with discretion, for he shall never be moved.

⁶ The righteous shall be had in everlasting remembrance;

⁷ He will not be afraid of evil tidings, his heart is ready to trust in the Lord.

⁸ His heart is firm, and will not shrink, until he looketh down upon his enemies.

⁹ He hath disbursed abroad, he hath given to the poor, and his righteousness endureth for ever and ever; his horn shall be exalted in glory.

¹⁰ The sinner shall see it, and be angry, he shall gnash with his teeth, and melt away; the desire of the sinner shall perish.

Psalm 112

Alleluia.

PRAISE the Lord, ye servants; O praise the Name of the Lord.

² Blessed be the Name of the Lord, from this time forth and for evermore.

³ From the rising up of the sun, unto the going down of the same, the Lord's Name is praised.

⁴ The Lord is high above all nations; His glory is above the heavens.

⁵ Who is like unto the Lord our God, that dwelleth on high,

⁶ And beholdeth the humble things that are in heaven and earth?

⁷ He raiseth up the beggar out of the dust, and lifteth the cripple out of the dump;

⁸ That He may set him with the princes, even with the princes of His people.

⁹ He maketh the barren woman to keep house, a joyful mother of children.

Psalm 113

Alleluia.

WHEN Israel came out of Egypt, the house of Jacob from among a strange people,

² Judah was His sanctuary, and Israel His dominion.

³ The sea saw it, and fled; Jordan was driven back.

⁴ The mountains skipped like rams, and the little hills like lambs.

⁵ What aileth thee, O thou sea, that thou fleddest? Thou Jordan, that thou wast driven back?

⁶ Ye mountains, that ye skipped like rams, and ye little hills, like lambs?

⁷ The earth quaked at the presence of the Lord, at the presence of the God of Jacob,

⁸ Who turned the hard rock into pools of water, and the flinty stone into a gushing spring.

⁹ Not unto us, O Lord, not unto us, but unto Thy Name give the glory, for the sake of Thy mercy and Thy truth,

¹⁰ Lest the heathen should say, Where is now their God?

¹¹ But our God is in heaven and on earth; He hath done all whatsoever He pleased.

¹² The idols of the heathen are silver and gold, even the work of men's hands.

¹³ They have mouths, and speak not; eyes have they, and see not.

¹⁴ They have ears, and hear not; noses have they, and smell not.

¹⁵ They have hands, and handle not; feet have they, and walk not, neither speak they through their throat.

¹⁶ May they that make them become like unto them, and all such as do put their trust in them.

¹⁷ The house of Israel hath trusted in the Lord; He is their helper and defender.

¹⁸ The house of Aaron hath trusted in the Lord; He is their helper and defender.

¹⁹ They that fear the Lord have put their trust in the Lord; He is their helper and defender.

²⁰ The Lord hath been mindful of us, and hath blessed us; He hath blessed the house of Israel; He hath blessed the house of Aaron.

²¹ He hath blessed them that fear the Lord, both small and great.

²² May the Lord increase you more and more, you and your children.

²³ Ye are the blessed of the Lord, Who made heaven and earth.

²⁴ All the whole heavens are the Lord's; but the earth hath He given to the children of men.

²⁵ The dead praise not Thee, O Lord, neither all they that go down into hell.

²⁶ But we who live will bless the Lord, from this time forth and for evermore.

Psalm 114

Alleluia.

I WAS filled with love, because the Lord will hear the voice of my supplication.

² Because He hath inclined His ear unto me, therefore will I call upon Him as long as I live.

³ The pains of death compassed me round about, and the perils of hell gat hold upon me; I found grief and sorrow, and I called upon the Name of the Lord.

⁴ O Lord, deliver my soul; gracious is the Lord, and righteous, yea, our God is merciful.

⁵ The Lord preserveth the simple; I humbled myself, and He saved me.

⁶ Turn again then into thy rest, O my soul, for the Lord hath prospered thee.

⁷ For He hath delivered my soul from death, mine eyes from tears, and my feet from stumbling.

⁸ I will be well-pleasing before the Lord in the land of the living.

Psalm 115

Alleluia.

I BELIEVED, so I spake; but I was greatly humbled.

² I said in my confusion, All men are liars.

³ What shall I render unto the Lord, for all that He hath rendered unto me?

⁴ I will take the cup of salvation, and call upon

the Name of the Lord.

⁵ I will pay my vows unto the Lord in the presence of all His people.

⁶ Precious in the sight of the Lord is the death of His saints.

⁷ O Lord, I am Thy servant; I am Thy servant, and the son of Thine handmaid; Thou hast broken my bonds in sunder.

⁸ I will offer unto Thee a sacrifice of thanksgiving, and will call upon the Name of the Lord.

⁹ I will pay my vows unto the Lord in the presence of all His people,

¹⁰ In the courts of the Lord's house, even in the midst of thee, O Jerusalem.

Psalm 116

Alleluia.

O PRAISE the Lord, all ye nations; praise Him, all ye peoples,

² For His merciful kindness is ever more and more towards us, and the truth of the Lord endureth for ever.

Psalm 117

Alleluia.

O GIVE thanks unto the Lord, for He is good, for His mercy endureth for ever.

² Let the house of Israel now say that He is good, for His mercy endureth for ever.

³ Let the house of Aaron now say that He is good, for His mercy endureth for ever.

⁴ Let all them that fear the Lord now say that He is good, for His mercy endureth for ever.

⁵ I called upon the Lord out of grief, and He heard me at large.

⁶ The Lord is my helper, and I will not fear what man shall do unto me.

⁷ The Lord is my helper, and I shall look down upon mine enemies.

⁸ It is better to trust in the Lord, than to put any confidence in man.

⁹ It is better to trust in the Lord, than to put any confidence in princes.

¹⁰ All nations compassed me round about, but in the Name of the Lord have I driven them back.

¹¹ They kept me in on every side, but in the Name of the Lord have I driven them back.

¹² They came about me like bees on a honeycomb, and burned even as a fire among the thorns, and in the Name of the Lord have I driven them back.

¹³ Hard pressed, I turned to fall, and the Lord catcheth me.

¹⁴ The Lord is my strength, and my song, and is become my salvation.

¹⁵ The voice of joy and salvation is in the dwellings of the righteous; the right hand of the Lord hath brought mighty things to pass.

¹⁶ The right hand of the Lord lifted me up; the

right hand of the Lord hath brought mighty things to pass.

¹⁷ I shall not die, but live, and declare the works of the Lord.

¹⁸ With chastening hath the Lord chastened me, but He hath not given me over unto death.

¹⁹ Open unto me the gates of righteousness, that, having gone into them, I may give thanks unto the Lord.

²⁰ This is the gate of the Lord, the righteous shall enter into it.

²¹ I will thank Thee, for Thou hast heard me, and art become my salvation.

²² The stone which the builders refused, is become the head stone of the corner.

²³ This is the Lord's doing, and it is marvelous in our eyes.

²⁴ This is the day which the Lord hath made, let us rejoice and be glad therein.

²⁵ Save me now, O Lord! O Lord, make haste.

²⁶ Blessed is he that cometh in the Name of the Lord; we have blessed you out of the house of the Lord.

²⁷ God is the Lord, and hath appeared unto us; appoint a festival with branches, even unto the horns of the altar.

²⁸ Thou art my God, and I will give thanks unto Thee; Thou art my God, and I will exalt Thee; I will thank Thee, for Thou hast heard me, and wast for me unto salvation.

²⁹ O give thanks unto the Lord, for He is good; for His mercy endureth for ever.

Psalm 118

Alleluia.

Octave 1: א ALEPH

B LESSED are the blameless in the way, who walk in the Law of the Lord.

² Blessed are they that search into His testimonies; with their whole heart shall they seek after Him.

³ For they who do no wickedness have walked in His ways.

⁴ Thou hast charged that we shall diligently keep Thy commandments.

⁵ O that my ways were so directed, as to keep Thy statutes!

⁶ Then should I not be confounded, when I consider all Thy commandments.

⁷ I will thank Thee with an unfeigned heart, when I shall have learned the judgments of Thy righteousness.

⁸ I will keep Thy statutes; O forsake me not utterly.

Octave 2: ב BETH.

H OW shall a young man correct his way? By keeping Thy words.

¹⁰ With my whole heart have I sought Thee; O estrange me not from Thy commandments.

¹¹ Thy words have I hid within my heart, that I should not sin against Thee.

¹² Blessed art Thou, O Lord; teach me Thy statutes.

¹³ With my lips have I declared all the judgments of Thy mouth.

¹⁴ I have had as great delight in the way of Thy testimonies, as in all riches.

¹⁵ I will ponder Thy commandments, and understand Thy ways.

¹⁶ I will study Thy statutes; I will not forget Thy words.

Octave 3: ג Gimel.

REWARD Thy servant; give me life, and I shall keep Thy words.

¹⁸ Open Thou mine eyes, that I may recognize the wondrous things of Thy Law.

¹⁹ I am a pilgrim upon earth, O hide not Thy commandments from me.

²⁰ My soul hath been consumed with longing for Thy judgments at all times.

²¹ Thou hast rebuked the proud; cursed are they that do err from Thy commandments.

²² O take from me rebuke and contempt, for I have sought Thy testimonies.

²³ For princes did sit and speak against me, but

Thy servant occupied himself in Thy statutes.

²⁴ For Thy testimonies are my consolation, and Thy statutes are my counsel.

Octave 4: ד DALETH.

MY soul cleaveth to the dust; O give me life, according to Thy word.

²⁶ I acknowledged my ways, and Thou heardest me; O teach me Thy statutes.

²⁷ Make me to understand the way of Thy statutes, and I shall ponder Thy wondrous works.

²⁸ My soul nodded off in weariness; sustain Thou me in Thy words.

²⁹ Take from me the way of injustice, and by Thy Law have mercy upon me.

³⁰ I have chosen the way of truth, and Thy judgments have I not forgotten.

³¹ I have stuck unto Thy testimonies, O Lord; confound me not.

³² I ran the way of Thy commandments, when Thou didst enlarge my heart.

Octave 5: ה HE.

MAKE the way of Thy statutes a Law unto me, and I shall always seek it.

³⁴ Give me understanding, and I shall delve into Thy Law; yea, I shall keep it with my whole heart.

³⁵ Set me on the path of Thy commandments, for therein hath been my desire.

³⁶ Incline my heart unto Thy testimonies, and not to covetousness.

³⁷ O turn away mine eyes, lest they behold vanity; give me life in Thy way.

³⁸ O stablish Thy word in Thy servant unto fear of Thee.

³⁹ Take away my rebuke, which I have considered, for Thy judgments are good.

⁴⁰ Behold, I have desired Thy commandments; O give me life in Thy righteousness.

Octave 6: ו VAU.

L ET Thy loving mercy come also unto me, O Lord, even Thy salvation, according unto Thy word.

⁴² So shall I have an answer for them that rebuke me, for I have trusted in Thy word.

⁴³ And take not the word of Thy truth out of my mouth utterly, for in Thy judgments have I hoped.

⁴⁴ So shall I always keep Thy Law; for ever, and for ever and ever.

⁴⁵ And I walked abroad, for I sought Thy commandments.

⁴⁶ I spake of Thy testimonies also before kings, and I was not ashamed.

⁴⁷ And my study was in Thy commandments, which I greatly loved.

⁴⁸ My hands also did I lift up unto Thy commandments, which I have loved, and I occupied myself in Thy statutes.

Octave 7: ז ZAYIN.

O REMEMBER Thy word unto Thy servant, by which Thou hast given me hope.

⁴⁹ The same hath comforted me in my humbleness, for Thy word hath given me life.

⁵¹ The proud have brazenly transgressed, yet have I not shrinked from Thy Law.

⁵² I remembered Thine everlasting judgments, O Lord, and was comforted.

⁵³ Grief hath taken me, because of the sinners that forsake Thy Law.

⁵⁴ Thy statutes have been my songs in the place of my pilgrimage.

⁵⁵ I have remembered Thy Name, O Lord, in the night-season, and have kept Thy Law.

⁵⁶ This befell me, because I sought Thy statutes.

Octave 8: ח HETH.

T HOU art my portion, O Lord; I said, I would keep Thy Law.

⁵⁸ I entreated Thy countenance with my whole heart; have mercy upon me, according to Thy word.

⁵⁹ I considered Thy ways, and turned my feet unto Thy testimonies.

⁶⁰ I made ready, and was not ashamed to keep Thy commandments.

⁶¹ The cords of sinners have bound me, but I have not forgotten Thy Law.

⁶² At midnight I rose up to give thanks unto Thee, because of Thy righteous judgments.

⁶³ I am a part of all them that fear Thee, and of them that keep Thy commandments.

⁶⁴ The earth, O Lord, is full of Thy mercy; O teach me Thy statutes.

Octave 9: ט ТЕТН.

T HOU hast dealt graciously with Thy servant, O Lord, according unto Thy word.

⁶⁶ O teach me goodness and correction and understanding, for I have believed Thy commandments.

⁶⁷ Before I submitted, I sinned; therefore have I kept Thy word.

⁶⁸ Thou art good, O Lord, and of Thy goodness teach me Thy statutes.

⁶⁹ The injustice of the proud increased against me, but I will look into Thy commandments with my whole heart.

⁷⁰ Their hearts have curdled like milk, but I have studied Thy Law.

⁷¹ It is good for me that Thou didst humble me, that I may learn Thy statutes.

⁷² The Law of Thy lips is better unto me, than thousands of gold and silver.

Octave 10: ' JOD.

THY hands have made me and fashioned me; O give me understanding, and I shall learn Thy commandments.

⁷⁴ They that fear Thee shall see me and be glad, because I have put my trust in Thy word.

⁷⁵ I have understood, O Lord, that Thy judgments are righteousness, and justly didst Thou humble me.

⁷⁶ But let Thy mercy comfort me, according to Thy word unto Thy servant.

⁷⁷ O let Thy loving mercies come unto me, and I shall live, for Thy Law is my consolation.

⁷⁸ Let the proud be confounded, for they have unfairly behaved lawlessly against me, but I will be occupied in Thy commandments.

⁷⁹ Let such as fear Thee turn unto me, and them that know Thy testimonies.

⁸⁰ O let my heart be blameless in Thy statutes, that I be not ashamed.

Octave 11: ⁷ CAPH.

MY soul hath longed for Thy salvation; I have trusted in Thy word.

⁸² Mine eyes longed for Thy word, saying, O when wilt Thou comfort me?

⁸³ For I am become like a wine-skin in the frost, yet did I not forget Thy statutes.

⁸⁴ How many are the days of Thy servant? When wilt Thou avenge me of them that persecute me?

⁸⁵ The law-breakers told me tales, but not so Thy Law, O Lord.

⁸⁶ All Thy commandments are true; they persecuted me unjustly; O be Thou my help.

⁸⁷ They had almost made an end of me upon earth, but I have not forsaken Thy commandments.

⁸⁸ O give me life according to Thy mercy, and so shall I keep the testimonies of Thy mouth.

Octave 12: ל LAMED.

O LORD, Thy word abideth for ever in heaven.
⁹⁰ Thy truth is from generation to generation; Thou hast laid the foundation of the earth, and it abideth.

⁹¹ By Thine ordinance doth the day continue, for all things serve Thee.

⁹² For if my delight had not been in Thy Law, I should have perished in my humbleness.

⁹³ I will never forget Thy statutes, for in them Thou hast given me life.

⁹⁴ I am Thine, O save me; for I have sought Thy statutes.

⁹⁵ The sinners laid wait for me to destroy me, but I have understood Thy testimonies.

⁹⁶ I have seen the limit of all perfection, but Thy commandment is exceeding broad.

Octave 13: מ MEM.

O HOW I have loved Thy Law, O Lord; it is my study all day.

⁹⁸ Thou through Thy commandment hast made me wiser than mine enemies, for it is mine for ever.

⁹⁹ I have understood more than all my teachers, for Thy testimonies are my study.

¹⁰⁰ I have become wiser than an elder, because I sought Thy commandments.

¹⁰¹ I have refrained my feet from every evil way, that I may keep Thy word.

¹⁰² I have not turned aside from Thy judgments, for Thou didst appoint a Law for me.

¹⁰³ O how sweet are Thy words unto my throat; yea, sweeter than honey unto my mouth.

¹⁰⁴ Through Thy commandments I understood, therefore have I hated every way of untruth.

Octave 14: נ NUN.

T HY Law is a lamp unto my feet, and a light unto my paths.

¹⁰⁶ I have sworn, and steadfastly resolved, to keep Thy righteous judgments.

¹⁰⁷ I was greatly humbled; give me life, O Lord, according to Thy word.

¹⁰⁸ Make acceptable the free-will offerings of my mouth, O Lord, and teach me Thy judgments.

¹⁰⁹ My soul is always in Thy hand, and I have not forgotten Thy Law.

¹¹⁰ The sinners laid a snare for me, yet I swerved not from Thy commandments.

¹¹¹ Thy testimonies have I claimed as my inheritance for ever, for they are the joy of my heart.

¹¹² In return, I have inclined mine heart to perform Thy statutes always.

Octave 15: ס SAMECH.

I HATED the law-breakers, but Thy Law have I loved.

¹¹⁴ Thou art my helper and my defender; I have trusted in Thy words.

¹¹⁵ Depart from me, ye wicked, and I will put the commandments of my God to the test.

¹¹⁶ O stand up for me according to Thy word, that I may live, and let me not be disappointed of my hope.

¹¹⁷ Help me, and I shall be saved, and I shall ever delight in Thy statutes.

¹¹⁸ Thou hast despised all them that depart from Thy statutes, for their intent is iniquitous.

¹¹⁹ All the sinners of the earth I accounted as transgressors, therefore have I loved Thy testimonies.

¹²⁰ Nail my flesh to the fear of Thee, for I was afraid of Thy judgments.

Octave 16: ע AYIN.

I HAVE done judgment and justice; O give me not over unto them that do me wrong.

¹²² Vouch for Thy servant unto good; let not the proud slander me.

¹²³ Mine eyes are wasted away with looking for Thy salvation, and for the word of Thy truth.

¹²⁴ O deal with Thy servant according unto Thy mercy, and teach me Thy statutes.

¹²⁵ I am Thy servant; O give me understanding, that I may know Thy testimonies.

¹²⁶ It is time for the Lord to act; for they have made void Thy Law.

¹²⁷ Therefore have I loved Thy commandments more than gold and topaz.

¹²⁸ Therefore have I held straight to all Thy commandments; I have hated every wrong way.

Octave 17: פ PE.

THY testimonies are wonderful, therefore hath my soul searched them out.

¹³⁰ The manifestation of Thy words shall give light and understanding unto the simple.

¹³¹ I opened my mouth and sighed, because I was longing for Thy commandments.

¹³² O look Thou upon me, and have mercy upon me, according to the judgment of them that love Thy Name.

¹³³ Direct my steps according to Thy word, and let not any wickedness have dominion over me.

¹³⁴ O deliver me from the calumny of men, and I shall keep Thy commandments.

¹³⁵ Make Thy face to shine upon Thy servant, and teach me Thy statutes.

¹³⁶ Mine eyes gushed out streams of water, because I kept not Thy Law.

Octave 18: צ Tzaddi.

RIGHTEOUS art Thou, O Lord, and true are Thy judgments.

¹³⁸ Thou hast enjoined as Thy testimonies exceeding righteousness and truth.

¹³⁹ Thy zeal hath used me up, because mine enemies have forgotten Thy word.

¹⁴⁰ Thy word is well tempered, and Thy servant hath loved it.

¹⁴¹ I am young, and of no account, yet have I not forgotten Thy statutes.

¹⁴² Thy righteousness is righteousness for ever, and Thy Law is truth.

¹⁴³ Grief and want have found me, yet are Thy commandments my comfort.

¹⁴⁴ The righteousness of Thy testimonies is everlasting; O give me understanding, and I shall live.

Octave 19: ק COPH.

I CRIED with my whole heart, Hear me, O Lord, and I will seek Thy statutes.

¹⁴⁶ I cried unto Thee, Save me, and I shall keep Thy testimonies.

¹⁴⁷ I got up in the dead of night and cried, I trusted in Thy word.

¹⁴⁸ Mine eyes were open before dawn, that I might be occupied in Thy words.

¹⁴⁹ Hear my voice, O Lord, according unto Thy mercy; give me life, according unto Thy judgment.

¹⁵⁰ They drew nigh that persecute me with wickedness; they are far gone from Thy Law.

¹⁵¹ Thou art nigh at hand, O Lord, and all Thy ways are truth.

¹⁵² I have known long since from Thy testimonies, that Thou hast established them for ever.

Octave 20: ר RESH.

O SEE my humbleness, and spare me, for I have not forgotten Thy Law.

¹⁵⁴ Judge Thou my cause, and deliver me; give me life, because of Thy word.

¹⁵⁵ Salvation is far from sinners, for they sought not Thy statutes.

¹⁵⁶ Thy mercies are many, O Lord; give me life, according unto Thy judgment.

¹⁵⁷ Many there are that trouble me, and persecute me, yet have I not swerved from Thy testimonies.

¹⁵⁸ I looked upon them that did not understand, and grieved, because they kept not Thy words.

¹⁵⁹ See how I have loved Thy commandments, O Lord; give me life, according to Thy mercy.

¹⁶⁰ The beginning of Thy words is truth, and all the judgments of Thy righteousness endure for evermore.

Octave 21: ש SHIN.

PRINCES have persecuted me without a cause, but my heart standeth in awe of Thy words.

¹⁶² I am as glad of Thy words, as one that findeth great spoils.

¹⁶³ I have hated and loathed untruth, but Thy Law have I loved.

¹⁶⁴ Seven times a day have I praised Thee, because of Thy righteous judgments.

¹⁶⁵ Great peace have they who love Thy Law, and nothing can trip them up.

¹⁶⁶ I have looked for Thy salvation, O Lord, and I have loved Thy commandments.

¹⁶⁷ My soul hath kept Thy testimonies, and loved them exceedingly.

¹⁶⁸ I have kept Thy commandments and Thy testimonies, for all my ways are before Thee, O Lord.

Octave 22: ת TAU.

L ET my petition come before Thee, O Lord; give me understanding, according to Thy word.

[170] Let my supplication come before Thee, O Lord; deliver me, according to Thy word.

[171] My lips shall break out in song, when Thou hast taught me Thy statutes.

[172] My tongue shall proclaim Thy words, for all Thy commandments are righteous.

[173] Let Thine hand be ready to save me, for I have chosen Thy commandments.

[174] I have longed for Thy salvation, O Lord, and Thy Law is my delight.

[175] My soul shall live, and shall praise Thee, and Thy judgments shall help me.

[176] I have gone astray like a sheep that is lost; O seek Thy servant, for I have not forgotten Thy commandments.

Psalm 119

A Song of Ascents.

W HEN I was in trouble I called upon the Lord, and He heard me.

[2] O Lord, deliver my soul from lying lips, and from a deceitful tongue.

[3] What shall be given unto thee, or what shall be aimed at thee, against a false tongue?

[4] Even the sharp arrows of the mighty, with hot burning coals.

⁵ Woe is me, for my wandering hath been prolonged; I have dwelt among the tents of Kedar.

⁶ Long did my soul wander; with them that hate peace I was peaceable,

⁷ But when I spake unto them, they fought against me without a cause.

Psalm 120

A Song of Ascents.

I LIFTED up mine eyes unto the hills; from whence will my help come?

² My help cometh even from the Lord, Who hath made heaven and earth.

³ Suffer not thy feet to slip, nor Him that keepeth thee to slumber.

⁴ Behold, He that keepeth Israel shall neither slumber nor sleep.

⁵ The Lord Himself shall keep thee; the Lord is thy shelter upon thy right hand;

⁶ The sun shall not burn thee by day, neither the moon by night.

⁷ The Lord shall keep thee from all evil; yea, the Lord shall preserve thy soul.

⁸ The Lord shall preserve thy going out, and thy coming in, from this time forth, and for evermore.

Psalm 121

A Song of Ascents.

I WAS glad when they said unto me, Let us go into the house of the Lord.

2 Our feet stood in thy gates, O Jerusalem.

3 Jerusalem is built as a city, whose sharing is in common.

4 For thither did the tribes go up, even the tribes of the Lord, the testimony of Israel, to give thanks unto the Name of the Lord.

5 For there sat the thrones of judgment, even the thrones of the house of David.

6 O pray for the peace of Jerusalem, and for prosperity to them that love thee.

7 Let there be peace in thy power, and prosperity within thy palaces.

8 For my brethren and neighbors' sake I spake peace concerning thee.

9 Because of the house of the Lord our God, I sought thy good.

Psalm 122

A Song of Ascents.

U NTO Thee have I lifted up mine eyes, O Thou that dwellest in heaven.

2 Behold, even as the eyes of servants are upon the hand of their masters, and as the eyes of a maid are upon the hand of her mistress, even so are our eyes upon the Lord our God, until He have pity upon us.

³ Have mercy upon us, O Lord, have mercy upon us, for we have had our fill of humiliation.

⁴ Our soul is fed up with the scornful reproof of the wealthy, and the disparaging of the proud.

Psalm 123

A Song of Ascents.

IF the Lord Himself had not been on our side, may Israel now say,

² If the Lord Himself had not been on our side, when men rose up against us, then would they have swallowed us up alive;

³ When their wrath was kindled upon us, then would the waters have drowned us.

⁴ The stream would have gone over our soul;

⁵ The roiling waters would have gone even over our soul.

⁶ Blessed be the Lord, Who hath not given us over for a prey unto their teeth.

⁷ Our soul escaped even as a bird out of the snare of the fowler; the snare was broken, and we were delivered.

⁸ Our help is in the Name of the Lord, Who hath made heaven and earth.

Psalm 124

A Song of Ascents.

THEY that trust in the Lord are as mount Zion; he that liveth in Jerusalem shall never be shaken.

² The hills are round about her; even so is the Lord round about His people, from this time forth for evermore.

³ For the Lord shall not suffer the rod of sinners to rest upon the lot of the righteous, lest the righteous stretch forth their hand unto wickedness.

⁴ Do well, O Lord, unto those that are good and true of heart.

⁵ As for such as turn aside unto craftiness, the Lord shall lead them forth with the workers of wickedness; peace be upon Israel.

Psalm 125
A Song of Ascents.

WHEN the Lord turned again the captivity of Zion, then were we like unto them that are comforted.

² Then was our mouth filled with joy, and our tongue with merry-making; then shall they say among the nations, The Lord hath done great things for them.

³ Yea, the Lord hath done great things for us already, whereof we rejoice.

⁴ Turn our captivity, O Lord, as the streams in the south.

⁵ They that sow in tears, shall reap in joy.

⁶ They went on their way and wept, sowing their seed, but they shall return in joy, bearing their sheaves.

Psalm 126
A Song of Ascents.

EXCEPT the Lord build the house, they labor in vain that build it; except the Lord keep the city, the watchman waketh but in vain.

² It is but lost labor that ye haste to rise up early, and so late take rest, and eat the bread of carefulness, when He shall give His beloved sleep.

³ Lo, children are the legacy of the Lord, the reward of the fruit of the womb.

⁴ Like as arrows in the hand of a giant, even so are the children of them that were cast out.

⁵ Blessed is he that hath his quiver full of them; they shall not be ashamed when they speak with their enemies in the gate.

Psalm 127
A Song of Ascents.

BLESSED are all they that fear the Lord, who walk in His ways.

² For thou shalt eat the fruit of thy labors; blessed art thou, and it shall be well with thee.

³ Thy wife shall be as a fruitful vine upon the walls of thine house;

⁴ Thy children like newly-planted olive trees round about thy table.

⁵ Lo, thus shall the man be blessed that feareth the Lord.

⁶ The Lord from out of Zion shall bless thee, and thou shalt see the good of Jerusalem all the days of thy life.

⁷ Yea, thou shalt see thy children's children. Peace be upon Israel.

Psalm 128
A Song of Ascents.

MANY a time have they fought against me from my youth up, may Israel now say;

² Yea, many a time have they fought against me from my youth up, but they have not prevailed against me.

³ The plowers plowed upon my back; they made long furrows.

⁴ But the righteous Lord hath hewn the necks of the sinners clean through.

⁵ Let them be confounded and turned backward, as many as have evil will at Zion.

⁶ Let them be even as the grass growing upon the house-tops, which withereth afore it be plucked up;

⁷ Whereof the mower filleth not his hand, neither he that bindeth up the sheaves his bosom.

⁸ Neither do they who go by say so much as, The blessing of the Lord be upon you, we have blessed you in the Name of the Lord.

Psalm 129

A Song of Ascents.

OUT of the depths have I cried unto Thee, O Lord; Lord, hear my voice.

² Let thine ears be attentive unto the voice of my supplication.

³ If Thou shouldest mark iniquities, O Lord; Lord, who shall stand? For with Thee there is forgiveness.

⁴ For Thy Name's sake have I waited for Thee, O Lord, my soul hath waited for Thy word; my soul hath hoped in the Lord.

⁵ From the morning watch until the night, from the morning watch, let Israel hope in the Lord.

⁶ For with the Lord there is mercy, and with Him is plenteous redemption, and He shall redeem Israel from all his iniquities.

Psalm 130

A Song of Ascents.

LORD, my heart is not haughty, nor mine eyes lofty,

² Neither have I exercised myself in great matters, nor in wonders too high for me.

³ If I had not been humble-minded, but had lifted up my soul, like as a child that is weaned against his mother, so wouldst Thou have done unto my soul.

⁴ Let Israel trust in the Lord, from this time forth and for evermore.

Psalm 131

A Song of Ascents.

REMEMBER, O Lord, David, and all his meekness;

² How he sware unto the Lord, and vowed a vow unto the God of Jacob,

³ I will not go into the tabernacle of mine house, or climb up into the couch of my bed;

⁴ I will not suffer mine eyes to sleep, or mine eye-lids to slumber, or the temples of my head to take any rest,

⁵ Until I find out a place for the Lord, an habitation for the God of Jacob.

⁶ Lo, we heard of it at Ephratha, and we found it in the fields of the wood.

⁷ We will go into His tabernacle; we will bow down toward the place where His feet have stood.

⁸ Arise, O Lord, into Thy rest; Thou, and the Ark of Thy holiness.

⁹ Thy priests shall be clothed with righteousness, and Thy saints shall rejoice.

¹⁰ For Thy servant David's sake, turn not away the face of Thine anointed.

¹¹ The Lord hath made a faithful oath unto David, and He shall not shrink from it, Of the fruit of thy loins shall I set upon thy throne.

¹² If thy sons will keep My covenant, and these testimonies that I shall teach them, their sons also shall sit upon thy throne for evermore.

¹³ For the Lord hath chosen Zion; He hath desired it for an habitation for Himself.

¹⁴ This is My rest for ever and ever; here will I dwell, for I have desired it.

¹⁵ Blessing, I will bless her catch; I will satisfy her poor with bread.

¹⁶ I will clothe her priests with salvation, and her saints shall be glad with joy.

¹⁷ There shall I make the horn of David to grow; I have prepared a lamp for Mine anointed.

¹⁸ His enemies shall I clothe with shame, but upon him shall My holiness flourish.

Psalm 132

A Song of Ascents.

BEHOLD, what is so good, or what is so fine, but for brethren to dwell in unity?

² It is like the myrrh upon the head, that runneth down upon the beard, even Aaron's beard, and goeth down to the fringes of his clothing,

³ Like as the dew of Hermon, which falleth upon the hills of Zion; for there hath the Lord ordained blessing, and life for evermore.

Psalm 133

A Song of Ascents.

BEHOLD now, bless ye the Lord, all ye servants of the Lord, that stand in the house of the Lord, even in the courts of the house of our God.

² Lift up your hands by night in the sanctuary, and bless the Lord.

³ The Lord bless thee out of Zion, Who hath made heaven and earth.

Psalm 134
Alleluia.

O PRAISE ye the Name of the Lord; O ye servants, praise the Lord,

² Ye that stand in the house of the Lord, in the courts of the house of our God.

³ O praise the Lord, for the Lord is good; O sing unto His Name, for it is good.

⁴ For the Lord hath chosen Jacob unto Himself, and Israel for His own possession.

⁵ For I have seen how great the Lord is, and that our Lord is above all gods.

⁶ All, whatsoever the Lord pleased, that hath He done, in heaven, and in earth, and in the seas, and in all deep places,

⁷ Bringing forth the clouds from the ends of the world, He made lightnings into rain, Who bringeth the winds out of His treasuries,

⁸ Who smote the first-born of Egypt, both man and beast.

⁹ He sent signs and wonders into the midst of thee, O Egypt, upon Pharaoh, and upon all his servants.

¹⁰ He smote many nations, and slew mighty kings;

¹¹ Sihon, king of the Amorites, and Og, the king of Bashan, and all the kingdoms of Canaan;

¹² And gave their land to be an inheritance, an inheritance unto Israel His people.

¹³ O Lord, Thy Name endureth for ever, and Thy memory from generation to generation,

¹⁴ For the Lord will judge His people, and be entreated concerning His servants.

¹⁵ The idols of the heathen are but silver and gold, the work of men's hands.

¹⁶ They have mouths, and speak not; eyes have they, and they see not.

¹⁷ They have ears, and yet they hear not, neither is there any breath in their mouths.

¹⁸ Let them that make them become like unto them, and all them that put their trust in them.

¹⁹ O house of Israel, bless ye the Lord; bless the Lord, ye house of Aaron; bless the Lord, ye house of Levi.

²⁰ Ye that fear the Lord, bless the Lord.

²¹ Blessed be the Lord out of Zion, who dwelleth at Jerusalem.

Psalm 135

Alleluia.

O GIVE thanks unto the Lord, for He is good, for His mercy endureth for ever.

² O give thanks unto the God of gods, for His mercy endureth for ever.

³ O give thanks unto the Lord of lords, for His mercy endureth for ever;

⁴ Who alone doeth great wonders, for His mercy endureth for ever;

⁵ Who by wisdom made the heavens, for His mercy endureth for ever;

⁶ Who fixed the earth upon the waters, for His mercy endureth for ever;

⁷ Who made the great lights, for His mercy endureth for ever;

⁸ The sun to rule the day, for His mercy endureth for ever;

⁹ The moon and the stars to govern the night, for His mercy endureth for ever;

¹⁰ Who smote Egypt with her first-born, for His mercy endureth for ever;

¹¹ And led forth Israel from among them, for His mercy endureth for ever;

¹² With a mighty hand and upstretched arm, for His mercy endureth for ever;

¹³ Who divided the Red Sea in two parts, for His mercy endureth for ever;

¹⁴ And led Israel through the midst of it, for His mercy endureth for ever;

¹⁵ But overthrew Pharaoh and his host in the Red Sea, for His mercy endureth for ever;

¹⁶ Who led His people through the wilderness, for His mercy endureth for ever;

¹⁷ Who smote great kings, for His mercy endureth for ever;

¹⁸ Yea, and slew mighty kings, for His mercy endureth for ever;

¹⁹ Sihon, king of the Amorites, for His mercy endureth for ever;

²⁰ And Og, the king of Bashan, for His mercy endureth for ever;

²¹ And gave their land for an inheritance, for His mercy endureth for ever;

²² An inheritance unto Israel His servant, for His mercy endureth for ever;

²³ For in our humbleness the Lord remembered us, for His mercy endureth for ever;

²⁴ And hath delivered us from our enemies, for His mercy endureth for ever;

²⁵ Who giveth food to all flesh, for His mercy endureth for ever.

²⁶ O give thanks unto the God of heaven, for His mercy endureth for ever.

Psalm 136

David's, by Jeremiah.

BY the waters of Babylon, there we sat down and we wept, when we remembered Zion.

² Upon the willows in the midst thereof did we hang our harps.

³ For there they that had taken us captive asked us for the words of a song, and they that led us away for a melody, saying, Sing us one of the songs of Zion.

⁴ How shall we sing the Lord's song in a strange land?

⁵ If I forget thee, O Jerusalem, let my right hand be forgotten.

⁶ Let my tongue cleave to the back of my throat, if I remember thee not, if I prefer not Jerusalem above my chief joy.

⁷ Remember the children of Edom, O Lord, in the day of Jerusalem, how they said, Down with it, down with it, even to the foundation thereof.

⁸ O daughter of Babylon, thou cursed one, blessed shall he be that shall do unto thee, as thou hast done unto us.

⁹ Blessed is he that shall seize and dash thine infants against a rock.

Psalm 137

A Psalm of David, by Haggai and Zechariah.

I WILL give thanks unto Thee, O Lord, with my whole heart, and before the angels will I sing praise unto Thee, for Thou hast heard all the words of my mouth.

² I will worship toward Thy holy temple, and give thanks unto Thy Name, because of Thy mercy and Thy truth, for Thou hast magnified Thy holy Name above all.

³ In whatsoever day I may call upon Thee, quickly hear me; Thou shalt fortify me in my soul by Thy strength.

⁴ Let all earthly kings give thanks unto Thee, O Lord, for they have heard the words of Thy mouth.

⁵ Yea, let them sing in the byways of the Lord, for great is the glory of the Lord.

⁶ For the Lord is high, yet hath He respect unto the lowly, and the high He knoweth from afar off.

⁷ Though I walk in the midst of trouble, Thou shalt refresh me; Thou hast stretched forth Thy hand upon the furiousness of mine enemies, and Thy right hand hath saved me.

⁸ The Lord shall make payment for me; O Lord, Thy mercy is for ever; despise not the works of Thy hands.

Psalm 138

Unto the end, David's, a Psalm of Zechariah
in the Dispersion.

O LORD, Thou hast examined me, and known me; Thou hast known my down-sitting, and mine up-rising.

² Thou hast understood my thoughts from afar off.

³ Thou hast searched into my path and my lot, and all my ways hast Thou foreseen.

⁴ For there is no guile in my tongue; Lo, O Lord, Thou hast known

⁵ All things, the last and the first; Thou hast made me and hast laid Thy hand upon me.

⁶ Thy knowledge is too wonderful for me; it is too hard, I cannot attain unto it.

⁷ Whither shall I go then from Thy Spirit? Or whither shall I flee from Thy presence?

⁸ If I climb up into heaven, Thou art there; if I go down to hell, Thou art there also.

⁹ If I take up my wings early, and dwell in the uttermost parts of the sea,

¹⁰ Even there also shall Thy hand lead me, and Thy right hand shall hold me.

¹¹ And I said, Peradventure the darkness shall hide me, and the night is light in my pleasures.

¹² For the darkness shall be no darkness with Thee, and the night shall be as bright as the day, for as is the darkness thereof, even so is the light of it.

¹³ For Thou hast made my reins; Thou didst take me from my mother's womb.

¹⁴ I will give thanks unto Thee, for Thou hast fearfully worked wonders; marvelous are Thy works, and that my soul knoweth right well.

¹⁵ My bones are not hid from Thee, which Thou didst make in secret, and my substance in the nether regions of the earth.

¹⁶ Thine eyes did see my unformed being, and in Thy book shall all be enrolled; in a day shall they be fashioned, when as yet there are none of them.

¹⁷ But Thy friends have been very dear to me, O God; their powers have been greatly strengthened.

¹⁸ I will count them, and they will be more in number than the sand; I woke up, and I am still with Thee.

¹⁹ Wilt Thou slay the sinners, O God? Depart

from me, ye blood-thirsty men!

²⁰ For Thou shalt speak against contriving; they shall take Thy cities in vain.

²¹ Have I not hated them, O Lord, that hate Thee, and pined away because of Thine enemies?

²² With a perfect hatred have I hated them; they have been to me as enemies.

²³ Examine me, O God, and know my heart; test me, and understand my ways.

²⁴ And look well if there be any way of wickedness in me; and lead me unto the way everlasting.

Psalm 139

Unto the end, a Psalm of David.

SAVE me, O Lord, from the evil man; from the wicked man deliver me,

² Who have imagined a lie in their heart, and stirred up strife all day.

³ They have sharpened their tongues like a serpent, adder's poison is under their lips.

⁴ Keep me, O Lord, from the hands of the sinner; save me from the wicked men, who have purposed to trip up my steps.

⁵ The proud have laid a snare for me, and spread a net abroad with cords for my feet.

⁶ They set traps in my way.

⁷ I said unto the Lord, Thou art my God; hear, O Lord, the voice of my supplication.

⁸ Lord, O Lord, Thou strength of my salvation,

Thou hast overshadowed my head in the day of battle.

⁹ Give me not over to the sinner, O Lord, because of my desire; they have plotted against me; forsake me not, lest they be too proud.

¹⁰ Let the mischief of their own lips fall upon the head of them that compass me about.

¹¹ Let hot burning coals fall upon them; Thou shalt cast them down into the torments, and they shall not stand.

¹² A garrulous man shall not prosper upon the land; evil shall hunt the wicked person unto extinction.

¹³ I know that the Lord will uphold the cause of the helpless, and avenge the poor.

¹⁴ Verily, the righteous shall give thanks unto Thy Name, and the just shall dwell in Thy presence.

Psalm 140

A Psalm of David.

LORD, I have cried unto Thee, hear me; receive the voice of my supplication when I cry unto Thee.

² Let my prayer be set forth in Thy sight as incense, and let the lifting up of my hands be an evening sacrifice.

³ Set a watch, O Lord, over my mouth, and a door of restraint before my lips.

⁴ Incline not my heart unto evil words, to imagine

excuses for sins with men who work wickedness; yea, I will have no doings with their elect.

⁵ The righteous shall chasten me with mercy, and reprove me, but let not the oil of the sinner anoint my head, for my prayer is yet more against their good favor.

⁶ Their judges were swallowed up close by the rock; they will hear my words, for they have prevailed.

⁷ As a clod of earth is broken upon the ground, so were their bones strewn beside hell.

⁸ For unto Thee, Lord, O Lord, are mine eyes; in Thee have I put my trust; O take not my soul away.

⁹ Keep me from the snare that they have laid for me, and from the traps of them that do wickedness.

¹⁰ The sinners shall fall into their own net; I am alone, until I have gone by.

Psalm 141

An Instruction of David, when he was in the cave praying.

I CRIED unto the Lord with my voice; with my voice unto the Lord did I make supplication.

³ I will pour out my petition before Him; I will declare before Him my trouble.

⁴ When my spirit would falter within me, then Thou knewest my paths; in this way wherein I walked have they privily laid a snare for me.

⁵ I looked upon my right hand and saw, and there was no man that would know me; I had no

place to flee unto, and there was no one looking out for my soul.

⁶ I cried unto Thee, O Lord; I said, Thou art my hope; Thou art my portion in the land of the living.

⁷ Consider my petition, for I am brought very low; O deliver me from my persecutors, for they have become too strong for me.

⁸ Bring my soul out of prison, that I may give thanks unto Thy Name; the righteous await me, until Thou shalt requite me.

Psalm 142

A Psalm of David, when Absalom his son pursued him.

O LORD, hear my prayer, consider my supplication in Thy truth; hearken unto me in Thy righteousness,

² And enter not into judgment with Thy servant, for before Thee shall no man living be justified.

³ For the enemy hath persecuted my soul; he hath smitten my life down to the ground; he hath laid me in the darkness, as those that have been long dead,

⁴ And my spirit is despondent within me, and my heart within me is vexed.

⁵ I remembered the days of old; I mused upon all Thy works; I exercised myself in the works of Thy hands.

⁶ I stretched forth my hands unto Thee; my soul gasped unto Thee as a thirsty land.

⁷ Hear me soon, O Lord, for my spirit faltereth; turn not Thy face from me, or I shall be like unto them that go down into the pit.

⁸ O let me hear Thy mercy in the morning, for in Thee have I trusted; tell me, O Lord, the way that I should walk in, for I lift up my soul unto Thee.

⁹ Deliver me from mine enemies, O Lord, for I have fled unto Thee.

¹⁰ Teach me to do Thy will, for Thou art my God. Thy good Spirit shall lead me into the land of righteousness.

¹¹ For Thy Name's sake, O Lord, quicken me by Thy truth; Thou shalt bring my soul out of trouble.

¹² And of Thy mercy Thou shalt slay mine enemies, and destroy all them that vex my soul, for I am Thy servant.

Psalm 143

A Psalm of David, concerning Goliath.

BLESSED be the Lord my God, Who teacheth my hands to war, and my fingers to fight;

² My mercy and my refuge, my protector and my deliverer, my defender, and I have trusted in Him; Who subdueth my people under me.

³ Lord, what is man, that Thou hast had such respect unto him? Or the son of man, that Thou so regardest him?

⁴ Man is like to vanity; his days as a shadow pass away.

⁵ Bow the heavens, O Lord, and come down; touch the mountains, and they shall smoke.

⁶ Flash forth the lightning, and scatter them; shoot out Thine arrows, and vex them.

⁷ Send down Thine hand from above; rescue me, and deliver me out of the great waters, from the hand of the strange children,

⁸ Whose mouths speak vanity, and their right hand is the right hand of untruth.

⁹ I will sing a new song unto Thee, O God; upon a psaltery of ten strings will I sing unto Thee,

¹⁰ Who givest salvation unto kings, who deliverest David Thy servant from the evil sword.

¹¹ Deliver me, and rescue me from the hand of the strange children, whose mouths speak vanity, and their right hand is the right hand of untruth,

¹² Whose sons are like newly planted saplings in their youth; their daughters are refined, adorned like unto a temple.

¹³ Their garners are full, overflowing with all manner of store; their sheep are fruitful, abundant in their issue, and their cattle are fat.

¹⁴ There is no falling down of fences, no trespassing, neither is there clamor in their streets.

¹⁵ The people that are in such a case have been called blessed, but blessed are the people whose God is the Lord.

Psalm 144

David's Psalm of praise.

I will exalt Thee, O my God, my King, and I will bless Thy Name for ever, yea, for ever and ever.

² Every day will I bless Thee, and I will praise Thy Name for ever, yea, for ever and ever.

³ Great is the Lord, and highly to be praised, and of His greatness there is no end.

⁴ Generation and generation shall praise Thy works, and declare Thy power.

⁵ They shall speak of the glorious majesty of Thy holiness, and tell of Thy wondrous works;

⁶ And of the might of Thy terrifying acts shall they speak, and tell of Thy greatness.

⁷ The memory of the abundance of Thy kindness shall they gush forth, and exult in Thy righteousness.

⁸ The Lord is merciful and gracious, long-suffering, and of great kindness.

⁹ The Lord is good unto all, and His mercies are upon all His works.

¹⁰ Let all Thy works praise Thee, O Lord, and let Thy saints bless Thee.

¹¹ They shall speak of the glory of Thy kingdom, and talk of Thy power,

¹² To make known unto the sons of men Thy power, and the glorious majesty of Thy kingdom.

¹³ Thy kingdom is an everlasting kingdom, and Thy dominion endureth throughout all ages; the

Lord is faithful in all His words, and holy in all His works.

¹⁴ The Lord upholdeth all such as fall, and lifteth up all those that be bowed down.

¹⁵ The eyes of all look unto Thee, O Lord, and Thou givest them their food in due season.

¹⁶ Thou openest Thine hand, and fillest every living thing with benevolence.

¹⁷ The Lord is righteous in all His ways, and holy in all His works.

¹⁸ The Lord is nigh unto all them that call upon Him, to all such as call upon Him in truth.

¹⁹ He will fulfill the desire of them that fear Him, and He will hear their prayer, and save them.

²⁰ The Lord preserveth all them that love Him, but all the sinners will He consume.

²¹ My mouth shall speak the praise of the Lord, and let all flesh bless His holy Name for ever, yea, for ever and ever.

Psalm 145

Alleluia. Of Haggai and Zechariah.

PRAISE the Lord, O my soul;
² While I live will I praise the Lord; I will sing unto my God as long as I have being.

³ O put not your trust in princes, in the sons of men, in whom there is no salvation.

⁴ His spirit shall go forth, and he shall return again to his earth; in that day all his thoughts shall perish.

⁵ Blessed is he that hath the God of Jacob for his helper, whose hope is in the Lord his God;

⁶ Who made heaven and earth, the sea, and all that therein is, Who preserveth truth for ever;

⁷ Who rendereth judgment for the wronged, Who giveth food unto the hungry; the Lord looseth the fettered;

⁸ The Lord giveth wisdom to the blind; the Lord raiseth up the fallen; the Lord loveth the righteous;

⁹ The Lord preserveth the proselytes; He defendeth the fatherless and the widow, but the way of sinners shall He destroy.

¹⁰ The Lord shall reign for ever, Thy God, O Zion, unto generation and generation.

Psalm 146

Alleluia. Of Haggai and Zechariah.

O PRAISE the Lord, for a psalm is a good thing; let our praise be sweet unto our God.

² The Lord Who doth build up Jerusalem, He shall gather together the dispersed of Israel,

³ Who healeth those that are broken in heart and bindeth up their wounds.

⁴ Who telleth the number of the stars, and calleth them all by their names.

⁵ Great is our Lord, and great is His power, and of His wisdom there is no end.

⁶ The Lord Who receiveth the meek, but Who humbleth the sinners down to the ground.

⁷ O begin unto the Lord in thanksgiving; sing unto our God upon the harp,

⁸ Who doth clothe the heaven with clouds, Who prepareth rain for the earth; Who maketh the grass to grow upon the mountains, and herb for the use of men;

⁹ Who giveth the cattle their fodder, and the young ravens that call upon Him.

¹⁰ He hath no pleasure in the strength of an horse, neither doth He favor any man's legs.

¹¹ The Lord favoreth them that fear Him, and that put their trust in His mercy.

Psalm 147

Alleluia. Of Haggai and Zechariah.

PRAISE the Lord, O Jerusalem! Praise thy God, O Zion!

² For He hath strengthened the bars of thy gates; He hath blessed thy children within thee;

³ Who maketh peace in thy borders, and filleth thee with flour of wheat;

⁴ Who sendeth forth His Word unto the earth; His Word runneth very swiftly;

⁵ Who giveth His snow like wool, and scattereth the hoar-frost like ashes;

⁶ Who scattereth His hail like bread; who is able to abide His frost?

⁷ He shall send out His Word, and melt them; His Wind shall blow, and the waters will run;

⁸ Who declareth His word unto Jacob, His statutes and ordinances unto Israel.

⁹ He hath not dealt so with every nation, neither hath He revealed His judgments unto them.

Psalm 148

Alleluia. Of Haggai and Zechariah.

O PRAISE the Lord from the heavens; praise Him in the heights.

² Praise Him, all ye His angels; praise Him, all ye His hosts.

³ Praise Him, sun and moon; praise Him, all ye stars and light.

⁴ Praise Him, ye heaven of heavens, and thou water that art above the heavens.

⁵ Let them praise the Name of the Lord; for He spake, and they came to be; He commanded, and they were created.

⁶ He hath established them for ever, and for ever and ever; He hath set an ordinance, and it shall not pass away.

⁷ Praise the Lord from the earth, ye dragons, and all deeps;

⁸ Fire and hail, snow and ice, the stormy wind, fulfilling His word;

⁹ Mountains and all hills, fruitful trees and all cedars;

¹⁰ Beasts and all cattle, creeping things and feathered fowls;

¹¹ Kings of the earth and all peoples, princes and all judges of the world;

¹² Young men and maidens, old men and children;

¹³ Let them praise the Name of the Lord, for His Name only is exalted; His praise is above heaven and earth.

¹⁴ And He shall exalt the horn of His people; this is a song for all His saints, for the children of Israel, for the people that draw nigh unto Him.

Psalm 149

Alleluia.

O SING unto the Lord a new song; His praise is in the church of the saints.

² Let Israel be glad in her Maker, and let the children of Zion exult in their King.

³ Let them praise His Name in the dance; let them sing praises unto Him with timbrel and psaltery.

⁴ For the Lord hath pleasure in His people; and shall lift up the meek unto salvation.

⁵ The saints shall boast in glory, and they will rejoice upon their beds.

⁶ Let the exultations of God be in their throats, and sharp two-edged swords in their hands,

⁷ To do vengeance among the heathen, and rebuke among the peoples;

⁸ To bind their kings in chains, and their nobles with manacles of iron.

⁹ To do among them the judgment written. This glory shall be to all His saints.

Psalm 150

Alleluia.

O PRAISE God in His sanctuary, praise Him in the firmament of His power.

² Praise Him for His mighty acts, praise Him according to the magnitude of His greatness.

³ Praise Him with the sound of the trumpet, praise Him upon the psaltery and harp.

⁴ Praise Him with the timbrel and dance, praise Him upon the strings and pipe.

⁵ Praise Him upon the well-tuned cymbals, praise Him upon the cymbals of jubilation.

⁶ Let every thing that hath breath praise the Lord.

Psalm 151

This psalm was specially written by David,
when he fought in single combat against Goliath, and is
outside the number of the 150 psalms. Not read in church.

I WAS small among my brethren, and the youngest in my father's house; I tended my father's sheep.

³ My hands made an organ, and my fingers fashioned a psaltery.

⁴ And who will tell my Lord? The Lord Himself, He shall hear it.

⁵ He Himself sent His Angel, and took me from my father's flock, and anointed me with the oil of His anointing.

⁶ My brethren were tall and fair, but the Lord took no pleasure in them.

⁷ I went forth to meet the Philistine, and he cursed me by his idols.

⁸ But I took the sword from him and cut off his head; and I took away reproach from the sons of Israel.